Strategic Positioning in Voluntary and Charitable Organizations

Routledge Studies in the Management of Voluntary and Non-Profit Organizations

SERIES EDITOR: STEPHEN P. OSBORNE, *University of Edinburgh, UK*

Strategic Positioning in Voluntary and Charitable Organizations

Celine Chew

Routledge
Taylor & Francis Group
New York   London

First published 2009
by Routledge
711 Third Avenue, New York, NY 10017

Simultaneously published in the UK
by Routledge
2 Park Square, Milton Park, Abingdon, Oxfordshire OX14 4RN

First issued in paperback 2014

Routledge is an imprint of the Taylor & Francis Group, an informa business

Typeset in Sabon by IBT Global.

Library of Congress Cataloging in Publication Data
Chew, Celine.
Strategic positioning in voluntary and charitable organizations / Celine Chew.
p. cm. -- (Routledge studies in the management of voluntary and non-profit organizations ; 12)
Includes bibliographical references and index.
1. Nonprofit organizations--Management. 2. Charities--Management. 3. Strategic planning. I. Title.

HD62.6.C495 2009
658.4'012--dc22   2008042894

ISBN13: 978-1-138-87944-7 (pbk)
ISBN13: 978-0-415-45304-2 (hbk)

To my late father who taught me the importance
of hard work, perseverance and humility

Contents

Contents

List of Illustrations

FIGURES

TABLES

List of Abbreviations

CAF	Charities Aid Foundation
EU	European Union
NCVO	National Council for Voluntary Organizations
NHS	National Health Service
SCVO	Scottish Council for Voluntary Organizations
UK	United Kingdom
US	United States of America

Foreword

Strategic positioning, as a management and marketing approach, has been well practised by private sector organizations since the 1960s. In contrast, voluntary and charitable organizations have only recently begun to recognize the relevance of positioning as a means to differentiate themselves in their increasingly competitive operating environment. These organizations and their global equivalents that provide public services are operating in demanding conditions, which have challenged their resource attraction and resource allocation. Of particular significance is the impact of governmental policies on the delivery of public services and wider external environmental drivers on charitable organizations' strategic positioning and their relationships with other voluntary and non-profit organizations and those in the public and private sectors.

However, there is a lack of research on whether or not voluntary and charitable organizations are responding to the changing environment in terms of their strategic positioning, and if so, how they are responding. Moreover, there remains a scarcity of literature on strategic positioning at the organizational level in non-profit and non-market contexts.

This book is based on original research that examines, for the first time, the extent to which contemporary theoretical perspectives and interpretation of strategic positioning depicted in the existing literature can be used to explain the positioning activities of charitable organizations within the wider voluntary and non-profit sector. Whilst the book is based on empirical research in the UK context, its findings and conclusions are applicable to voluntary and charitable organizations that are operating in increasingly competitive environments outside the UK. Specifically, this book provides:

- a conceptual understanding of the relationship between strategic positioning at the organizational level and its related concepts of strategic position and positioning strategy in charitable and non-profit contexts;
- empirical evidence detailing, for the first time, the extent of strategic positioning, the anatomy of a positioning strategy, and the process of developing a positioning strategy in charitable organizations that are involved in the provision of public services;

- an analysis of the key factors that influence the choice of a positioning strategy in the charitable context, and the depiction of these factors in an original integrating model;
- an exploration into the extent to which existing strategy/marketing literature on strategic positioning is applicable in the charitable context.

The research adopts a multidimensional perspective in examining the strategic positioning activities at the organizational level in the charitable context. It utilizes a three-stage methodological approach to develop an original theoretical model, integrating the key factors that influence the choice of positioning strategy in charities.

This book rekindles the existing paucity of critical analysis on the adoption of blanket for-profit approaches in the management of voluntary and charitable organizations. The development of a new theoretical model and the mapping of strategic positioning activities in charitable organizations therefore make this book an important addition to both voluntary sector management studies and the strategy management/marketing literature on positioning in non-profit organizations within and outside the UK. It also aims to encourage the development of theoretical models and conceptual frameworks that can better accommodate non-market and non-profit management contexts.

ABOUT THE AUTHOR

Celine Chew *BBA, MBA, FLMI (distinction), PhD* is a Chartered Marketer, a Fellow of the UK Higher Education Academy, a Fellow of the Life Management Institute (LOMA), an Associate of the Centre for Business Relationships, Accountability, Sustainability and Society (BRASS) in Cardiff University, a founding member of the International Research Society for Public Management (IRSPM) and a Book Reviews Editor of *Public Management Review*. Dr Chew teaches strategy and non-profit marketing in Cardiff University, UK. Her research interest focuses on the interface between strategy, marketing, social enterprise and public policy in non-profit and public service organizations. Prior to her academic career, Dr Chew has held senior management positions in international business, marketing and management consultancy in the Asia Pacific region.

Acknowledgments

This book is the culmination of four years of empirical research, a legion of assistants and plenty of sweat and tears along the way. To acknowledge everyone who has helped me in completing this book would be impossible. However, a number of people have been especially valued and they are detailed in the following.

I owe my continuing enthusiasm and passion for researching third sector and public service organizations to Professor Stephen Osborne, whose insights, expertise, input, and friendship have been invaluable. His constant encouragement and support have been magnanimous, both for the research upon which this book is based and in completing this book.

My twin sister, Cheng, has been instrumental in my decision to embark on this journey. She has always been there for me in good and difficult times on this journey, and has often brought out the courage in me to do the right thing.

My thanks also go to several colleagues who have provided invaluable comments and suggestions on the draft book chapters and this research, in particular, Dr. Tony Ellson, Professor Mary Tschirhart, Professor Alex Murdock, Professor Ian Bruce, Professor Gillian Wright, Professor Pete Alcock, Dr. Paul Davis, Dr. Karen West, and Mike Tricker.

Special thanks must go to Kim Loo for her untiring efforts in helping me polish the book chapters and the final manuscript to the form that follows. Debbie Harris has been indispensable in helping me during the last stage of completing the manuscript. Terry Claque, Thomas Sutton, Terence Johnson, and their colleagues from Routledge have been most supportive and helpful throughout.

I would also like to thank the following publishers for their permission to use and reproduce selective and/or adapted material from their publications in this book: Pearson Education Ltd. (Table 2.1 in Chapter 2), Taylor and Francis Ltd. (Figure 2.2 in Chapter 2), Institute of Local Government Studies, University of Birmingham (Table 2.2 and Figure 2.1 in Chapter 2), The National Council for Voluntary Organizations (Tables 3.1, 3.3, and 3.4 in Chapter 3), and The Chartered Institute of Public Finance and Accountancy and Blackwell Publishing (Figure 7.1 in Chapter 7).

Preliminary and emerging findings from the research upon which this book is based have been presented in a number of academic conferences between 2004 and 2007. These have included the annual conferences of the International Research Society for Public Management (IRSPM), the 2006 European Group of Public Administration (EGPA), and the 2004 Research Colloquium jointly organized by Aston University and Birmingham University where I received the Best Paper Award. Comments from conference participants have been invaluable.

Parts of Chapter 2 are based upon material authored by myself and published in an article in *Local Governance* 29, no. 4 (2003): 288–323. Chapters 4 and 5 are drawn from material authored by myself and published in Aston Business School Research Working Paper Number RP 05/06 and from an article in *Public Management Review* 8, no. 2 (2006): 333–350. Similarly, Chapters 5, 6, and 7 are taken from material authored by myself and published in Aston Business School Research Working Paper Number RP06/24 and Number RP07/01, in *Public Money & Management* and *Nonprofit & Voluntary Sector Quarterly* (the latter two with Stephen P. Osborne).

Finally, this book would not have been possible without the participation of the survey respondents, the coordinators and interviewees in the case study organizations, and the panel of academic experts, charity practitioners, and doctoral researchers who have shared their experiences and provided valuable insights in the research upon which this book is based. They must, however, remain anonymous, but I am grateful to all of them for their time and support.

As always, responsibility for the content of this book lies with me alone.

1 Strategic Positioning, the Voluntary and Charitable Sector, and Public Services

This book concerns the strategic positioning of charitable organizations or charities as part of the wider voluntary and non-profit sector. Specifically, it focuses on the organizational-level positioning of charities that are involved in the provision of public services, either as their core social mission or in partnership with statutory bodies.

> The charity's identity has to reflect faithfully its role, and the role depends heavily on the positioning of the charity in the public's mind in relation to local and national statutory services, commercial organizations and particularly other charities. (Bruce 1998: 215)

This topic is an important one. The application of positioning as a strategic management and marketing contrivance by private sector organizations has been well researched. Strategic positioning is increasingly being advocated for non-profit organizations as part of the plethora of management and marketing approaches to help them differentiate in an increasingly challenging and competitive external environment. However, little has been researched into whether charitable organizations are positioning themselves in their changing environments, and if so, how they are undertaking this.

This book is based on original research that will contribute to new knowledge and theory in positioning at the organizational level in the non-profit and non-market contexts. It utilizes empirical evidence from UK charitable organizations and their environmental contexts to examine the extent to which contemporary theoretical perspectives and interpretation of strategic positioning depicted in the existing literature can be used to explain the positioning activities of charitable organizations within the wider voluntary and non-profit sector. Whilst this book is based on empirical evidence from the UK charity context, its findings and conclusions are applicable to voluntary and charitable organizations that are operating in increasingly competitive environments elsewhere. It rekindles the scarcity of critical analysis on the adoption of blanket for-profit management approaches in the non-profit and non-market contexts.

OPERATING ENVIRONMENT OF VOLUNTARY
AND CHARITABLE ORGANIZATIONS

The operating environment of charitable organizations is increasingly competitive and has been described by some authors, on the one hand, as closely resembling the private sector environment. They compete for new/continuing revenue and scare resources, and operate within particular legal and regulatory boundaries. They are influenced by changes in the economic, technological, and political environments, and they interact with different groups of stakeholders in the process of providing/delivering their services (Bruce 1998; Sargeant 1999; Keaveney and Kaufmann 2001). Specifically, Saxton's (2003) study into how charities in the UK are managed concluded that the key success indicators adopted by their senior executives closely resemble those of commercial (for-profit) organizations. NCVO (2006a) has raised a growing concern that voluntary and charitable organizations are becoming more like private sector firms because they are generating an increasing proportion of their income from service fees and contracts rather than from voluntary sources (donations and grants).

Charities are also increasingly embarking on social enterprise or trading activities to support their social missions. For instance, earned income from trading and non-voluntary sources of British charities reached £13.3 billion in 2005, or an increase of 46 per cent from a decade ago. This increase contrasted with a decrease of 9 per cent and 39 per cent in voluntary income and investment income respectively over the same period (NCVO 2006a, 2007). In a similar vein, income from fees paid for services delivered by US charities and non-profit organizations have increased 145 per cent since the late 1970s (Hudson 2003).

On the other hand, it has been acknowledged by other authors that the context in which charities operate has several dissimilarities to that of commercial (for-profit) organizations, such as primacy of non-profit-orientated mission/purpose, tension between mission and needs/interests of stakeholders, nature of the offering, the need for resource attraction and resource allocation, resource dependency, and predominance of non-market pressures in managerial decision-making (Octon 1983; Lovelock and Weinberg 1989; Bovaird and Rubienska 1996). This perspective is well summarized by Horne and Laing (2002):

> Although possessing different ethos and cultures, voluntary and statutory sector organizations operating in post-industrial societies share common market challenges. Both are confronted with a need to serve multiple markets, an indirect-payment receipt linkage, the primacy of non-economic objectives, and the delivery of offerings comprising both private and public benefits. (829)

It has been well documented that the public policy context and wider operating environment of charities operating in the UK, US, and in the developed economies of Europe and Asia Pacific have become increasingly competitive in the third millennium (Deakin 2001; Hudson 2003; NCVO 2004a, 2004b; CAF 2005; Anheier 2005; Seddon 2007). Charities and other voluntary sector organizations are being propelled into the forefront of public service policy development and delivery (Anheier 2005; NCVO 2004b, 2005a, 2006b). For instance, The Association of Chief Executives of Voluntary Organizations (ACEVO) in the UK reported that many charities were ready to deliver large-scale public services with more charities willing to take on this role in the future (Society Guardian 2005).

Charities also perceive their greatest competition from the growing number of other charities and voluntary organizations for financial and other resources (Chew 2006a, 2006b). Moreover, charities are partnering private sector organizations in social enterprise and trading activities to diversify their income sources in order to sustain their public service missions (Andreasen and Kotler 2003). The blurring of boundaries between charitable, voluntary, public, and private sectors is thus likely to continue and will further increase competition for financial, human, and physical resources (Anheier 2005; NCVO 2005b, 2006b). These developments have put greater pressures on charities to manage their operations to effectively satisfy both their short-term survival needs and their longer-term strategic positioning (Chew 2005, 2006b). They have also created new challenges for charitable organizations in resource attraction, resource allocation, and in managing new patterns of relationships with public and private sector organizations (Deakin 2001). CAF (2004) reports that British charitable organizations are maintaining a relatively high level of public support for donated income. However, the public is moving away from supporting individual charities to supporting causes (Maple 2003). Therefore, charities would need to work harder to distinguish themselves more clearly in order to retain public support for both the cause and the organization that is promoting and delivering it.

PROFESSIONALIZATION OF CHARITY MANAGEMENT

These external environmental pressures have persuaded a growing number of charities to embark on 'professionalization' of management practice, including the use of strategic management and marketing planning (Leat 1995a; Sargeant 1995; Bruce 1998). A number of larger charities have embarked on positioning/repositioning strategies to distinguish themselves in more challenging and competitive environments. These approaches are designed to help them address the problems of raising and maintaining funding to compete with other charities, and arguably with organizations in the private and public sectors. NCVO (2004a) suggests that those charities that are increasingly involved in public services delivery need to review their strategic positions within the changing political, economic, and social landscape.

Strategic positioning is based on the notion of differentiating the charitable organization and its service offerings from those of the competition (Lauffer 1984), and could provide it with the framework for developing appropriate communication strategies to promote their value propositions to the target audiences in some distinctive way (Lovelock and Weinberg 1989; Kotler and Andreasen 1996; Andreasen and Kotler 2008). Charitable organizations have been advised to regularly examine their existing strategic positions as compared to other service providers to see how distinct they are to their target audiences, and to develop appropriate positioning strategies, in particular, to guide their fundraising and communications activities (Sargeant 1999).

STRATEGIC POSITIONING IN THE CHARITABLE CONTEXT

Despite the growing recognition of the importance of positioning as a management tool, cases of positioning by British charities were only discussed in the non-profit and charity marketing/strategy literature from the mid-1990s (e.g., Wray 1994; Saxton 1996; Bruce 1998; Kennedy 1998; Maple 2003). Interestingly, the concept of positioning was popularized in private sector marketing during the 1960s and 1970s with pioneers such as Alpert and Gatty (1969), and Trout and Ries (1972), who emphasized the communications role of positioning for commercial (for-profit) organizations.

Whilst there are now many textbooks and conceptual articles on strategic management and marketing for non-profit organizations in general, empirical research into the area of strategic positioning in the non-profit context has remained sparse and has focused on tactical issues such as fundraising, promotion and communications in charity management (Balabanis, Stables, and Phillips 1997). This book argues that the majority of theoretical underpinnings of strategic positioning have been derived from the commercial strategy/marketing literature.

A more prominent issue is the scant literature on strategic positioning as it applies to charities, and the current lack of empirical research on how these organizations have responded, in terms of their strategic positioning, to the changing political, economic, social, and competitive landscape. Moreover, reported cases of positioning tend to focus on larger charities and are arguably anecdotal or post hoc descriptions. Notable exceptions include Hibbert's (1995) empirical study on the market positioning of British medical charities, and Hibbert and Horne's (1996) conceptual discussion, which questions the conventional donor decision process in charitable giving. Hibbert's study (1995) reveals that British charities lacked clearly defined positions in the market, thereby making it hard for them to differentiate their positioning message from other charities. Hibbert and Horne (1996) suggest that many charities experience low awareness levels from external audiences. This lack of attention to organizational positioning in the charity sector could pose a major longer-term problem for resource attraction and in building the charity's brand identity (Bruce 1998). The relevant target audiences persist in recognizing the 'cause' but not the specific charity delivering the service.

Crucially, this book fills a notable gap in the existing literature and research with a critical examination of the strategic positioning of charities at the organizational level. Strategic positioning at the organizational level is defined in this book as a management decision process in order to identify the strategic position of the organization, and to develop a positioning strategy to differentiate it effectively from other providers (Chew 2005). Positioning at the organizational level is distinct from, but provides direction for positioning at the other (operational) levels, such as product positioning and brand positioning (Hooley, Saunders, and Piercy 1998; Fill 2002).

The literature review in Chapter 2 will explain strategic positioning at the organizational level further, and will show that contemporary strategy/marketing literature provides a variety of definitions and applications for the concept of positioning as they relate to both commercial (for-profit) and non-profit organizations. However, there remains no single universally accepted definition for this concept (Kalafatis, Tsogas, and Blankson 2000; Attia 2003). The process of positioning helps to create the strategic position of the organization and its offerings in the marketplace (Kotler 1994). From the organization's perspective, its own strategic position can explicitly or implicitly identify the key direction for creating its distinctiveness.

The strategic position also provides guidance in developing the positioning dimensions (key strengths and core competences) of the organization to distinguish itself from other providers. This strategic position embodies the 'strategic intent' or overriding ambition of the organization to reach its desired position (Hamel and Prahalad 1989: 64). Strategic intent for positioning by commercial (for-profit) organizations is often viewed in the extant literature as focusing on competitive goals, in particular, striving for a leadership position by outmanoeuvering their rivals. However, there is currently a lack of research into the understanding of strategic intent for positioning in organizations other than for-profit ones.

This book presents empirical evidence, which initiates an exploration into the strategic positioning activities of charitable organizations and their motives for undertaking positioning. Furthermore, it investigates the strategic positioning of charities from their perspective. It will also be explained in Chapter 2 that there are at least two views of the organization's strategic position—the organization's and that of the external target audience. Much of the existing, albeit limited, empirical research on positioning in the charitable context emphasizes the perception of external audiences, in particular, those of providers of funds such as donors, on the charity's market position (e.g., Hibbert 1995). Andreasen, Goodstein, and Wilson (2005) suggest that all too often non-profit organizations neglect monitoring whether their organization's strategic position, as perceived by the external audiences, is the same as their perception of it. Whilst both views of the organization's position are important, this book argues that the organization's determination of its strategic position is fundamental in shaping the external audience's perspective of its distinctiveness compared to other providers.

PURPOSE AND CONTRIBUTIONS OF THIS BOOK

The lack of empirical research and theoretical/conceptual models that can accommodate the diverse voluntary sector and guide strategic positioning practice in charitable organizations have provided the motivation to create this book. This book, and the study upon which it is based, reopens a noted paucity of empirical research on how voluntary and charitable organizations have strategically positioned themselves in a changing external operating environment and policy context.

Two main research objectives are established to guide this study: to explore the extent to which charitable organizations undertake strategic positioning activities, and to examine the key factors that influence the positioning strategy in charitable organizations.

The contributions of this book are therefore in three ways. First, it will investigate the extent to which charitable organizations are undertaking strategic positioning activities. This examination will focus on UK charities, in particular those that are involved in public service delivery. It will be the first to provide, through the combined evidence of an exploratory survey and in-depth case studies, an empirical mapping of strategic positioning activities in the voluntary and charitable context. This mapping will include the process of developing a positioning strategy, the type of positioning strategies adopted by charities, the key components of their positioning strategy, and the factors that influence their choice of a positioning strategy. The experiences of the case study organizations in their positioning activities will also provide useful insights for managers who are involved in planning and/or implementing organizational positioning in charities and the wider voluntary sector.

Second, it will adopt a multidimensional approach to explore and synthesize the alternative theoretical perspectives on the concept of strategic positioning, which will provide an understanding of how these could be applied to explain positioning in the non-profit sector. This book argues that strategic positioning in the charitable context is a multifaceted concept and requires a multidimensional approach to researching it. To serve as guidance to the empirical part of the research, it will provide a conceptual clarification of the concept of strategic positioning, and the relationship between strategic positioning and its sister concepts, such as strategic position and positioning strategy. Whilst much of the existing literature and theoretical perspectives on positioning have been derived from the study of commercial (for-profit) organizations, this book will provide a potential contribution to general theories on positioning in the strategic management and marketing literatures from the study of charitable organizations.

Third, it will develop an original theoretical model that is shaped from empirical evidence from this research. This model integrates and explains, for the first time, the multidimensional factors that influence an organizational-level positioning strategy in charitable organizations. It is argued in this book that this model can better explain the influencing factors on the positioning strategy of charitable organizations due to the grounded approach in developing it. The findings from this study will highlight the inadequacy of existing marketing/strategy literature on positioning to fully explain strategic positioning in non-profit and non-market contexts. In this respect, the research and integrating model provide distinct additions to both voluntary and non-profit management studies in the UK and elsewhere, while providing an alternative perspective to researching charity positioning in contemporary marketing/strategy literature.

ORGANIZATION OF THIS BOOK

The book is organized in three parts. Figure 1.1 presents the organization of this book, its planned research outputs, and major contributions.

The first three chapters represent the conceptualization stage of the research. Following this introduction chapter, Chapter 2 will explore the existing literature on the theoretical perspectives of strategic positioning from both contemporary strategic management and marketing literature, and those that have been adopted for non-profit organizations in general, and charitable organizations specifically. It discusses topics relating to strategic positioning at the organizational level, the process of developing a positioning strategy, and the role of positioning.

Three broad theoretical perspectives will be reviewed in terms of their orientation, key focus, and potential influence on positioning strategy decisions. An initial organizing conceptual framework results from this review identifying the components of a positioning strategy and the key influencing factors in the charitable context. These constituents will be compared with the resultant model of influencing factors that will be shaped from the empirical findings in the second and third stages of the study. The model and its constituents will be detailed fully in Chapter 7 of this book. Chapter 3 will explore the evolving policy context and other external environmental conditions in which voluntary and charitable organizations in the UK operate. It reviews the voluntary/charity management literature to identify drivers for the relevance of strategic positioning and adoption of strategic management and marketing approaches in the charitable context. This provides an appreciation of their unique organizational and environmental contexts in which the empirical part of this study was based.

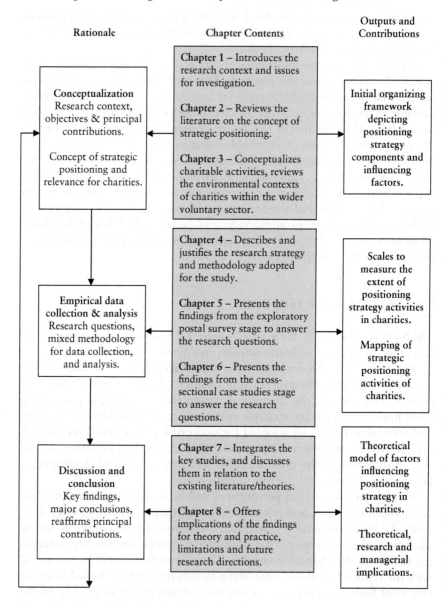

Figure 1.1 Organization of this book.

The next three chapters, namely, Chapters 4, 5, and 6, will introduce the research questions that will guide the two empirical stages of this study and describe the methodology and empirical findings based on the general welfare and social care charitable subsectors in the UK. Chapter 4 outlines the three-stage methodology adopted for this study, which derives its strength from both the quantitative and qualitative research meta-frameworks. The empirical stages, which were carried out between 2004 and 2006, included an exploratory postal survey stage and a multiple cross-sectional case studies stage. A mixed methodology of data collection and analysis was used to adequately address the research objectives and questions that had been established for the study.

Chapter 5 will present the empirical findings from the exploratory postal survey stage. The main objectives were to explore and describe the strategic positioning activities in a sample of general welfare and social care charities and to answer the research questions established for this stage of the study. The findings from this stage will produce an initial mapping of the positioning activities of charities, which is a key contribution of this book. The survey utilized a self-administered postal questionnaire in order to collect primary data for analysis. Due to the lack of existing scales to measure the extent of strategic positioning in the charitable context, two scales were developed specifically in this study to measure the extent of positioning strategy and strategic marketing planning activities. An initial picture of the influencing factors in the charitable context emerged at this stage. The largely descriptive data was analyzed using frequency tables, cross-tabulations, and chi-square tests for significance.

Emerging themes arising from the survey findings will provide guidance for an in-depth investigation at the next empirical stage. Chapter 6 presents the empirical evidence from the cross-sectional case studies stage. The main objective here was to investigate in further depth the strategic positioning activities of charities in three broad themes: the process of strategic positioning, the anatomy of a positioning strategy, and the key factors influencing positioning strategy in the charitable context. Four case studies will be examined to answer the research questions established for this stage of the study. Multiple sources of evidence were gathered in the case studies. The use of multiple methods and sources of data at different stages of this research provided both methodological and data triangulation and were aimed at enhancing the reliability and validity of the findings (Denzin 1978b; Jick 1979; Mingers and Brocklesby 1995). The three broad themes will be evaluated both through the intra-case and cross-case analyses in order to build a more robust model that integrates the external, internal, and mediating influencing factors into a broader explanatory framework.

Following the empirical part of the study, the book will conclude in the last part, which comprises two chapters. Chapter 7 draws together the key findings derived from the postal survey stage and case studies stage presented in Chapters 4 to 6 of this book and discusses them in relation to the existing literature and theories reviewed in Chapters 2 and 3. It will synthesize the findings to address the two main research objectives established for this study. Importantly, it unveils and explains an original theoretical model that has been shaped from the empirical findings of this research. The model integrates the multidimensional factors that influence a positioning strategy in the charitable context. This is another key contribution of the book towards positioning theory and charity management practice. Chapter 8 will conclude this book by summarizing the major conclusions of this study and discussing the major implications of the research findings for contemporary positioning theory and practice. These have import both for future research about voluntary and charitable organizations and their management.

2 Strategic Positioning, Strategic Position, and Positioning Strategy

The chapter is intended to review the key literature about strategic positioning in both the contemporary strategic management and marketing literatures, and those that have been adopted for non-profit organizations in general, and charitable organizations specifically. The aim is to identify gaps in the extant literature/research in relation to strategic positioning at the organizational level in the charitable context, and to locate this study within the wider context of the management literature. This review is part of the first stage of a three-stage methodology utilized in this study, namely, the conceptualization stage.

This chapter begins with an overview of the origins of positioning in order to appreciate its historical role in the management of organizations and how this has progressed from consumer product marketing to its contemporary role in strategy development. This is followed by a conceptualization of strategic positioning at the organizational level, which is distinct from positioning for products and brands, and to differentiate it from its sister concepts of strategic position and positioning strategy. The process of developing a positioning strategy is explored from the perspectives of two schools of thought, namely, the marketing perspective and the strategic management perspective.

Three other theoretical perspectives on strategic positioning are next discussed in terms of their orientation, key focus, and potential influence on positioning strategy decisions in the charitable context. This review leads to an initial organizing conceptual framework that identifies the key components of a positioning strategy and proposes the key factors influencing positioning strategy in the context of charitable organizations. A final section will summarize the review of selective literatures conducted in this chapter and will highlight the gaps in empirical research in strategic positioning at the organizational level in the charitable context.

THE ORIGINS AND EVOLVING ROLES OF POSITIONING

The evolving roles of positioning in the organization can be traced in the literature at different phases in the development of marketing and strategic management in the developed markets of the US, UK, and Western Europe. However, most of the theoretical underpinnings of positioning found in the literature have been derived from the context of commercial (for-profit) organizations, which this section will draw upon to provide the necessary background for our understanding of the concept of positioning and its role in the strategic planning and development process.

Although positioning has been widely discussed and used in contemporary commercial (for-profit) marketing and strategy formulation, there remains no single universally accepted definition of the concept (Blankson and Kalafatis 1999; Kalafatis, Tsogas, and Blankson 2000). Moreover, the concept of positioning has been defined in a number of ways in the extant literature (Maggard 1986; Aaker 1989; Arnott 1992; Attia 2003). Of particular interest is the term 'positioning,' which is often used generically to denote other seemingly similar, but arguably disparate concepts, such as, 'strategic positioning' and 'position' (Blankson 1999; Chew 2003), and different levels of positioning within the organization (Chew 2006b). These definitions will be reviewed more comprehensively in the next section of this chapter.

The concept of positioning is rooted in private sector marketing and can be traced back to the 1960s. The post-war era saw the explosive growth in demand for consumer products. During this period, positioning was popularized in consumer product marketing by pioneers such as Alpert and Gatty (1969). They identified positioning as the differentiation of brands according to consumers' perceptions. They studied differences in consumers' perceptions of the organization's products/brands when these were positioned differently using technology as the differentiating dimension over similar products in the marketplace. The focus of positioning at that time was therefore on the consumer perspective of the organization's product positioning, which was relative to similar offerings in the marketplace.

Throughout the 1970s and early 1980s, as part of the organization's effort to differentiate its offerings in increasingly competitive market environments, several authors popularized positioning by linking it to advertising, communication, and image promotional strategies (e.g., Smith and Lusch 1976; Brown and Sims 1976; Engels 1980; Aaker and Myers 1987). Some authors, such as Trout and Ries (1972) and Ries and Trout (1986), remained focused on the consumer perspective of the organization's position. They argued that 'positioning is something that you do with the consumer's mind' (ibid.: 2), with little conscious efforts on the part of the organization to create or modify its offerings. These authors emphasized the creative use of marketing techniques, such as advertising to promote the organization's products to external audiences. However, there was increasing interest among other researchers on the managerial aspects of positioning, in particular, how to develop strategy to strengthen the organization's position in competitive markets. For instance, Cravens (1975) identified positioning as a means of selecting an appropriate marketing strategy, while

Brown and Sims (1976) established the importance of competitor analysis and identifying needs of target consumers as part of the positioning process. Kotler (1980) was one of the earliest scholars to link positioning for products to the wider strategic marketing planning process. Kotler's (ibid.) strategic planning model emphasized the central role of marketing planning in the corporate planning process, and stressed how organization-wide goals could be achieved through the implementation of specific marketing activities. In summary, the marketing perspective of positioning, which placed the product and the consumer at the heart of strategy, dominated positioning theory and research during this period.

The 1980s and 1990s saw the development of positioning theory, with research being increasingly focused on improving the competitive advantage and performance of commercial (for-profit) organizations as part of their strategy development process. Hofer and Schendel (1978: 25) defined competitive advantage for commercial (for-profit) organizations as 'the unique position an organization develops vis-à-vis its competitors.' Porter (1980, 1985) is one of the earliest scholars who argued for the creation of competitive advantage in positioning strategy in order to differentiate the organization from competitors in various industries/sectors. His generic or core positioning strategies are based on creating particular competitive advantages in response to different industry influences. The Porterian perspective on positioning will be reviewed in more detail in a later section of this chapter. Other scholars (e.g., Crawford 1985; Doyle and Saunders 1985) continued the marketing tradition of defining positioning by determining the ways in which products were differentiated in order to identify its key role in developing a competitive marketing strategy.

From the mid-1990s two further strands in positioning theory and research emerged; namely, the resource-based view within the strategic management perspective, and positioning for service organizations (e.g., Lovelock, Vandermerwe, and Lewis 1996; Zineldin 1996; Zeithaml and Bitner 1996; Kalafatis, Tsogas, and Blankson 2000; Zineldin and Bredenlow 2001). The resource-based view argues that competitive advantage is created within the organization as opposed to being located in the external environment/industry. It stresses organizational resources as potential sources of competitive advantage and de-emphasizes the role of external industry influences on the organization's position (e.g., Barney 1991; Grant 1991; Amit and Schoemaker 1993).

The emergence of the resource-based perspective on positioning arose at a time when a strong interest in the process of strategic planning and development in organizations was already apparent. However, there were conflicting orientations of positioning among scholars who shared this perspective. For instance, Mintzberg (1995) defined strategy as a 'position,' in other words, means of locating an organization within its operating environment (ibid.: 17). This external orientation reinforced the view shared earlier by Hofer and Schendel (1978: 4) who suggested that strategy, as a position, becomes the 'match between the organization and its environment.' On the other hand, Thompson (1967) argued that the strategic position of the organization is a place in the product-market domain/environment where resources are concentrated, thus reinforcing the resource-based view that emphasizes the role of organizational resources in creating positional advantage in a competitive market. The resource-based perspective on strategic positioning will be reviewed in more detail in a later section in this chapter.

Moreover, during this period, the marketing perspective of positioning also took on a more 'integrative' stance regarding the sources of competitive advantage in commercial (for-profit) organizations. Several scholars (e.g., Hooley, Broderick, and Moller 1998; Hooley, Saunders, and Piercy 1998; Hooley et al. 2001; Juga 1999; Chang and Singh 2000) acknowledged that an integrative approach that incorporated both external environmental influences and internal organizational capabilities in developing positioning strategy was needed.

Strategic positioning continues to be widely promoted in the marketing and strategic management literature into the new millennium, both at the organizational level (e.g., Hooley et al. 2001; Hooley, Saunders, and Piercy 2004; Johnson, Scholes, and Whittington 2006) and at the product/service and brand levels (e.g., McCarthy and Norris 1999; Bhat and Reddy 1998; Kotler 2000; Blankson and Kalafatis 2001). At the same time, there is a growing recognition that strategic positioning is more than gaining competitive advantage over rival providers through operational means, such as advertising and product segmentation, but could be influenced by the organization's vision, its mission, and its culture (Hatch and Schultz 2001; Ellson 2004).

Interest in the research of positioning in service organizations heightened from the 1990s simultaneously with the further theoretical development in services marketing and management. There was a general agreement among scholars that positioning for services was more complex and, in some cases, often more difficult to implement than physical products (Blankson and Kalafatis 2001). This argument was based on the consensus that services have distinctive characteristics, making them fundamentally different from physical goods (Dibb and Simkin 1993; Devlin, Ennew, and Mirza 1995; Zeithaml and Bitner 1996). Positioning for services would require the development of unique organizational capabilities, such as human resources and skills (Skaggs and Youndt 2004), and therefore could influence the type of positioning strategy that service organizations adopt (Ellis and Mosher 1993; Blankson and Kalafatis 1999). Devlin, Ennew, and Mirza (1995) suggest that the distinctive characteristics of services have implications for the process of positioning, such as the importance of developing trust, reliability, and personalized interaction with service users as differentiating dimensions in the positioning strategy.

In the non-profit marketing literature, Lauffer (1984) and Lovelock and Weinberg (1989) were among the earliest, albeit few, scholars to advocate strategic marketing planning and positioning as part of the marketing strategy for non-profit organizations. It was only during the 1990s that cases of positioning had become recognized as an area of discussion in the charity marketing/strategy literature, and from that point positioning as a management practice was prescribed to British charities to help them preserve their distinctiveness in a changing operating environment (e.g., Wray 1994; Saxton 1996; Bruce 1998; Frumkin and Kim 2001; Hudson 2002: Maple 2003). The majority of these authors supported the usefulness of positioning in charities, especially by helping them to differentiate their cause/offerings in an increasingly challenging and competitive external environment. The operating environment of charities will be reviewed in Chapter 3. As it will also be discussed in Chapter 3, there is general agreement among scholars that significant dissimilarities exist between the organizational characteristics of charitable organizations and commercial (for-profit) organizations. Arguably, these dissimilarities, coupled with the service-orientation of charities would have implications for managing these organizations.

However, the literature on positioning in voluntary and non-profit organizations tends to describe this concept in similar ways to the contemporary marketing/strategy literature (e.g., Lovelock and Weinberg 1989; Sargeant 1999; Kotler and Andreasen 1996; Andreasen and Kotler 2003). This has prompted a growing number of non-profit management scholars to acknowledge the need for adaptation in the type of positioning strategy for charities. For instance, Frumkin and Kim (2001) argued that positioning around the non-profit mission is a distinctive way for voluntary and non-profit organizations to differentiate themselves in the competitive marketplace, and is a more effective way of attracting donations from the public compared to positioning based on efficiency or lower cost/price. Wray (1994) and Saxton (1996) suggested a variety of alternative positioning strategies that British charities could adopt to differentiate themselves in an increasingly competitive fundraising environment. Andreasen, Goodstein, and Wilson (2005) argue that sectoral differences are potential barriers when transferring business concepts in their entirety from the for-profit sector to the non-profit sector, whilst others argue for the adaptation of these concepts in the charitable context (McLeish 1995; Maple 2003). Moore (2000) suggests that private sector strategy models advocated for non-profit organizations fail to take into account the social purpose–driven mission and different funding avenues of the latter. Moreover, the values-critical culture of charities and non-profits create special challenges for them when adopting business models, emphasizing operational efficiency and short-term performance goals in the government-contracting market (Frumkin and Andre-Clark 2000).

In summary, since the 1960s, the original role of positioning as an advertising and promotional technique has evolved to become a fundamental element of the corporate/marketing strategy development process in contemporary organizational management. Despite this evolution there remains little literature and a paucity of empirical research on positioning in voluntary and non-profit organizations in general, and charities specifically. Moreover, the reported cases of positioning in charities have been largely anecdotal or post hoc descriptions. Notable exceptions include Hibbert (1995), who studied the market positions of British medical charities as defined by external audiences, and Kennedy (1998), who explored the effects of positioning on the corporate strategy in a large British charity. Both researchers concluded that charities lacked distinctive positions making it difficult for them to clearly differentiate their organization from the other charities providing similar services or who operated in the same subsector. The next section builds on the preceding overview of positioning by reviewing the specific definitions of positioning and establishing the focus for strategic positioning in this study.

CONCEPTUALIZING STRATEGIC POSITIONING, STRATEGIC POSITION, AND POSITIONING STRATEGY

This section will draw out the various perspectives of strategic positioning by reviewing specific literatures on positioning that are aimed at private sector organizations and those that are prescribed for non-profit organizations. The intention is to clarify the relationship between related concepts of strategic positioning, strategic position, and positioning strategy. As highlighted in the preceding section there is no commonly accepted definition of the concept of positioning for commercial (for-profit) organizations or non-profit ones.

A review of contemporary strategy and marketing literatures suggests that there is a general confusion in the use of the term 'positioning.' Kalafatis, Tsogas, and Blankson (2000) argue that several terms used by authors, such as positioning (Kotler 1999), product positioning (Harrison 1987), market positioning (Greenley 1989), and competitive positioning (Hooley, Broderick, and Moller 1998; Hooley, Saunders, and Piercy 1998) have apparent definitional differences but are substantially superficial. In other words, authors tend to refer to the same concept using various terminologies. An added confusion is that positioning has also been used interchangeably with the term 'position' (e.g., Smith and Lusch 1976) and 'positioning strategy' (e.g., Lovelock and Weinberg 1989).

Crucially, literature has shown the few attempts made to distinguish between different levels of positioning, namely, at the organizational level and at the product/brand level, and to also identify the relationship between strategic positioning, strategic position, and positioning strategy. This section aims to provide a clearer conceptualization and differentiation between these concepts to be adopted for this study.

Strategic Positioning

The term 'positioning' is often used interchangeably in contemporary strategy/marketing literature to mean 'strategic positioning' because of the perceived role it plays in strategy development. Zineldin and Bredenlow (2001) define strategic positioning for commercial (for-profit) organizations as:

> A process of defining and maintaining a distinctive place in the marketplace for an organization and/or its product offerings so that the target market/prospect understands and appreciates what the organization stands for in relation to its competitors. (484)

Porter (1996: 62) suggests that strategic positioning means "performing different activities from rivals or performing similar activities in different ways." The main goal of strategic positioning for private sector organizations from a marketing perspective is arguably to create some form of differential advantage that would be valued by their target consumers in a competitive environment (Hooley 2001). Kalafatis, Tsogas, and Blankson (2000), however, emphasized positioning at the heart of corporate strategy and not of sales tactics. Positioning at the corporate level requires managers to take deliberate and proactive actions to identify and develop the organization's competitive position based on its operational and experiential dimensions, rather than promotional efforts. They (ibid.) argue that the marketing perspective of positioning that is focused primarily on the consumer's perception of the organization or its offerings does not provide sufficient guidance on the choice of positioning strategies available to the organization.

There are at least two levels of positioning in the organization, namely, at the organizational level and the product/brand level (Hooley, Saunders, and Piercy 1998). Webster (1992) adds a third dimension to positioning, namely, positioning at the operational (or tactical) level. These authors, however, were in agreement that strategic positioning at the organizational level is a long-term process of developing the organization's overall competitive advantage in the marketplace. The role of strategic positioning at this level is to identify the organization's place in its environment, which depends on its mission and distinctive/core competences (Prahalad and Hamel 1990). Hooley (2001) argues that this role requires managers to make strategic decisions, such as, the choice of the target users/consumers and the differential advantage for their positioning strategy. Webster (1992) suggests that the role of marketing for an organizational-level strategic positioning is to communicate the strategic position of the organization to its internal and external audiences.

Positioning at the product/brand or operational level involves identifying how the organization's offerings are perceived by its users/consumers relative to other competing products or brands and then developing appropriate marketing mix strategies that support their positions in the marketplace. The organizational-level positioning necessarily influences (directs or constrains) on the product/brand-level positioning (ibid.: 309). Positioning at the organizational level is therefore distinct from but provides direction for positioning at the other (lower) levels in the organization.

Additionally, the distinctiveness of services provided by service organizations and non-profit organizations compared to physical goods suggests that organizational-level positioning is more important for services than product or brand positioning (Devlin, Ennew, and Mirza 1995). This is because creating differentiation advantage based on product features is limited, even impractical for service and mission-critical organizations (ibid.: 121). Chew (2005) distinguishes between strategic positioning at the organizational level and positioning at the operational level in charities. Strategic positioning is defined as "a managerial decision-process to develop an organization level positioning strategy that aims to effectively differentiate the organization from other non-profits or service providers" (ibid.: 4). The aim is to identify the charity's place (its strategic position) in its environment, which is shaped by its mission and distinctive or core competences (Chew 2006a, 2006b).

Strategic Position

The process of strategic positioning helps to create the strategic position of the organization and its offerings in the marketplace (Kotler 1994). Johnson, Scholes, and Whittington (2006) suggest that the strategic position of an organization is the outcome of decisions made at the corporate level, and is influenced by the external environment, availability of internal resources, and core competences, and the expectations of various internal and external stakeholders. The organization's strategic position explicitly or implicitly identifies the key direction for its core positioning strategy and provides guidance in developing its positioning dimensions (its distinctiveness) based on key strengths and core competences in order to differentiate itself from other providers (Chew and Osborne 2008a). Chapter 1 highlighted that the strategic intent or overriding ambition for strategic positioning should be embodied in the organization's strategic position. Arguably, this enables commercial (for-profit) organizations to strive for a competitive position by winning over rival providers (Hamel and Prahalad 1989: 64). However, the strategic intent for charitable and non-profit organizations is less clear because of the lack of research on this topic.

Kotler and Andreasen (1996) argue that many voluntary and non-profit organizations fail to succeed because their target audiences do not really know who they are or how they are different from other voluntary/non-profit organizations. Having a clear strategic position can help these organizations to differentiate themselves from others in the eyes of their target audiences to whom they depend on for service users, volunteers, and financial support. Bruce (1998) goes further to suggest that the strategic positions of UK charities should be defined in terms of both the organization's purpose and their offerings in any strategic plan. He argues that the identity and position of a charity are inextricably linked, and charities would need to consider the basis on which they compete within a chosen subsector or segment for funding and public attention.

The literature also suggests that there are at least two parties' views of an organization's strategic position: that belonging to the organization and that of its external target audience. The process of strategic positioning within the organization creates its strategic position, which is communicated through a chosen positioning strategy to the various target audiences (Reddy and Campbell 1993; Hooley 2001; Fill 2002). The resulting strategic position refers to the organization's 'place' in the marketplace from its own perspective (Attia 2003). The other view of the organization's position is from the external audience's perspective. This 'market' perspective may or may not be similar to that of the organization. For instance, Reddy and Campbell (1993) cautioned that strategic positioning can take place without the deliberate efforts of the organization. In other words, the external audience, such as the consumer or even the competitor, could assign a position to the organization vis-à-vis other competitors' positions in the marketplace. The strategic position of the organization is therefore relative (Hooley 2001). Andreasen, Goodstein, and Wilson (2005) argue that regular monitoring of the external target audience's perspective of the organization's strategic position is necessary to ensure consistency between how the organization views itself and how the external audience views it.

Figure 2.1 depicts the relationship between strategic positioning, strategic position of the organization, and its positioning strategy. It highlights the importance of consistency between the strategic position developed within the organization and communicated to its target audiences through the

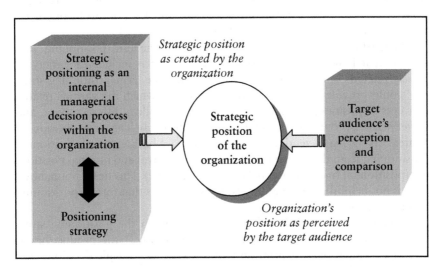

Figure 2.1 Relationship between strategic positioning, strategic position, and positioning strategy at the organizational level. Adapted: Chew (2003, Figure 1) *Reprinted with permission.*

positioning strategy, and the strategic position of the organization as perceived by its target audience (Attia 2003; Chew 2003).

Positioning Strategy

In order to investigate the factors that could influence the choice of positioning strategy in the charitable context in this study, it is necessary to operationalize positioning strategy by identifying its key components. Identifying these components will also provide a general framework in which different positioning strategies could be developed. As with the general confusion in the literature about the terms 'positioning' and 'position' highlighted earlier in this chapter, there is also little consensus among scholars as to the components that constitute a positioning strategy. Furthermore, there is a paucity of empirical research in this topic (Blankson and Kalafatis 2001), in particular, in the context of organizations other than for-profit ones.

An early delineation of the key decisions of a positioning strategy was proposed by Doyle (1983, cited in Brooksbank 1994: 10). The components of a positioning strategy comprise of three interrelated sub-components: choice of target consumer, choice of competitor, and choice of differential advantage through which the organization should compete. However, this definition was limiting because it reflected the pre-1990s notion of positioning that was mainly concerned with product positioning to satisfy consumers' needs as discussed earlier in this chapter. Moreover, it did not address organizational-level positioning for services and non-profit organizations. Nevertheless, this conceptualization of positioning strategy has been adopted by marketing scholars for commercial (for-profit) organizations (e.g., Brooksbank 1994; Kotler 1999), and for non-profit organizations (e.g., Lovelock and Weinberg 1989).

Maggard's (1986) examination into the use of the term 'positioning' suggests that it is not a single, distinct concept, but it includes a variety of closely related concepts. Maggard suggests that the term 'positioning strategy' could provide a conceptual vehicle through which the various related concepts of positioning, such as segmentation, product differentiation, and target markets, could be coordinated more effectively. The term 'positioning strategy' is also sufficiently broad to encompass both external positioning (positioning from the external audience's perspective) and internal positioning (positioning from the organization's perspective). This description, however, is not helpful in defining the strategic decisions that form a positioning strategy for this study.

Crucially, Webster (1992) distinguished between the positioning strategy decisions at the organizational level and those at the product/brand level. Positioning the organization requires making strategic decisions that necessarily influence the scope of the organization's operations and its use of organizational resources to create 'distinctive competences' (ibid.: 11). The organizational mission and its corporate values can also influence positioning strategy at the organizational level. This view is supported by Porter (1996), who emphasizes the fundamental role of senior managers by determining generic or core positioning strategies for their organization. In contrast, positioning at the product/brand level involves marketing decisions that create competitive product/brand attributes that can be promoted and communicated to the organization's various target external audiences (Webster 1992). This distinction offers an important starting point to the understanding of the overlapping influences of strategic management and marketing thoughts in developing positioning strategy at the organizational level.

A generic or core positioning strategy provides the broad framework within which the organization decides more specific positioning activities. Porter (1980) advocates 'differentiation positioning,' 'focus positioning,' and 'lower-cost leadership' as three generic or core positioning strategies for commercial (for-profit) organizations. Organizations adopting differentiation positioning establish some positively distinctive ways in which their offerings meet the needs of their target audiences and are demonstrably valued by them. Focus or niche positioning is focusing on serving a particular group of users/beneficiaries, geographic area, or providing a type of service better than other providers of similar service. Lower-cost leadership is where the organization leads the market by setting low prices.

Interestingly, there have been few efforts in the literature to identify the components of a positioning strategy in voluntary and non-profit organizations. Lovelock and Weinberg (1989) were among the earliest, albeit few, scholars to date to do so. However, their depiction of positioning in non-market contexts is very similar to that adopted by marketing scholars for commercial (for-profit) organizations and tends to perpetuate the marketing perspective on the role of positioning.

> Positioning plays a critical role in the formulation of marketing strategy [for non-profit organizations] . . . Once chosen, a positioning strategy forms the framework on which to build and coordinate the elements of the marketing mix. (Lovelock and Weinberg 1989: 88)

Positioning strategy decisions, according to Lovelock and Weinberg (ibid.), involve the choice of target audience, identification of strategic positions of competing providers, and choice of a desired position that distinguishes the organization from other providers. Their definition, however, is not very helpful for this present study because it does not provide adequate guidance on how the desired strategic position could be selected or what factors could influence the choice of positioning strategy in the charitable context. There is general consensus in the marketing literature that the key target audience for positioning by for-profit organizations is often the 'customer' who pays for the product/service (Hooley, Saunders, and Piercy 1998; Kotler 1994; Webster 1994). This simplistic notion of the 'customer' is difficult to apply to non-profit organizations. Bruce (1995, 1998) argues that charities have at least four 'customer groups': beneficiaries/users, supporters, intermediaries, and other stakeholders. Other authors (e.g., Mason 1984; Andreasen and Kotler 2003) suggest that 'customers' of non-profits include both external and internal target audiences who are involved in their resource allocation and resource attraction activities.

Hooley, Broderick, and Moller (1998) and Hooley, Saunders, and Piercy (1998) provide a clearer conceptualization of the components of a positioning strategy. Their depiction of a 'competitive' positioning strategy involves determining the choice of target audience (where the organization will compete) and the choice of 'positioning dimensions' upon which the organization develops its distinctive advantage (how the organization will compete). Their conceptualization reflects the contributions of the marketing perspective and strategic management (resource-based view) perspective in explaining how positioning strategy is developed within organizations.

Positioning dimensions are conceptually defined by Hooley, Broderick, and Moller (1998: 106) as the infinite number of different ways in which an organization might position itself as part of its positioning strategy. Positioning dimensions are unique differentiators based on major organizational strengths that are distinctive of the organization, and which can provide long-term strategic advantages (Chew 2003, 2006a). A range of positioning dimensions have been suggested in the literature for commercial (for-profit) organizations such as low or high price, superior quality, innovation, benefits, and bespoke services (Kotler 1999; Hooley, Broderick, and Moller 1998; Hooley, Saunders, and Piercy 1998) and for non-profit organizations such as specialization, ancillary/support services, relationship with influential stakeholders or parent organization, responsiveness to users needs, and service quality (Lovelock and Weinberg 1989; McLeish 1995; Kotler and Andreasen 1996; Saxton 1996). MacMillan's (1983) matrix of competitive positions emphasizes positioning at the product/service (programme) level for non-profit organizations, which are subservient to their missions and corporate strategies. Competitive position is defined by MacMillan as 'the degree to which the organization has, or is acknowledged as having, superior potential to support the programme' (65). A strong or weak competitive position is determined by assessing the degree to which the organization and/or its products/services satisfy a range of criteria compared to other competing non-profits. These include geographic location, market share, stakeholder loyalty, quality of service delivery, technical and organizational skills, fundraising ability, and cost efficiency in its operations. These criteria resemble positioning dimensions that have been prescribed for both commercial (for-profit) organizations and non-profit organizations, as discussed earlier.

However, positioning dimensions require appropriate resources and capabilities if they are to sustain the generic or core positioning strategy over time (Hooley, Broderick, and Moller 1998; Hooley, Saunders, and

Piercy 1998; Hooley et al. 2001). Different positioning dimensions will draw heavily on the availability of resources and capabilities in the organization. For instance, an emphasis on superior or high quality service would require excellent service delivery and relationship management skills, while a lower-cost positioning would require good cost control and cost-efficient supply chain/distribution capabilities (Hooley, Broderick, and Moller 1998; Hooley, Saunders, and Piercy 1998). The decision of which positioning dimensions to develop implies making long-term strategic choices by senior management (Porter 1985). Whilst the strategic position of an organization could evolve over time, the initial choice of the organization's strategic position could constrain or limit future positioning choices (Porter 1996; Zineldin and Bredenlow 2001). However, there is a lack of empirical studies to identify the components of a positioning strategy of charitable organizations. This study aims to fill this gap.

Summary

The preceding review of the existing literature on the relationship between strategic positioning, strategic position, and the components or strategic decisions that make up a positioning strategy highlights a general lack of conceptual frameworks/models to guide research and practice in organizational-level strategic positioning in the charitable context. Moreover, there is at present a lack of empirical research to examine the strategic positioning goals and activities of charities in a structured way. This study aims to fill a modest part of these gaps.

Given the general consensus in both contemporary strategy/marketing and the non-profit management literature on the significant role that positioning plays in strategy formulation today, the term 'strategic positioning' will be adopted in this study to explore the extent to which charitable organizations undertake positioning at the organizational level as opposed to positioning at the product/brand level. The term 'strategic position' will also be adopted, extending the meaning of strategic positioning in this study. Positioning strategy decisions for charitable organizations are strategic ones, which are comprised of three interrelated components: choice of the generic or core positioning strategy, their key target audiences, and the choice of positioning dimensions used to differentiate the organization from other providers and support the core positioning strategy (Chew 2006a).

PROCESS OF DEVELOPING A POSITIONING STRATEGY

Developing a positioning strategy is a deliberate, proactive, and iterative process, which necessarily involves decisions at the conceptual and strategic levels (Kalafatis, Tsogas, and Blankson 2000). Zineldin and Bredenlow (2001) go further to assert that developing a positioning strategy is an essential key activity of corporate management and that strategic positioning decisions are too important to be determined at the operational levels in the organization. The scant literature on positioning in non-profit organizations tends to describe the process of developing positioning strategy in similar ways as found in the commercial (for-profit) marketing/strategy literature. Two broad schools of thought on the process of developing positioning strategy in non-profit organizations are evident in the extant literature, namely, the marketing perspective and the strategic management perspective.

Marketing Perspective of Positioning

The first school of thought advocates the marketing perspective of positioning, which argues that positioning strategy is a key component of the strategic marketing planning process for non-profit organizations in a similar way as for commercial (for-profit) ones (e.g., Lovelock and Weinberg 1989; Kotler and Andreasen 1996). Positioning strategy in this context is the outcome of the strategic marketing planning process, which is aligned with organizational goals, internal resource capabilities, and external market opportunities (Lovelock, Vandermerwe, and Lewis 1996; Hooley, Saunders, and Piercy 1998; Hooley et al. 2001). This perspective emphasizes the leading role of marketing in the organization's strategic planning process. For instance, Hooley, Saunders, and Piercy's (1998) conceptualization of competitive positioning suggests that corporate management needs to be increasingly market-led to cope with the changing external environment. The role of marketing in this context is to: identify and communicate target audiences' needs and wants, determine the organization's strategic (competitive) position, and implement the positioning strategy of the organization (Hooley et al. 2001).

Although there has been growing empirical evidence since the 1990s that revealed voluntary and charitable organizations are increasingly practising marketing (Rees 1998), the evidence also suggests that the extent of marketing adoption in charitable organizations at the strategic level remains low, for example, Cousins (1990) on marketing planning, Sargeant (1995) on segmentation for fundraising, and Balabanis, Stables, and Phillips (1997) on market orientation in British charities, and tends to revolve around short-term tactics such as fundraising and public relations (Bruce 1998: 87). Rees (1998) compared the adoption of marketing research and practice in the US and UK non-profit sectors. Rees (ibid.) also noted a paucity of conceptual and empirical studies into the appropriateness of private sector marketing models and techniques for voluntary and non-profit organizations in the UK, which needs to be critically addressed.

> [T]he UK lags behind the US in not-for-profit marketing and it will soon be emulating the US. Marketing in the UK not-for-profit sector need not evolve in the same way as the US. . . . the problems and issues

encountered in the US are now being experienced in the UK. Examples include: calls for more empirical research; the question of ethics especially in health care marketing; modification of language and the true marketing orientation of not-for-profit sector managers. (Rees 1998: 126)

Strategic Management Perspective of Positioning

The second school of thought is anchored in contemporary strategic management literature, which argues that identifying and creating the organization's strategic position is part of the corporate strategy planning process. This perspective recognizes the leading role of strategic positioning in driving strategy formulation at the organizational level rather than at the functional levels where marketing is arguably located.

Strategic management has three main elements ... [It] includes understanding the strategic position of an organization, strategic choices for the future and turning strategy into actions. (Johnson, Scholes, and Whittington 2006: 16)

The process of reviewing the external environmental trends, internal organizational capabilities, and the expectations of stakeholders results in the identification of the organization's strategic position (Johnson, Scholes, and Whittington 2006). The aim is to find a 'strategic fit' between organizational strengths and external opportunities (ibid.: 61). The strategic management literature suggests that the importance of strategic planning, development, and implementation has long been advocated to voluntary and non-profit organizations (Shapiro 1973; Drucker 1990; Bryson 1995).

Several authors have posited that strategic management should be more, not less, important for charities (e.g., Landry et al. 1985, cited in Courtney 2002; Handy 1990; Lyons 1996; Hudson 2002). British charities, in particular, began to explore the potentialities of adopting and adapting strategic planning models and techniques since the 1980s to help them manage and develop their organizations in an increasingly challenging external operating environment (Leat 1995a; Courtney 2002). Whilst recognizing the crucial differences between charitable organizations and organizations in the public and private sectors, Hudson (2002) argues that charities, like other organizations, require a structured process for regularly revisiting their missions and strategic positions. The outcome of the external and internal strategic reviews in the charity's corporate strategy planning process is its strategic position.

Reviewing strategy is a process of monitoring changes in the external environment and developments within the organization in order to gain a deeper understanding of the organization's strategic position.

This may involve reviewing the mission, the objectives or the strategies the organization is pursuing, or any combination of all three. (Hudson 2002: 126)

The enthusiasm for adopting 'professional' management approaches coincided with the growth in the number of charities from the 1970s and into the new millennium, which was a response to the changing role of the voluntary sector, meeting needs that arose and that were not being adequately dealt with by the government/public sector agencies, and the changing relationship with public and private sector organizations (Courtney 2002; CAF 2004). Chapter 3 will review the relevant literature on the development of strategic orientation in charity management in more detail.

However, it is less clear from the extant literature/research whether the marketing perspective or strategic management perspective on developing positioning strategy is theoretically more appropriate for charitable organizations. Moreover, there is little empirical evidence to date to suggest that charities are practising strategic positioning in similar ways as prescribed for commercial (for-profit) organizations. This present study aims to fill a small part of this research gap by examining the strategic positioning activities in the charitable context using empirical evidence in British charities.

DELIBERATE PROCESS VERSUS EMERGENT PROCESS

In addition to different roles that positioning strategy plays in the process of strategic positioning, which were reviewed earlier, the extant literature also highlights the on-going academic discourse on how strategy is, or could be, developed. A review of the relevant literature on this topic helps us understand and explain the empirical findings on the process of developing positioning strategy in the later chapters of this book.

Johnson, Scholes, and Whittington (2006: 41) offer three alternative 'strategy lenses' for viewing strategy and its development in organizations: the 'design lens,' 'the experience lens,' and the 'ideas lens.' Their theoretical underpinnings are based on different organizational theories and assumptions. This subsection synthesizes the various literatures on this topic and Table 2.1 summarizes a comparison of their key features.

The design lens views strategy development as the deliberate positioning of the organization through a 'rational, analytical, structured and directive process' (Johnson, Scholes, and Whittington 2006: 42). This perspective suggests that a positioning strategy of an organization is the result of the process of strategic positioning, which attempts to match organizational strengths and resources with opportunities in the external environment (Porter 1980, 1985). Organizations are viewed as having rational structures, systems, and mechanisms by which strategies are developed and implemented (Learned et al. 1969; Andrews 1971). They have hierarchies and systems that are

Table 2.1 Alternative Theoretical Lenses on Strategy Development

	Design Lens	*Experience Lens*	*Ideas Lens*
Main arguments	• Strategy is developed through a deliberate positioning effort. • Rational, step-by step process to optimize economic performance.	• Strategy is developed through a combination of individual and collective efforts. • Incremental and experiential process.	• Strategy emerges through variety in and around the organization. • Innovative and experimental process.
Assumptions about organizations	• Mechanistic, hierarchical, and rational systems.	• Cultural based on past experiences, success and legitimacy.	• Complex and diverse organic systems.
Role of top management	• Strategic decision-makers.	• Enactors of experience.	• Coaches of content; pattern recognizers.
Underpinning theories	• Organizational economics; decision sciences.	• Institutional and culture theories; psychology.	• Complexity and evolutionary theories.
Scholars/ advocates	• Learned et al. (1969); Ansoff (1965); Andrews (1971); Porter (1980; 1985).	• Simon (1960); Lindblom (1959); Quinn (1978); Mintzberg and Waters (1985); Schein (1992).	• Behn (1988); Hamel and Prahalad (1990); Mintzberg (1978, 1995).

Adapted: Johnson, Scholes, and Whittington (2006, Exhibit 1.iv) *Reprinted with permission.*

controlled in a rational way through targets and performance appraisals. It is the responsibility of senior managers, in particular, the chief executive, to develop the organization's mission and determine its key strategic directions (Ansoff 1965). This 'design lens' perspective is useful for managers as a starting point to evaluate and plan their strategies. However, this perspective alone is insufficient to guide strategy development in more complex environments (Johnson, Scholes, and Whittington 2006).

The experience lens views strategy development as the outcome of individual and collective experiences, and their 'taken-for-granted assumptions' (Schein 1992). Positioning strategy is thus the outcome of an incremental process of traditions, past experiences, and assumptions of people within the organization (Johnson, Scholes, and Whittington 2006: 45). It is developed in an adaptive and incremental way, building on the existing strategy and changing gradually. Managers' understanding of their organization's strategic position is heavily influenced by their collective experiences. Questioning and challenging these experiences is crucial for organizations to avoid 'strategic drift,' where the positioning strategy progressively fails to support the strategic position of the organization and, consequently, performance is adversely affected (Johnson, Scholes, and Whittington 2006: 27).

Lindblom (1959), Simon (1960) and Quinn (1978) argue that the deliberate and rational decision-making process is inappropriate for addressing complex organizational problems, in particular, in increasingly uncertain operating environments. Using public sector organizations as illustrations for his argument, Lindblom (1959) suggests that managers 'muddle through' in their attempt to develop strategy in situations where the availability of resources and information is uncertain. Quinn (1978) reinforces the experience lens' perspective of positioning strategy formulation by arguing that formal strategic plans could also be part of the incremental process of strategic change. Strategic planning process occurs 'from the bottom up,' that is, at lower levels of the organization in response to top management's defined goals and assumptions (ibid.: 15).

This critique is echoed by Mintzberg and Waters (1985), who suggest that the rational systematic process ignores incremental and emergent strategies as alternative outcomes to the strategy development process. They emphasize the importance of existing competencies of the organization, such as culture and past experiences. Furthermore, Mintzberg (1978) shows that a strategy developed in a dynamic environment is more likely to emerge from patterns of past experiences. Strategy formulation in such situations is not a regular or well-sequenced process. Rather, it may occur in bursts of unplanned or reactive actions due to the dynamic nature of the organization's operating environment. However, in practice, both preplanned (deliberate) and emergent strategies are capable of being realized ones in the process of strategy development (ibid.: 946).

The main limitation of the experience lens stems from its assumption that strategy is heavily influenced by internal organizational culture, which is based on managers' experiences, past successes, and desire for legitimacy. These in-built 'taken-for-granted' ways of doing things in the organization could provide a false sense of security for the organization when significant strategic changes are needed (Johnson, Scholes, and Whittington 2006: 49). On a positive side of the balance sheet, a unique organizational culture could be a core competence for the organization (Prahalad and Hamel 1990) and, therefore, a source of competitive advantage for its positioning strategy (Amit and Schoemaker 1993).

The ideas lens suggests that strategy emerges from innovation through variety and diversity, which exists in and around the organization (Johnson, Scholes, and Whittington 2006: 49). Its main argument is that organizations are complex and open systems, and need to be in contact with and responsive to a changing external environment (Pfeffer and Salancik 1978). Eisenhardt and Sull (2001) argue it is unlikely that the organization's competitive advantage would be sustainable over the long term in a highly unstable and competitive operating environment. Consequently, its positioning strategy could emerge as patterns of successes from experimentation of different ideas and innovations. Behn's (1988) concept of 'management by groping along' reflects this perspective of strategy development. Behn's view is similar to that of Lindblom's (1959) for public non-profit sector managers. Both scholars criticized the inappropriateness of the rational and the systematic approach (the design lens) for strategy development in public services organizations. However, according to Behn (1988: 658), strategy is more likely to be developed by experimentation and learning as the organization strives towards achieving its mission or policy objectives rather than merely anticipating environmental changes. In such a scenario, having a strong organizational culture could limit creativity and provide fewer opportunities for developing ideas and innovations (Johnson, Scholes, and Whittington 2006).

The ideas lens enables a deeper appreciation of innovative strategies in organizations in order to cope in highly unstable external environments. However, tensions could arise within the organization between the need to continually adapt to the changes in the external environment and to maintain ordered patterns of behaviour. Mintzberg (1987) argues that managers are like 'craftsmen' in strategy development, where they reconcile their desire for quantum-leap changes and the need for continuity. This situation is particularly relevant to charitable organizations that are operating in increasingly challenging external environments.

Chapter 3 will review in more detail the operating environment of charities. The distinguishing features of innovativeness and flexibility of charitable organizations, which enable them to cope with changes in the environment, are increasingly being challenged by the need to sustain legitimacy to different stakeholders, in particular, those parties that they depend on for funding and other critical resources. This phenomenon is reflected in Osborne's (1996b) study, which shows that the innovative capacity of British voluntary and non-profit organizations was significantly influenced by a combination of institutional forces (among other factors) at different levels: societal level (e.g., the impact of governmental perceptions and legislations), industry/subsector level (e.g., the influence of key resource providers such as local authorities), and within the organizations (e.g., its mission, established culture, and traditions). These forces could result in 'legitimate innovation' in voluntary and non-profit organizations where they portray their organizational activities as innovative in order to satisfy the institutional expectations of various parties (Osborne 1998: 179).

Summary

This section has synthesized the relevant literature on how strategy could be developed. It has noted that no one particular theoretical perspective can adequately accommodate the process of strategy development in different environmental and organizational situations. This review, nevertheless, provides useful insights into the possible ways to explain positioning strategy formulation in non-competitive environments.

THEORETICAL PERSPECTIVES ON FORCES SHAPING A POSITIONING STRATEGY

The preceding sections in this chapter have so far highlighted that much of the theoretical underpinnings of strategic positioning described in the existing literature were derived from the context of commercial (for-profit) organizations. This section will draw upon three broad theoretical perspectives on the forces that could shape positioning strategy in order to provide the necessary conceptual background for the identification of influencing factors in the charitable context. The three theoretical perspectives are:

- competitive industry forces/market-orientation perspective (Porter 1980, 1985; Hooley, Broderick, and Moller 1998; Hooley, Saunders, and Piercy 1998: Hooley et al. 2001)
- resource-based view in the strategic management literature (Wernerfelt 1984; Grant 1991; Barney 1991; Amit and Schoemaker 1993; Peteraf 1993)
- stakeholder perspective and insights from the resource dependence theory (Pfeffer and Salancik 1978; Freeman 1984; Clarkson 1995; Mitchell, Agle, and Wood 1997)

Table 2.2 provides a summary of the alternative theoretical perspectives identified in this section and their proposed influence on positioning strategy decisions.

Competitive Industry Forces/Market-Orientation Perspective

This perspective comprises two related theoretical views that are arguably orientated towards the external environment in different ways when identifying forces that shape the organization's positioning strategy. They are: Porter's (1980) industry forces model and the market-orientation perspective.

Porter's Industry Forces and Generic Positioning Strategies

Porter's (1980) competitive industry forces model uses external environmental or industry forces to explain and predict why some business industries or sectors are inherently more 'profitable' than others. He suggests that commercial (for-profit) organizations should be proactive in order to optimize performance in the marketplace by effectively positioning themselves vis-à-vis these forces. Organizations operating in an industry or sector produce the same principal offering that are close substitutes for each other (Porter 1980: 5). Porter argues that five main forces, namely, existing competitors, demands of consumers, relative power of suppliers, threat of new entrants, and alternative offerings combine to shape the nature and level of competitive intensity in any given industry/sector. Competitive intensity in the organization's industry/sector can affect the organization's ability to carry out particular types of strategies and therefore limit managerial choices (Porter 1991). In strategic terms, the organization's main goal is to find a strategic position in its operating environment that it can best defend against or influence the external forces in its favour.

Porter (1980) argues that three alternative generic or core positioning strategies, namely, 'differentiation positioning,' 'focus positioning,' and 'lower-cost leadership,' are available to organizations to cope with the different dynamics arising from the industry forces. These generic positioning strategies have already been defined earlier in this chapter. Each generic positioning strategy requires different organizational resources and supporting structure in order to perform effectively (ibid.: 40). The theoretical assumptions of this model support the open-systems theory of organizations, which emphasizes the intimate and dynamic exchange relationships between an organization and its supporting operating environment (Katz and Kahn 1978). These relationships are not static but dynamic. Changes in the operating environment lead to demands for change in the organization, and even efforts to resist those demands result in internal organizational changes (ibid.: 31).

Although Porter's industry forces model and generic positioning strategies are derived from the context of commercial (for-profit) organizations, there have been attempts to adapt his model for the charitable context. For instance, McLeish (1995: 215) highlights the importance of identifying the charitable organization's comparative position vis-à-vis other providers of similar services in the sector that it operates. This environmental analysis, he argues, will help the charity determine its strengths and weaknesses in relation to other service providers. Certain elements of the model could be useful to charities by alerting them to the potential impact of external environmental forces on their strategic opportunities and threats. The model also underlines the proactive role of managers when making strategic choices in determining the strategic position of their charitable organization.

Other charity marketing authors suggest that differentiation positioning and focus positioning are more appropriate for charities (e.g., Wray 1994; Bruce 1998). Additionally, Saxton (1996) conceptualized four alternative generic positioning strategies for charities, which are arguable adaptations of Porter's (1980) generic strategies. They are: (a) externally driven, (b) niche (focus) by issue/emotional cause or by geography, (c) differentiation by customer group, by product, or by belief, and (d) awareness. However, there is currently a lack of empirical research to support these propositions.

Table 2.2 Summary of Theoretical Perspectives on Forces Influencing a Positioning Strategy

Theoretical Perspectives	Key Authors	Orientation and Key Focus	Level of Analysis	Potential Influence on Positioning Strategy Decisions
Industry competitive forces shape organizational competitiveness	Porter (1980, 1985)	External orientation—Focus is on industry (sectoral) forces that collectively determine the degree of competitive intensity. Industry forces shape organization's generic positioning strategy and competitive advantage.	Organization level with locus of control in industry.	What generic/core positioning strategy? Which target audience?
Market orientation and competitive positioning	Kohli and Jaworski (1990); Narver & Slate (1990); Hooley et al. (1998a,1998b)	External orientation—Focus is on identifying and satisfying external and customer needs/wants; also focus on market intelligence gathering dissemination in particular on competitors' strategies. Creation of competitive position is a key outcome of the strategic marketing planning process, which links the various components of market analysis, competitor analysis and internal organizational analysis.	Organizational level	What generic/core positioning strategy? Which target audience? What positioning dimensions relative to competitors to be used?

Resource-based view	Penrose (1959); Wernerfelt (1984); Hansen & Wernerfelt (1989); Barney (1991); Grant (1991); Amit & Schoemaker (1993)	Internal orientation—Organizations possess inimitable resources that can be sources of competitive advantage, which form the bases for building and defending strategic positions. Resource-based view focuses on managerial identified sources of organizational assets and capabilities as key sustainable sources of competitive advantage relative to competitors.	Organizational level	What positioning dimensions to use to support the generic/core positioning strategy and that can be sustained by distinctive competences.
Stakeholder theory and resource dependence theory	Freeman (1984); Pfeffer & Salancik (1978); Clarkson (1995); Mitchell, Agle, and Wood (1997)	External orientation and internal orientation—Stakeholder theory focuses on satisfying the interests of external and internal stakeholders in order to enjoy successful performance; Resource dependence theory focuses on influential external stakeholders who control critical resources that are needed for the organization's survival and who have the power to control its strategic decisions and behaviour.	Organization level with managers as the centre of relationships with external and internal stakeholders.	What generic/core positioning strategy? What positioning dimensions should be used that satisfy the interests and gain the support of various stakeholders.

Source: Chew (2003, Table 1) *Reprinted with permission.*

Market Orientation and Competitive Positioning

Market orientation has evolved in the marketing literature since the 1990s to reflect the philosophy and behaviour of organizations that have emphasized identification and satisfaction of the 'customer's' needs/wants (Narver and Slater 1990; Kohli and Jaworski 1990). The concept consists of three behavioural components, as identified for commercial (for-profit) organizations: customer orientation, competitor orientation, and interfunctional coordination (Kohli and Jaworski 1990: 6). Accordingly, market orientation emphasizes specific marketing-related activities in the organization, which facilitate the operationalization of the marketing concept.

The marketing perspective of developing a positioning strategy has already been reviewed earlier in this chapter. It views the creation of a strategic (competitive) position as the outcome of the strategic marketing process. Hooley, Saunders, and Piercy (1998: 103) argue that competitive positioning is intimately related to the concept of market orientation because it defines how the organization will compete by identifying its target audiences and the competitive advantage that will be pursued in serving them. However, this competitive advantage must be built on the organization's distinctive resources and capabilities (Hamel and Prahalad 1994; Webster 1994). This latter point is shared by the resource-based view of creating distinctive advantage in strategy formulation.

Since the 1990s, there have been a number of empirical studies on the effects of market orientation and organizational performance in the UK context (e.g., Diamantopoulos and Hart 1993; Greenley 1995; Doyle and Wong 1998; Harris 2001). However, there is a paucity of empirical research into the direct link between market orientation and strategic positioning at the organizational level for both commercial (for-profit) and non-profit organizations. Notable exceptions include Hult and Ketchen's (2001) study into the link between market orientation as an organizational capability, which revealed a positive effect on this relationship on the performance of large US multinational corporations, and Langerak's (2003) study into the effects of market orientation on the choice of generic positioning strategies adopted by manufacturing firms in the Netherlands. Although these studies were based on non-UK organizational contexts, they nevertheless highlight the important influence of organizational resources deployed to create specific positioning dimensions to differentiate the organization from other providers of similar service.

From the mid-1990s, market-orientation studies have emerged in voluntary and charitable contexts in an attempt to conceptualize and operationalize market orientation in the non-market context (e.g., Balabanis, Stables, and Phillips 1997; Liao, Foreman, and Sargeant 2001; Vazquez, Alvarez, and Santos 2002). However, there remains an overall lack of empirical research on the relationship between market orientation and strategic positioning in the charitable context.

Resource-Based View and Positional Advantage

The resource-based perspective provides an alternative understanding of how positional advantage could be created within organizations. Since the introduction of the term 'resource-based view' by Wernerfelt (1984), several studies have further developed the resource-based view's contribution in strategy development (e.g., Barney 1991; Grant 1991; Peteraf 1993; Amit and Schoemaker 1993).

The resource-based perspective of positional advantage has been developed in earlier works of economists, such as Penrose (1959), who recognized the significance of a commercial (for-profit) organization's heterogeneous resources on its performance. It emerged in the strategic management literature during the 1980s to counter the Porterian view that external industry forces play a determining role in shaping competition and the organization's positioning strategy. Hansen and Wernerfelt's (1989) empirical work highlighted the influence of organizational factors in strategy formulation, in particular, the role of internal resources and capabilities as building blocks of strategy, rather than the role of external industry factors. The resource-based view facilitates an understanding of the resources and capabilities that underpin the creation of positioning dimensions in alternative positioning strategies that may be considered by the organization (Fahy and Smithee 1999). However, it also recognizes the presence of industry factors, and therefore represents a bridge between internal organizational-based and external environmental-based perspectives in explaining competitive advantage in strategic positioning (Collis and Montgomery 1995).

Various types of advantage-generating resources have been suggested in the strategic management literature, such as resources that provide value to consumers (Barney 1991; Collis and Montgomery 1995), those that have the ability to resist duplication by competitors (Dierickx and Cool 1989; Reed and DeFillippi 1990), and those that are sustainable over time (Grant 1991). Several typologies of advantage-generating resources and their definitions have also been proposed in the literature, which is selectively highlighted in this subsection (see Fahy 2000 for a fuller discussion). For instance, Grant (1991: 118) suggests that the organization's resources are distinct from its capabilities. The former consists of tangible sources of assets such as capital equipment, patents, finance, and brand name, while the latter are intangible sources of advantage such as managerial skills, leadership, teamwork, coordination, culture, or organizational routines. Other scholars, such as Barney (1991: 101), have identified three categories of resources: physical capital (e.g., equipment, building, geographic location, access to materials), human capital (e.g., managers' and staff's skills, experience, training, judgement, and relationships), and organizational capital (e.g., formal and informal planning, controlling and coordinating systems). Hooley, Saunders, and Piercy (1998) suggest that organizational resources comprise of assets and capabilities. They (ibid.) define organizational assets as the resource endowments that the organization has accumulated over time and can be deployed to create competitive advantage (ibid.: 99). Organizational assets comprise of both tangible and intangible resources. Capabilities, on the other hand, are the skills and competencies of individuals and groups in the organization that organize, manage, coordinate, and undertake specific sets of activities within and outside the organization (Hooley, Saunders, and Piercy 1998: 101). Scholars have suggested that intangible resources such as the organization's reputation and capabilities of managers are more important sources of generating competitive advantage than tangible resources (e.g., Amit and Schoemaker 1993; Hall 1992, 1993; Fahy 2000).

Stakeholder Perspective and Influence of Resource Dependency

Several authors have highlighted that one of the distinguishing features in the management of voluntary and charitable organizations compared to commercial (for-profit) organizations is the multiplicity in the number of stakeholders, and the greater complexity in their relationships with the non-profit organization (e.g., Lovelock and Weinberg 1989; Bryson 1995; Kotler and Andreasen 1996; Bruce 1998; Maple 2003). Another distinguishing feature is the greater dependency of charities on external stakeholders and the impact of resource dependency on their strategic choices (Saxon-Harrold 1990). It is therefore relevant for this study to consider the stakeholder perspective and the influence of resource dependency on the positioning strategy of charitable organizations.

Understanding Stakeholder Influence

The stakeholder theory advocated by Freeman (1984) provides an alternative perspective in understanding why and how organizations behave in ways that cannot be directly attributed to economic market forces (Key 1999). It also offers an understanding of other possible sources of influence in the organization's external and internal environments on its strategic choices and actions. Stakeholder theory depicts the organization to be at the controlling centre of the system. The challenge for managers is to balance the needs/wants of the organization and those of each stakeholder group in its strategic decision-making and selection (Miller and Lewis 1991). Freeman and Reed (1983: 91) and Freeman (1984: 46) provide both broad and narrow definitions of a stakeholder. The broad definition suggests a stakeholder as 'any group or individual who can affect or is affected by the achievement of an organization's objective.' Their narrow definition identifies stakeholders as 'those groups who are vital to the survival and success of the corporation.'

Clarkson (1995) argues that the organization is essentially a coalition of primary stakeholders whose continued participation is critical to its success. He distinguishes between primary stakeholders and secondary stakeholders.

Primary stakeholders are individuals or groups whose continuing participation is essential for the organization to survive as a going concern. A high level of interdependence is assumed to exist between the organization and its primary stakeholders. The role of managers is to satisfy the needs and demands of each primary stakeholder to ensure its survival and continued success. Secondary stakeholders are those who can influence or affect, or are influenced and affected by the organization's actions, but they are not directly involved in transactions with the organization, nor are they essential for its survival (Clarkson 1995: 107). Importantly, Donaldson and Preston (1995) remind us that it is important not to define stakeholders too broadly as this unnecessarily includes actors in the organization's environment, such as competitors and the media, that may have some impact on its activities but stand to gain no particular benefit from the organization's successful operations (ibid.: 86).

In the charitable context the satisfaction of key external stakeholders is crucial to ensuring organizational success, while the support and commitment of key internal stakeholders are vital for the successful strategic planning in non-profit organizations (Nutt and Backoff 1992; Schein 1992; Bryson 1995). For instance, the support and commitment of key internal stakeholders (e.g., employees, volunteers, unions) are important for strategic positioning to succeed in charities (Bruce 1998; McLeish 1995). Additionally, external parties (e.g., government funders, major corporate donors, suppliers, banks, and other non-profit organizations) that provide essential resources to the charitable organization could complement or collaborate in the charitable organizations' projects, and hence influence the outcome of these projects. However, according to the resource-based view, satisfying all the key stakeholders of an organization is particularly difficult—the task would depend on the type of resources that the organization is dependent on and the availability of these resources (Amit and Schoemaker 1993; Barney 1991; Grant 1991; Mahoney and Pandian 1992). Consequently, this could result in the rationing of resources directed to the needs/wants of particular stakeholder groups (Greenley and Foxall 1998).

Resource Dependence Theory

In terms of explaining stakeholders' influence on positioning strategy decisions, the resource dependence theory shares the view of the stakeholder theory that an organization is a coalition of varying interests, often having incompatible preferences and goals (Pfeffer and Salancik 1978). Power is one of the defining attributes of an influential stakeholder (Mitchell, Agle, and Wood 1997), with critical resources that an organization depends on for its sources of competitive advantage. This phenomenon can be explained further with the resource dependence theory, particularly when it is applied in the context of voluntary and charitable organizations and where there is often a greater number of stakeholders and complexity in relationships with them (Lovelock and Weinberg 1989; Bryson 1995; Kotler and Andreasen 1996; Bruce 1998; Maple 2003).

The resource dependence theory assumes that organizations are open-systems that are embedded in an environment comprised of other organizations upon which they are dependent for survival (Pfeffer and Salancik 1978). The key to organizations' survival is their ability to acquire and maintain resources from the external environment. Organizations survive, in part, through a learned ability to cope with environmental contingencies and negotiating exchanges to ensure needed resources are continued.

According to Pfeffer and Salancik (1978), resource dependence exists when one actor supplies another with a resource that is scarce (suppliers are few in number), less mobile, and is considered critical for the survival of the recipient. Pfeffer and Salancik define control as 'the ability to initiate or terminate actions at one's discretion' (1978: 259), and dependence as 'the product of the importance of a given input or output to the organization and the extent to which it is controlled by a relatively few number of organizations' (1978: 51). Therefore, certain external primary stakeholders may have the power to control the resources needed by the organization and exert influence on the organization's strategies. Moreover, Greenley and Foxall (1998) argue that a dominant external stakeholder may exert an excessive amount of power and influence on the organization's strategic autonomy. The implication is that the interest and demands of this dominant stakeholder take precedence over those of other stakeholders. This would affect the organization's performance objectives, which could be constrained or determined by the need to prioritize the dominant stakeholder's interest.

INTEGRATING THEORETICAL PERSPECTIVES ON FORCES INFLUENCING POSITIONING STRATEGY

There remains an on-going debate as to whether organizational resources (assets and capabilities) or market competitiveness contributes in shaping an organization's strategies, actions, and outcomes. Traditional strategy research and organization theory suggest that organizations can adapt their strategies and capabilities as their external environments change (Barnard 1938; Ansoff 1965; Andrews 1971; Hofer and Schendel 1978; Miles and Snow 1978; Porter 1980; Child 1972). However, the contemporary view among scholars is that both industry and organizational forces play important roles in determining competitive advantage of positioning strategy (Hooley, Broderick, and Moller 1998; Hooley, Saunders, and Piercy 1998; Fahy 2000). Henderson and Mitchell (1997) argue that there is reciprocal interaction at multiple levels of analysis between the external (industry) environment and internal organizational resources that shape strategy formulation and performance. At the same time, interaction between strategy and performance could influence both organizational capabilities and the competitive environment.

In terms of strategic positioning, Hooley, Broderick, and Moller (1998) and Hooley, Saunders, and Piercy (1998) suggest that both the industry/marketing (external-orientation) perspective and the resource-based view (internal-orientation) perspective are necessary for effective development and implementation of a positioning strategy. The marketing-orientation perspective argues that if strategy becomes too embedded in internal resources alone it runs the risk of ignoring the demands of changing turbulent markets and external environments. On the other hand, the resource-based view argues that positioning strategies would be more effective if they exploited the organization's resource endowments and capabilities. In addition, the earlier review in this section suggests that the stakeholder and resource dependence perspective also provide valuable insights into the influential roles of primary internal and external stakeholders on the organization's strategic choices and actions.

INITIAL ORGANIZING CONCEPTUAL FRAMEWORK OF INFLUENCING FACTORS

The review of the theoretical perspectives of forces influencing positioning strategy in the previous section provides the basis for proposing an initial multidimensional conceptual framework for this study. This section introduces and explains this conceptual framework for charitable organizations. Three broad groups of influences covering various factors are proposed: external environmental, internal organizational, and stakeholder influences (Chew 2006b). Figure 2.2 depicts the initial organizing conceptual framework.

External Environmental Influences

These comprise of factors external to the organization outside the management's direct control, such as industry competitive intensity (Porter 1980, 1985), economic conditions, technological changes, social-demographic changes, legal conditions, and the political environment (Learned et al. 1969; Andrews 1980; Mintzberg 1995). Critical trends in the external operating environment of charitable organizations could provide opportunities or impede their strategic directions and positioning. These include: social-demographic trends (e.g., changing age structure, changes in the demographics of service users and funders, and how their needs will change), legal-political changes (e.g., critical policy decisions and actions towards welfare reform, investment in education, and changes to charity laws), changes in the economic environment (recessionary or growth trends),

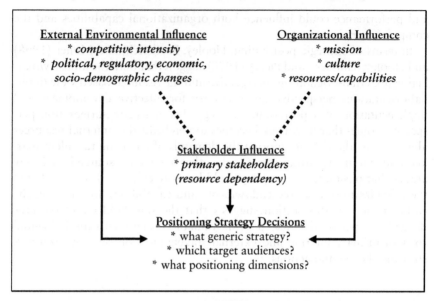

External Environmental Influence
* *competitive intensity*
* *political, regulatory, economic,*
  socio-demographic changes

Organizational Influence
* *mission*
* *culture*
* *resources/capabilities*

Stakeholder Influence
* *primary stakeholders*
  (resource dependency)

Positioning Strategy Decisions
* what generic strategy?
* which target audiences?
* what positioning dimensions?

Figure 2.2 Initial organizing framework for examining the key factors influencing a positioning strategy in charitable organizations. Source: Chew (2006b, Figure 1) *Reprinted with permission.*

and technological changes that make cost-effective electronic/internet capabilities available (Bruce 1998; Hudson 2002).

Competition for funding and other organizational resources from other charities, voluntary, private and public sector organizations have been suggested as a growing influence on strategic choices of charities (Saxon-Harrold 1990; Bruce 1998; CAF 2004). Kendall and Knapp (1996) argue that voluntary and non-profit organizations that delivery certain types of public services (e.g., social care, health care, housing) face increasing competition from commercial (for-profit) organizations and government agencies in the emerging 'quasi-markets' for the delivery of public services in British public policy. Charitable organizations have to compete for government funding and public service contracts. At the same time, public sector contracts/projects often have tougher budgetary and auditing controls to which charities would be required to adhere.

Saxon-Harrold's (1990) study on the organizational strategic choices of British voluntary and charitable organizations concluded that their strategies were less likely to be shaped by internal organizational forces than from external environmental forces, such as the degree of competition for resources and also the degree to which they are dependent on external parties, such as government, for funding. Competitive intensity was found to be high in the charitable subsectors where high degrees of similarity in goals and tasks existed between charities. Instances where a number of charities often target the same cause, service users/beneficiaries, or type of service offered, such as children services, elderly care, and general community services within the same geographical area (CAF 2004), remain evident in many charity subsectors today.

Internal Organizational Influences

These comprise of resources internal to the organization that managers have access to and can deploy to create competitive advantage through a positioning strategy. Three possible influencing factors are suggested: organizational mission, culture, and organizational resources.

Mission is defined as the fundamental purpose of a non-profit organization (Hudson 2002). It describes the rationale for its existence and what it does (ibid.: 102). In strategic management perspective mission helps to direct organizational efforts and resources to achieve its ideal view of the world: its vision. Hudson (2002) further argues that charities have a much stronger sense of mission than their counterparts in the private and public sectors. A charity's mission or purpose is one of the major characteristics that makes managing of the organization challenging because it has a powerful impact on strategic approaches and management choices (Leat 1995a). The legal status of a charity could further constrain it from changing its mission without causing serious damage to its purpose for existence.

In terms of strategic positioning, Frumkin and Kim (2001) suggest charities should position themselves around their mission. They argue that the essence of strategic positioning for voluntary and non-profit organizations is to find a strategic position that is difficult to imitate over the long term. Zineldin and Bredenlow (2001) show that vision, mission, and the strategic position of a service-orientated organization are interrelated. The vision and mission guide the organization's corporate planning and implementation of its strategic positioning activities. Mission could both facilitate and constrain positioning strategy choices in the charitable context.

Culture is part of the 'strategic orientation' of the organization (Hooley et al. 2001). Different strategic orientations affect strategy choice and strategy implementation differently (Greenley and Foxall 1997, 1998). Culture is a set of shared assumptions and understandings about organizational functioning (Deshpande and Webster 1989). Moreover, the culture of an organization sets the internal context within which strategic decisions are made (Webster 1994). Schein (1992) defines corporate culture as a set of basic assumptions, which are invented, discovered, or developed by a given group, while learning to cope with its problems of external adaptation and internal integration.

Two broad perspectives of culture have been suggested in the contemporary marketing/strategy literature. One view is that culture is something the organization has. The marketing perspective of positioning prescribes to this view. It advocates market orientation as a culture that should be cultivated by the organization (Deshpande and Webster 1989; Narver and Slater 1990; Kohli and Jaworski 1990; Webster 1992). The other view is advocated by the resource-based view within the strategic management literature. Under this perspective culture *is* the organization and therefore is difficult to imitate (Knights and Willmott 1987; Ogbonna 1993; Legge 1994). Amit and Schoemaker (1993) classify culture as a 'strategic asset' because it is a desirable source of competitive advantage for the organization due to the creation of causal ambiguity. Due to the intangible nature of organizational culture (e.g., its history, managers' ability to lead and manage change, team working ability, and innovative ability), it is often difficult to duplicate thereby ensuring a high degree of inimitability by competitors or other organizations providing similar services (Barney 1991).

Organizational Resources

It was established earlier in this chapter that organizational resources are important bases for developing the positioning dimensions of a positioning strategy that could differentiate the organization from other providers. This study uses the term 'resources' to include tangible and intangible assets and capabilities of a charitable organization (Hall 1992, 1993). Assets are the resource endowment that the charity has acquired or built over time and can be deployed to its positioning dimensions (Hooley, Broderick, and Moller 1998; Hooley et al. 2001). These include the charity's reputation, ownership of particular distribution or production capacity, and relationships with various stakeholders. On the other hand, capabilities are defined as those resources that facilitate the effective deployment of assets to establish the charity's distinctive positioning (Hooley, Broderick, and Moller 1998; Fahy 2000). These include specialized service expertise, knowledge of local community needs, application experience, and skills to utilize relevant technologies.

Marketing scholars have suggested that marketing capabilities are essential for creating competitive advantage in a positioning strategy. Day (1994), in particular, suggests 'outside-in,' 'inside-out,' and 'spanning' capabilities. First, outside-in capabilities are those skills and competencies, such as market research and customer relationship management. Networking capabilities that help the organization to operate more effectively in the external environment are also cited as outside-in capabilities (Cravens and Piercy 1994). Second, inside-out capabilities are the internal capabilities of the organization that have little value until "activated by forces in the external environment, such as market requirements, competitive challenges, and external opportunities" (Day 1994: 41). Finally, spanning capabilities are those skills and competencies that serve to integrate inside-out and outside-in capabilities, such as service delivery and new product/service development, where both understanding of the market requirements and internal competencies to fulfil them are required.

However, as highlighted earlier, there is general consensus among scholars that both external environmental factors and internal organizational resources and capabilities play a part in shaping strategy, positional advantage, and performance in organizations. Therefore, it is essential that charitable organizations acquire, develop, and nurture a portfolio of resources and capabilities rather than a narrow range in order to sustain their positioning strategy.

Stakeholder Influence

Stakeholder influence on positioning strategy is conceptualized as coming from primary (external and internal) stakeholders and to a lesser extent from secondary stakeholders. Various definitions of the term 'stakeholder' have been discussed earlier in this chapter. The key definitions are revisited in this subsection.

Primary Stakeholders

The initial conceptual framework proposes a more specific identification of primary stakeholders who could influence the positioning decisions of a charitable organization. This study adopts the definition of influential stakeholders offered by Clarkson (1995) and Mitchell, Agle, and Wood (1997) as 'those without whose continuing participation the charity cannot survive, and those who possess the power and legitimacy to influence organizational behaviour by virtue of their resource dependent relationships with the charitable organization.'

It is argued here that the particular context in which British charities operate would require them to incorporate a greater number of stakeholders' interests/needs and to manage a greater complexity of influences on their strategy development and decision-making process than in commercial (for-profit) organizations. Blois (1993) argues that all organizations have to deal with multiple constituencies, and rejects the claim of some authors that multiple stakeholders are the distinguishing feature of charitable organizations. In contrast, Leat (1995a) supports the notion that the number and type of stakeholders of charitable organizations are greater and more varied compared with those in commercial (for-profit) organizations. Moreover, particular groups of external stakeholders, such as government as a funder and regulator, have become increasingly influential as key external stakeholders of voluntary and charitable organizations.

British charitable organizations face additional regulatory influences from the Charity Commission and charity laws, which generally constrain their actions in certain ways that do not apply to commercial (for-profit) organizations. Furthermore, donors' and the general public's expectations may be higher for charities with high public profiles, in particular, when they campaign and fundraise for certain types of charitable causes (Leat 1995b).

Bruce (1998) suggests that the internal primary stakeholders of charities include employees and the board of trustees/management committee members. Other authors have suggested that not all stakeholders are equally active or important to different voluntary and non-profit organizations (e.g., Kotler and Andreasen 1996). Their influence can change in the level of salience from time to time, depending on situational factors (Mitchell, Agle, and Wood 1997).

Influential External Stakeholders and Resource Dependency

The resource dependence theory views organizations as inadequately self-sufficient in their resource needs and requiring resources from the external environment (Pfeffer and Salancik 1978). This situation can be appropriately applied to the voluntary and non-profit sector where many charities are dependent on external parties for resources for their survival, in particular, financial support from philanthropic donors and/or government (central and local) agencies (Saxon-Harrold 1990). Other studies on funding relationship and the impact of this on strategy suggest that the strategic autonomy of British charities tend to erode when they rely substantially on one or a few dominant funders (e.g., Leat, Smolka, and Unell 1981; Wortman 1982).

Based on the resource dependence theory it is further suggested here that certain primary external stakeholders in the charitable organization's operating environment on whom it relies for funding and other resources would have the power to directly influence its strategic decisions and actions. These stakeholders include local government agencies/authorities that provide financial resources (e.g., grants and public service contracts) and volunteers who serve as their trustees or fundraisers, and who deliver essential services to their beneficiaries.

CONCLUSIONS

This chapter has conducted a systematic review of strategic positioning and has synthesized the various literatures on it. A multidimensional approach was adopted in undertaking this review, which drew upon insights from various theories in strategy development, marketing, and resource-based views within the strategic management literature, stakeholder theory, and the resource dependence literature. Importantly, four points have surfaced from this review.

First, there is little existing literature and lack of empirical research on strategic positioning at the organizational level in voluntary and charitable organizations. Although, there has been general agreement among charity researchers that the type of positioning strategies for charities needs adapting for those advocated for commercial (for-profit) organizations, there remains a lack of conceptual and theoretical models to guide positioning research and management practice in the charitable context.

Second, much of the existing non-profit strategy/marketing literature tends to describe the concept of positioning, which espouses the role of strategic positioning, the process of developing a positioning strategy, and the benefits of positioning, for voluntary and charitable organizations in similar ways to those advocated in contemporary strategy/marketing literature for commercial (for-profit) organizations. There is currently a lack of empirical work determining whether these assertions are appropriate for charitable organizations where their positioning goal(s) or strategic intent may be dissimilar to those of commercial (for-profit) organizations.

Third, the existing contemporary literature on positioning suffers from a lack of conceptual clarity about the definition of strategic positioning at various organizational levels and its relationship with strategic position and positioning strategy in the organization. This chapter has clarified these relationships. It has also established the definitions of strategic positioning, strategic position, and the three key components of a positioning strategy to be adopted for this study.

Finally, multiple theoretical lenses are useful in providing alternative perspectives on the forces influencing positioning strategy. They highlight a general lack of adequate conceptual frameworks that can accommodate non-market and non-profit contexts. The alternative theoretical perspectives offer a starting point to organize an initial conceptual framework on influencing factors that guide this study. It depicts a combination of external environmental, internal organizational, and stakeholder influences on positioning strategy in the charitable context.

These points signal significant gaps in the existing literature for positioning theory development and empirical research in the charitable context. This present study aims to fill a small part of these gaps. In order to appreciate the research context in which the empirical stage of this study is embedded more fully, the next chapter will review the operating environment of charitable organizations.

3 Conceptualizing Charitable Sector and Charitable Activities

This chapter will provide an expanded review of the operating environment of charitable organizations, which was introduced in Chapter 1. Specifically it focuses upon the environment of charities in the UK. This review is necessary to better understand the contextual background in which the empirical stages of this study are embedded. It will be particularly useful to readers who may be less familiar with the UK voluntary and charitable context. The chapter begins with an overview of the charitable sector by briefly tracing its development within the wider voluntary and non-profit sector over six historical phases until the mid-1990s. This is followed by a conceptualization of the charitable sector using alternative criteria. Next, an overview of the changes in the public policy context and external operating environment in which charities have operated since New Labour came into government in 1997 is discussed. The chapter will then explore the emergence of strategic management and marketing approaches in the charitable sector from the early 1990s. Differences between the charitable and commercial (for-profit) organizational contexts are examined as part of this exploration. Four key drivers that have influenced the adoption of explicit competitive strategies and have elevated the importance of strategic positioning in charities are suggested. Overall, this chapter intends to provide a deeper appreciation of the research context upon which this study is based.

CONCEPTUALIZING THE CHARITABLE SECTOR AND CHARITABLE ACTIVITIES

This section provides further understanding of the charitable context within the wider sector of voluntary and non-profit organizations in the UK, and the various attempts in the literature to conceptualize the charitable sector and its activities. It is acknowledged in the extant literature that there remains no single agreed upon definition of the voluntary sector (Lane, Passey, and Saxon-Harrold 1994; Kendall and Knapp 1995, 1996; Courtney 2002), the types of organizations that should constitute the charity sector (e.g., registered charities, general charities, non-registered charities, non-registered voluntary action or community groups, quangos, and large government institutions) or how charities should be classified (Mintel 2001; NCVO 1996).

It is further observed that the literature on the voluntary and non-profit sector in the UK often relates to charitable organizations and charitable activities. This is understandable because the growth of the voluntary sector in the UK has been very much intertwined with the development of charitable giving and philanthropy in British history. Kendall and Knapp (1996) and Courtney (2002) provide detailed accounts of these historical developments, which this section draws on. Hudson (2003) compares the historical developments in the UK and US voluntary and charitable sectors and suggests that each country has adopted policies from the other over the past two decades. Six phases have been identified in the development of the provision of voluntary aid in Britain since 1600 until the mid-1990s. Each of these phases is briefly outlined in the following.

Origins (Medieval and Tudor Periods)

The Roman Catholic Church played a central position in the delivery of formal philanthropy during this period. Dissatisfaction with the Church by the fifteenth century spurred more secular forms of charitable giving. Organized mutual aid by various trades, such as guilds and livery companies, marked the beginning of the organized voluntary sector. The 1601 Statute on Charitable Uses, which defined what was and what was not charitable, was established during this period (Kendall and Knapp 1996).

Pre-Industrial Era (1660s to 1800)

This period was characterized by a more tolerant climate of charitable giving. Rodgers (1949: 8) described this era as the "golden age of philanthropy." The Tudor system of charity administration declined under the pressures of the Civil War. Several reforms to the national system of Poor Law administration were passed during the latter part of the eighteenth century, effectively removing previously harsh acts on repression of the poor. Many church schools for the poor that were often run by the Church of England were established and charitable hospitals were founded (Key Note 1997). Mutual aid increased with the formation of friendly societies and with other associates that acted as intermediaries between donors and beneficiaries.

Industrial Era (1800 to 1850)

During this period, there was a tightening up of the Poor Law (Poor Law Amendment Act) in 1834 and almsgiving to deter the "able-bodied poor" from receiving relief and to encourage commitment to the work ethic (Hill 1970, quoted in Kendall and Knapp 1996: 37). A range of evangelical and moral societies were developed, which reflected a more charitable ethos of the middle-class women. At the same time, a revolution among the working-class organizations, such as friendly societies and trade clubs, became more threatening to the ruling class.

Later Half of the Nineteenth Century

Davis Smith (1995) defines this phase as the heyday of British philanthropy because of the economic benefits to the population during the Industrial Revolution and the expansion of the British Empire. Proliferation of charitable activity coupled with an increase in charitable giving by the middle-class households characterized this period of growth in the charitable sector. This development was the first indication that charitable activities/causes were becoming mass-duplicated, and thus began to create problems of identity and differentiation for charities performing essentially similar services (Courtney 2002). The growing number of charities established during the Victorian period necessitated further reforms of the charity law. The 1853 Charitable Trusts Act was enacted, which created the Charity Commission with limited powers to monitor charitable activities.

1940s to 1970s (The Welfare State)

Relief of poverty and promotion of welfare were largely provided by charities that had little or no state regulation until the early 1940s. The welfare state and the provision of services by government and public bodies who provided support for those who were in need emerged during the post-war upheavals after the First and Second World Wars. The National Council of Social Services, now known as the NCVO, was set up in 1919 as a national coordinating body of charities and other voluntary and non-profit organizations.

Whilst charitable funds continued to grow during this period, serious concerns were raised about the limitations of charities in their attempts to deliver comprehensive services, such as health and education (Courtney 2002). Perceived weaknesses of charities, such as 'amateurism,' 'paternalism,' and 'insufficiency,' have been scrutinized (Salamon 1987), in particular, in the management of hospitals and the quality of medical care provided to armed force recruits at that time. Several recommendations by Beveridge (1948) in relation to creating a welfare state were implemented by the Labour Government of 1945–1951. The charitable sector's role in education and social services had been preserved but its health-care and income maintenance roles were removed through direct government provision of the NHS and National Insurance in 1946. The expanding role for government in provision of public services prompted a review of the legal environment for charities, which resulted in the 1960 Charities Act. This refined the legal powers of the Charity Commission in regulating charities and charged it with maintaining a central register of charities in the UK.

1970s to Mid-1990s (Blurring of Sectors in Public Service Delivery)

Significant shifts in the relationship between the charitable/wider voluntary sector and the public and private sectors in Britain characterized this period. The Wolfenden Committee report (1978) reinforced the welfare state tradition in providing public services, and at the same time legitimized the role of the voluntary and charitable sector as a partner that "complements, supplements, extends and influences the statutory system" in public service delivery (ibid.: 26, quoted in Kendall and Knapp 1996: 137). At the same time, the primacy of commercial (for-profit) organizations was emphasized. The Conservative Governments of 1979–1996 thus marked a sharp change in attitude towards government itself and the other major participants in public policy (Kendall and Knapp 1996). The presumption was that public services would be more efficiently delivered by the private sector or other sectors other than government. This ideology resulted in the transfer of many public services, such as health and social services, formerly performed by government to the private sector organizations, charities, and voluntary and non-profit organizations on a contractual basis, particularly from the beginning of the 1990s (Alcock 2003).

Since the 1990s, the expansion of the voluntary sector had gathered momentum due to the disillusionment of people with the public sector and the divestment of a range of public services by central government and local authorities to the voluntary and private sectors. Recognizing the growing importance of charities within the wider voluntary sector, NCVO set up a Charities Department in 1924 to encourage more efficient voluntary giving to charities. This was renamed the Charities Aid Foundation (CAF), which was given independent status as a registered charity in its own right in 1974. The 1960 Charities Act was repealed and replaced by the Charities Acts of 1992 and 1993, which provided the legal framework for charities operating in the wider voluntary sector in Britain to this date (Home Office 2006).

The significance of charities in the wider voluntary sector remains evident today. For instance, the NCVO's yearly *Almanac*, which reports on the status of the voluntary sector in the UK, focuses on the affairs of 'general charities' as the main composition of voluntary and non-profit organizations. General charities are defined by NCVO as registered charities but exclude those organizations that are considered part of the government apparatus, financial institutions considered to be part of the corporate sector, and organizations that deliver only private benefit (NCVO 2002b).

An estimated 153,000 general charities were registered in the UK as of 2002 (NCVO 2004a). This figure had increased to 165,000 in June 2006 (Charity Commission 2006). The five hundred largest charities attracted over 45 per cent of total annual income of all registered charities, which amounted to £35 billion in 2004 (Charity Commission 2004).

Salamon and Anheier (1992a: 142) argue that general charities are at the "centre of gravity" of the UK voluntary sector, which are formally registered as charities with the Charity Commission and given legal status and protection. The Charity Commission for England and Wales is established by law as the regulator of charitable status and registrar of charities in England and Wales. Scotland and Northern Ireland do not have the equivalent of the Charity Commission as in England and Wales. However, the Charities Register in Scotland and the Northern Ireland Council for Voluntary Action maintain a database of registered charities in Scotland and Northern Ireland respectively. Their definitions of registered charities are comparable to those used by the Charity Commission of England and Wales (NCVO 2002b).

Just as there have been various attempts to define the type of organizations that make up the essentially eclectic voluntary sector (Lane, Passey, and Saxon-Harrold 1994; Kendal and Knapp 1996; Courtney 2002), attempts to define the charitable sector are seen as equally problematic. This section reviews three alternative approaches to conceptualizing 'charity' and 'charitable purpose' in the UK context.

Legal Definition

English case law provides a legal framework within which the concepts of 'charity' or 'charitable' are interpreted. Section 96[1] of the Charities Act 1993 defines a 'charity' as:

> any institution, corporate or not, which is established for charitable purposes and is subject to the control of the High Court in the exercise of the court's jurisdiction with respect to charities.

This is consistent with the Charity Commission's statement of what is meant by 'charity' and 'charitable organization' in the UK.

> For an organization to be a charity it must fall within the law's understanding of "charity" and be subject to the jurisdiction of the High Court (Charities Act 1993, s.96[1]). For an organization to be a charity it must have purposes which are charitable by reference to case law. (Charity Commission 2001)

Organizations that are legally recognized as charities in England and Wales have to be registered with the Charity Commission, unless they are exempted or excepted by order or regulation, or whose income from all sources does not exceed £5,000 a year (Charities Act 2006, Chapter 3). Registered charities are required to submit their annual reports, which should include a statement of accounts for the financial year, to the Charity Commission within ten months from the end of that financial year (Charities Act 1993, Section 45).

Functional Definition

These legal interpretations of 'charity' do not provide sufficient guidance as to what is charitable nor do they identify which organizations qualify for charitable purposes. Due to this limitation, the functional definition is employed in addition to the legal one to provide further insights into this concept. The Charitable Uses Act 1601 (Statute of Elizabeth I) provided an illustrative list of 'charitable purposes,' whilst having no intention to define them at that time. In other words, a purpose would be considered charitable according to English Law provided it falls "within the spirit and intendment" of the Act's preamble, as decided by the courts (Kendall and Knapp 1996: 66).

Over the years, the illustrative list of charitable purposes has been developed by the law courts and expanded to include new purposes based on an interpretation of the preamble. For instance, in 1891 Lord Macnaghten updated the interpretation of the Charitable Users Act 1601 by classifying charitable purposes as falling into four categories or heads. These were refined in the Charities Act 1960 and later followed in the Charities Acts of 1992 and 1993. The four categories were: the relief of poverty, advancement of education, advancement of religion, and other purposes beneficial to the community (not falling under the aforementioned three categories).

An alternative perspective of the functions of voluntary and charitable organizations is offered by Handy (1990) who suggests three different functions of organizations that reside within the voluntary sector.

- Mutual Support—established by members for the purpose of providing mutual benefits, advice and encouragement, such as health and medical conditions, drug addiction, leisure activities, and benevolent activities.
- Service Delivery—arguably the biggest and most visible form of activity performed by charities for those in need, such as emergency rescue, services for the disabled, elderly, children, and young people. Many of these services are currently provided by charities, but were previously the sole responsibility of the public sector.
- Campaigning—specifically established to campaign for a general cause or to act as a pressure group in a particular interest, such as environmental issues and rights of minorities in a community.

These functions were expanded by Alcock (2003: 168) who depicted four different types of organizations found within the voluntary sector, namely, protective organizations (mutual support and benefits), service organizations (motivated by altruism and provide services to others), campaigning organizations, and representative organizations (promote general issues affecting large numbers of people or self-interest of members). However, this categorization of charities by functions is problematic because charities often perform multiple functions. For instance, many general welfare and social care charities in Britain deliver services directly to their beneficiaries, offer mutual support to members, and campaign for their causes in search for donations and public support (Chew 2006a, 2006b).

In addition, there are two further requirements for charitable purposes under prevailing charity laws in the UK. First, they must be exclusively charitable. Second, they must be for the benefit of the public, namely, the whole community or a considerable section of it (Kendall and Knapp 1996; Charity Commission 2005b). There was ambiguity in the definition of 'public benefit' as it applied to different charities under the Charitable Users Act 1601. The presence of 'public benefit' was presumed to be inherent in charitable organizations that were involved in the first three categories of public benefit, unless they were proven to the contrary. However, for organizations that have purposes that fell under the fourth category, namely, 'other purposes beneficial to the community,' public benefit must be demonstrated. Moreover, the test for public benefit was assessed on a case-by-case basis, and examined on its own merits.

The wider voluntary sector has evolved appreciably since the Charitable Uses Statute of 1601. It now includes organizations that are presently classified as charities but have expanded their scope of operations to include activities that are arguably for private benefit, such as mutual and self-help activities that provide benefits to individuals. CAF (2004: 19) reported that the changing shape and size of the charitable sector over the past decade was partly due to the growth of certain types of charitable organizations (e.g., hospices, faith-based charities representing immigrant groups), the creation of new charities through the contracting out of public services previously provided by central and local governments, and the development of new charitable organizational forms (e.g., social enterprises and partnerships with private and public sectors). For instance, the number of registered charities had risen from 120,000 in 1975 to over 190,000 by the end of 2006 (Charity Commission 2007b). Between six thousand and seven thousand new charities were registered each year since the mid-1990s (Charity Commission 2003, 2004, 2006, 2007b).

These perceived weaknesses in the definitions of charitable status and inconsistency in the assessment of 'public benefit' in charities prompted the Labour Government to initiate changes to the charity law.[1] These changes culminated in the enactment of the Charities Act 2006, which was given Royal Assent on 7 November 2006. It expands the list of charitable purposes from four to twelve. These are: advancement of health, citizenship or community development; arts/heritage/science; amateur sport; human rights/conflict resolution/reconciliation; environmental protection or improvement; animal welfare; and the relief of those in need by reason of youth, age, ill-health, disability, financial hardship, or other disadvantage. In addition, charitable purpose must now be demonstrated by organizations that purport to being charitable rather than being presumed under previous charity law. The Charity Commission is tasked with administering the test for public benefit in registered charities.

Structural-Operational Definition

The third approach to defining the charitable sector is the structural-operational definition. Salamon and Anheier (1992a) first introduced this approach to classify organizations that should be considered as voluntary and non-profit ones. This approach does not emphasize the purpose of the organization, but rather its structure and operations. Salamon and Anheier's (ibid.) five organizational features have been adopted by several authors in order to characterize voluntary and non-profit organizations (e.g., Osborne 1996a, 1996b, 1998; Courtney 2002) and particularly for general charities (NCVO 2002b). According to this definition, charitable organizations would need to:

- be institutionally independent from government and businesses (for-profit sector)
- be non-profit distributing although they can generate surpluses/profits in a given year of operations
- have their activities benefit the wider public, going beyond any membership; and demonstrate to some meaningful degree voluntary participation in the form of "non-compulsory" time (e.g., volunteers in operations and management), money (e.g., donations), and/or contributions in kind (Anheier 2005: 49)

In addition, NCVO's definition of general charities excludes organizations that are predominantly sacramental religious bodies or places of worship (NCVO 2002b).

LOCATING THE CHARITABLE SECTOR WITHIN THE WIDER VOLUNTARY AND NON-PROFIT SECTOR

Table 3.1 provides a conceptualization of the types of organizations that make up the charitable sector within the wider range of non-profit organizations in the UK. This conceptualization suggests that charities, as defined in this study, fall within the first three categories, namely, general charities, registered charities, and the wider sector of voluntary and community organizations that essentially provide public benefits and demonstrate voluntary value (Salamon and Anheier 1992a, 1992b; Osborne 1996a, 1996b, 1998; NCVO 2002b, 2006a).

Table 3.1 Conceptualizing Charitable Organizations within the Wider Sector of Voluntary and Non-Profit Organizations in the UK

Sector	Dominant Organizational Type	Purpose
General charities	Same as registered charities but excludes those that are part of the government apparatus, financial institutions considered to be part of the commercial (for-profit) sector, and those that deliver only private benefit (NCVO 1996; 2002b).	Preparation of national accounts required by the Office of National Statistics.
Charitable	Same as general charities but include registered charities, exempt and excepted charities that fall have to comply with requirement to register with the Charity Commission.	Legally recognized as undertaking activities that within the definition of charity law but do not satisfy the twelve categories of charitable under the Charities Act 2006.
Voluntary and community	Includes registered charities and non-charitable and non-profit organizations, which should demonstrate public benefit and have some aspect of voluntary value (Osborne 1996a, 1996b, 1998).	Mainly used for policy purposes, which recognizes the wider sector of voluntary organizations other than charities that operate for public benefit.
Non-profit	All non-profit organizations, such as general charities, registered charities, and those in the voluntary and non-profit sector, and include those for private benefit but non-commercial. Include quasi-non-governmental organizations and those excluded from general charities definition (Salamon and Anheier 1992a; Kendall and Knapp 1996).	International comparison (e.g., John Hopkins comparative non-profit sector).
Social economy	Includes cooperatives and mutual associations that serve a social purpose but may be commercial (for-profit). Social enterprises in the UK are included here. (NCVO 2002a; NCVO 2006b).	Widely used in Europe.
Civil Society	All organizations that do not operate in the pure public or private sectors (NCVO 2002a; Anheier 2005).	Promoting the participation of citizens in developing and implementing public policy and public service delivery.

Adapted: NCVO (2002b: 19, Table 3.2; 2006a: 14–15, Table 1). *Reprinted with permission.*

The earlier review in this section has highlighted the difficulty in defining and conceptualizing the charitable sector and charitable activity. It has been argued here that attempts to frame the sector using any one definitional criterion were not able to fully encapsulate the diverse nature of the organizations that make up the charitable sector. A significant part of the broad voluntary and non-profit sector is comprised of charities, whether general charities or registered charities. Whilst the focus of this study is on the strict legal definition of charities, nevertheless, it appreciates the diversity of the voluntary and non-profit sector and recognizes the practical difficulties of investigating the entire spectrum of these organizations in this research. The next section will show that charitable organizations strive to remain independent of government and the private sector, and yet are increasingly reliant upon them for funding and other resources in a challenging external operating environment.

Policy Context and External Operating Environment of Charitable Organizations

In its strategic analysis of the voluntary sector for 2003–2004, NCVO (2003) suggested that the major drivers for the uncertainty and change in the UK voluntary sector in the short and medium term would continue to stem from developments in the political-regulatory and socio-economic environments. This section reviews the key developments in the public policy context and the wider external environment in which British charities have been operating under the administration of New Labour since 1997. This period was selected in order to identify the more current environmental developments and their impact on the management of charities from that period and into the third millennium.

Evolving Policy Context Affecting Charitable Organizations Since 1997

Since New Labour was elected into government in 1997, the operating environment in which charitable and voluntary organizations exist can be characterized by an arguably enabling policy context that further promoted voluntary action and raised the profile of the voluntary sector in public policy development and service delivery (Alcock 2003; NCVO 2004a, 2004b). This development was part of the government's agenda to 'modernize' public services in the UK, especially in the areas of regeneration policy, tackling social exclusion, and improving the delivery of public services (Cabinet Office 1999). The government's increased enthusiasm from working with charities and other voluntary and non-profit organizations in policy development and service delivery within this new agenda for change has been evident in several ways. The major policy developments and their effects on charities in particular, and the voluntary sector in general, are highlighted in the following.

- The Deakin Commission (1996) and Kemp Commission (1997) reviewed the future of voluntary action in England and Scotland respectively. They concluded that charitable and voluntary organizations contribute significantly to public policy development and delivery and suggested that relations between these organizations and government should be formalized, i.e., through formal contractual agreements. A National Compact (Home Office 1998), based on recommendations of the Deakin Commission (1996) was thus created, establishing the framework for a formal working relationship between central government and charitable and voluntary organizations in delivering public services. It argues that these organizations have distinct advantages in delivering services more effectively to groups of people in need and those who are particularly difficult to reach by government or its agencies. The 'positional advantage' of charities includes their specialist/expert knowledge of a service or geography, innovative capacity, access to the wider community, and the ability to work closely with users, beneficiaries, and their families because of their independence of government (HM Treasury 2002: 16).
- The National Compact was later widened to include the establishment of a number of Local Compacts between local authorities and voluntary sector organizations operating in local areas (Osborne 2002; Osborne and McLaughlin 2004). Codes of Good Practice were published, including Funding and Procurement of Service Contracts and Grants to guide voluntary organizations and government agencies on the formation, funding, and implementation of service delivery agreements. However, a major criticism of the Compacts was that, whilst they offered guides to good practice, they were not legally binding on the parties involved (NCVO 2002a). Nevertheless, they have been generally welcomed by the charitable and voluntary organizations. The commitment of government, enshrined in the Compact, was to recognize and preserve charities' independence of government, irrespective of their funding relationship. This commitment was further reinforced by the newly enacted Charities Act 2006, which was discussed earlier in this chapter, to encourage the campaigning and advocacy roles of charities in pursuance of their charitable purposes.
- Against this backdrop for change, the government initiated a strategic review of charities and the wider voluntary and non-profit sector in September 2002 (Private Action, Public Benefit: A Review of Charities and the Wider Not-for-Profit Sector), which sought to modernize the prevailing charity law (Strategy Unit 2002). As it has been indicated earlier, the charity laws had failed to keep pace with the rapid developments in charity practice since the early 1960s. The charity law reforms thus entailed, clarifying the definition of 'charity' and 'charitable purposes' in the Charities Act 2006. In addition, they created new legal forms for charitable organizations that enabled charities to

undertake trading activities to further their charitable purposes (e.g., the Community Interest Company in 2005 and the Charitable Incorporated Organization, which will be legally available after 2008). The Charities Act 2006 also expanded the legal responsibilities of the Charity Commission in administering more rigid tests for 'public benefit' in charities.

- At the same time, a governmental 'Cross Cutting Review' was initiated in September 2002 by the Treasury, which identified a greater role in public services delivery by charities and the wider voluntary sector (HM Treasury 2002). The main purposes of this review were to analyze the contribution of the voluntary sector in public service delivery and to identify areas for improvement, especially funding, capacity building, and improving the range and quality of services offered by charitable and voluntary organizations. The government had committed funding for the voluntary sector through the creation of a one-time, three-year investment of £125 million 'Future Builders Fund' in 2004 to develop the capital assets and infrastructure in these organizations. Funding was provided especially for the smaller organizations in order to enable them to take on their public service delivery role more effectively (HM Treasury 2002). This development was aimed at encouraging working partnerships between government (central and local) authorities and charities/voluntary organizations. The funds were targeted specifically at organizations that were involved in the delivery of services in four key government areas: health and social care, crime and social cohesion, education and learning, services for children and young people.
- The government has also encouraged more people to donate to charitable causes by initiating a series of tax relief measures designed to increase donated income in the voluntary sector (NCVO 2002b). In 2000, 'Getting Britain Giving in the 21st Century' was launched. Using this mode, the £1,200 maximum limit on gifts made through the payroll-giving scheme to charities was removed and replaced by a three-year supplement of 10 per cent on donations. The minimum limit of £250 for gifts to attract income tax relief through gift aid[2] was removed. The procedures for using gift aid were also simplified to enable charities to receive tax relief contributions from donors more efficiently.

Therefore, it is evident that the past decade of an enabling policy environment has resulted in the broadening of the scope and scale of activities by charitable and voluntary organizations. Of particular significance was the expansion in the roles and contributions of the charitable sector since 2000 in public service delivery and policy development, which have, as argued by Alcock (2003), exceeded those at any time in the previous century. The key motivation for the increased interest and funding commitment of New Labour in the voluntary sector was to facilitate the modernization of public services, tackle poverty and social inclusion, and to improve the quality of life in Britain (HM Treasury 2002).

Osborne's (2003a) four models of government and voluntary organizations' relationship over the past century in the UK suggest that this relationship had shifted from one where the state and the voluntary sector acted independently of each other to one where both parties are assumed to have potential competencies in the governance, production, and delivery of public services. However, this apparent 'partnership' is arguably an unequal one in which central government articulates the role and sponsors the activities of voluntary organizations in public service delivery. Charities and the wider voluntary sector have thus become one of the main vehicles for government's pursuance of their policy objectives and agenda.

IMPACT OF POLICY CHANGES ON CHARITABLE ORGANIZATIONS

The effects of the various governmental policy initiatives on the voluntary sector reviewed earlier have been demonstrably felt at two levels (Blackmore 2004):

1. increased funding from government (central and local authorities)
2. increased consultation on policy issues that impacted government directly

The contribution from statutory funding (grants and contract fees) has increased appreciably over the past decade. During the period 2000–2001, voluntary and charitable organizations received £1.8 billion and £1.1 billion from central government and local authorities in England respectively, for delivering a range of public services, especially social services, development, and housing (HM Treasury 2002: 12–13). Over 38 per cent of the total annual income of general charities came from statutory sources in 2005 compared to 27 per cent a decade earlier (NCVO 2004a, 2007). 42 per cent of the top five hundred fundraising charities' annual new income in 2002 constituted statutory income (CAF 2004).

It will be shown later in Tables 3.3 and 3.4 that public sector funding has become the largest contributor of charities' total income ahead of individual donations in 2005 (NCVO 2007). Tax-effective giving initiatives have also benefited charities. They received over £2 billion in donations from individuals through these initiatives in 2002, including £437 million in tax relief paid back by the government (NCVO 2004a). Gift aid generated the bulk of this amount, which was £1.98 billion in 2002 (ibid.).

However, not all charities are involved or wished to be involved in delivering public services that are funded by the government. As highlighted earlier, the government's commitment to funding and development of charitable and voluntary organizations in the delivery of public services under the 2002 Treasury's 'Cross Cutting Review' targeted specific areas within its political agenda. The issue of independence of voluntary organizations in general, and charities specifically, was at the heart of concerns that arose from the changing climate of increasing funding for delivering public services under government contracts. The key defining characteristics of charities and voluntary organizations are their independence from the government, the private sector or other statutory agencies, and also their capacity to self-govern and make independent decisions.

Potential risks facing charities that are increasingly involved in delivering public services funded by statutory sources or working in partnership with government have been raised by academics and charity practitioners (e.g., Leat 1995b; Pharoah 2003; Blackmore 2004). Osborne and Ross (2001) identified two such risks—'isomorphism' (where the charity loses its distinctiveness and become more like its counterparts in the public and private sectors) and 'incorporatism' (where the charity sector itself becomes an arm of the government apparatus). Other authors have cautioned charitable organizations that increasingly deliver public services under contracts from government risk mission drift in their search for funds (NCVO 2004b; Alcock, Brannelly, and Ross 2004).

Blackmore (2004), however, argues that there is little empirical evidence to suggest that the risks to the independence of charitable and voluntary organizations have indeed become a reality. Working collaboratively or formally in partnerships with organizations from other sectors may be beneficial for voluntary and non-profit organizations, provided that they are clear about the benefits and risks of pursuing these relationships. For charities that have traditionally depended on external parties for resources and support, such as funders/donors, volunteers, the media, and businesses in general, the degree of interdependence between them and other organizations/sectors is perhaps more relevant to the debate in the current climate of change (Blackmore 2004: 41).

The idea of delivering services that are for 'public benefit' is, however, not new to charitable organizations. Many of the activities that are now classed as public services were set up by charities to fill unmet needs long before the state decided to play a greater role in public welfare provision (Blackmore, Bush, and Bhutta 2005). The boundaries between what is considered public and private goods/services blur where the same services are to be found in different sectors of societies that are in varying stages of development (Flynn 2002: 13). The Charity Commission advised charities that delivering public services is a key governance and management issue for them. Engaging with government in service provision should be done in a manner that does not compromise the charity's mission, its independence, and financial position.

Charities have always undertaken activities that are commonly regarded as "public services", and charities often pre-dated and pre-empted statutory provision. For example, highway maintenance, primary education and hospitals were all originally provided by charities. Lifeboat rescue services and hospice care are still provided by charities. Public perception of what government should provide changes over time, as do relative levels of provision by the charitable and public sectors. Delivering public services may not be appropriate for many charities, and trustees must make informed decisions about whether to engage in this service delivery. (Charity Commission 2005b)

OTHER EXTERNAL ENVIRONMENTAL TRENDS AND THE IMPACT ON CHARITABLE ORGANIZATIONS

Since the mid-1990s, the social, economic, and technological environments of charities have been characterized as both challenging and 'fragile' (NCVO 2003, 2004a, 2005b). In examining these trends for the charitable sector, it is impossible to be exhaustive. At the same time, there is little extant literature that analyzes these changes and their specific impact on charitable organizations in a comprehensive way. A notable exception is NCVO, which has published its annual *Voluntary Sector Strategic Analysis* since 2003. The review that follows will highlight selective key environmental trends and their impact on charitable activities since the 1990s and into the new millennium.

Social-Demographic Trends

Social-demographic changes have the potential to affect the activities of charitable organizations in various ways. A selective number of trends are reviewed here for the purpose of this study. These environmental developments have potential opportunities and threats for public services, particularly for organizations involved in delivering and funding them, whether they are charities, other voluntary organizations, or government.

An Ageing Population

The UK population is getting older. The proportion of people aged sixty-five and over constituted 16 per cent of the population in 2005 (National Statistics 2006). The number of people aged fifty and over is predicted to increase by 30 per cent from 18.3 million in 2000 to 23.8 million in 2020. Forty-five per cent of the population will be over the retirement age by 2020 (Future Foundation 2003). At the same time, British people above the age of fifty have significant spending power on leisure and services. This is expected to increase from 44 per cent in 2000 to 50 per cent of the population in 2020 (ibid.).

An ageing population poses considerable demands for particular services for the elderly such as health care, social care, specialized housing and residential care, and pension arrangements. As older people live longer they could require financing for nursing home/residential care, thereby reducing the traditional form of legacy income for charities or being written out altogether (Evans and Saxton 2003). Moreover, an increase in demand for older people in the job market, in particular part-time work, could reduce the number of older volunteers. This has been a traditional source of volunteers for British charities (NCVO 2005b).

Change in Family Structure

The structure of the family is also changing. The rise in the number of one-person households and the growing diversity of family structures are leading to a more fragmented and complex society where reliance on service provision rather than traditional support mechanisms is expected to further increase (NCVO 2003). Future Foundation (2003) refers to this trend as a move from the traditional 'horizontal family' (where several generations of the traditional family live together in a household) to the 'vertical family' (where the family has become smaller with fewer children and grandparents in the household). The trend towards a more complex form of 'vertical family' has developed because both parents enter into new relationships as a result of divorce and remarriage, and also due to the decrease of marriages (Future Foundation 1999, 2006). The proportion of married-couple households in the UK has decreased to less than 40 per cent in 1998 compared to 70 per cent of all households in the 1970s (Evans and Saxton 2003). Conversely, the number of single-person households has increased from less than 20 per cent in the 1970s to nearly 30 per cent by 2001 (ibid.). The resultant trend towards the growth of the single-parent family and extended step-families have several implications for alternative providers of social welfare and housing services other than the family (NCVO 2003). A more diverse and flexible range of skills are required of paid staff and volunteers in order to adequately meet the needs/concerns of the family within this changing structure.

Increased Mobility of the Population

Geographical and professional mobility has risen, specifically among the younger population (NCVO 2003). Geographical mobility includes legal migration into the UK from other parts of the EU and other countries. The enlargement of the EU has major implications for the movement of labour in the UK. Professional mobility has continued to put pressure on the job market, which averages 20 per cent to 25 per cent annual turnover in staffing over the past decade (ibid.). Delays in entering the job market because of educational and/or family priorities, and the decline in the traditional family structure (reviewed in the preceding subsection) could lead to increased mobility. This diversity has changed patterns in community participation, which tends to revolve around specific interests of different groups in the community rather than in communities of place (NCVO 2004a). The services of charities are being challenged within increasingly transient and diverse communities. Regional and local charities could contribute significantly to bridging gaps between the different communities of interest.

Social Attitudes and Values

NCVO (2004b) argues that notions of trust and confidence are central to understanding social attitudes and values that affect charities and their relationship with users/beneficiaries on the one hand, and funders/donors on the other. The shift towards a consumer society has not only shaped the attitudes of recipients of public services but expectations of providers and funders as well. These changing expectations mirror those of consumers in the private sector who desire quality, choice, information, and the right to compensation when things go wrong (Blackmore 2004: 12). Consumer activism is increasingly prevalent in economically developed societies, where more socially aware citizens and socially responsible corporations voice their concerns publicly, for instance for increased accountability by providers of public services. Charities and other voluntary organizations are not immune to consumer activism or intense media scrutiny. Eurobarometer (cited in NCVO 2004b: 25) reports that voluntary organizations including charities are still relatively well trusted by the UK public ahead of political parties, the press, the church, and the legal system.

Nevertheless, the impact on charitable organizations is evident from the changing relationships with the user/recipient of publicly funded services and with the public sector agencies that commissioned these services. For instance, there is growing pressure on charities to demonstrate accountability and performance for their charitable causes, and to the beneficiaries and communities they represent (Blackmore 2004). Yet many charities do not automatically value their beneficiaries because structurally, as argued by Bruce (1995), charities have a wide array of different audiences, where most attention is focused on donors and funders. The emphasis on the individual rather than society has also influenced purchasing patterns and brand loyalty, which has shaped donor/funder behaviour in the UK. Donors and funders become more discerning and choosy about the causes they wish to support. The trend that has seen the public's declining support in social issues and increasing concern for specific community interests may limit funding opportunities for some charitable causes in the future (NCVO 2004b).

A combination of complex social-demographic and policy changes over the last twenty years has thus complicated fundraising for charitable organizations. The trend is towards a more diversified portfolio of income sources for many charities in their efforts to maintain services to their users/beneficiaries (CAF 2004). (See also Tables 3.3 and 3.4 for sources of charity income).

Economic Conditions

NCVO (2005b) argues that since the late 1990s, the increasing fragility of the national economy has been a key strategic threat that charities and other voluntary organizations in the UK have had to face whilst entering the new millennium. The charities' experiences during the recessionary years in the early and late 1990s have, arguably, shaped their less optimistic expectations of the funding environment for the future. Taylor-Gooby's (1994) study 'Charities in Recession: Hard Times for the Weakest?' into the effects of the economic recession of the early 1990s on UK charities has great significance, revealing that, whilst many charities were having difficulties in fundraising during the recession, the level of demand for their services grew.

The extent to which different charities have experienced a decrease in income and an increase in demand with the recession were explained by variations in factors such as size, geography, and service subsector. The two sources of income that charitable organizations experienced the greatest decline in the economic recession were donations (individual and corporate) and grants from government (central and local). On the other hand, voluntary sector grants from trusts and foundations provided the biggest increase in funding to charities during this period. Larger charities (annual income exceeding £50,000) and smaller ones (annual income below £7,500) had coped best during economically challenging periods. For instance, Taylor-Gooby (1994) found that larger charities were able to utilize their stronger resource base, therefore enabling an increase in fundraising and marketing activities to bolster their generation of income during the recessionary periods. Smaller charities were buffered from the full effects because of their geographical or service focus. Mid-sized charities that operated in subsectors, such as social care, community and economic development, and the arts, experienced the greatest decline in income. They received most of their funding from local and central governments. Conversely, charities that were involved in "long-standing needs," such as social care, health, and education, experienced the least decline in demand for their services (ibid.: 106). Those operating in the southern parts of the UK experienced the greatest demand for their services because of cutbacks in funding from local authorities and the increase in unemployment during this period.

These findings are revealing because they showed empirically that charitable organizations were capable of responding rapidly to economically challenging conditions. For instance, those organizations that have experienced the largest decline in income and resource support in recessionary times tend to undertake the most radical changes in their attempts to survive. These included changes to their organization structures, cutbacks on service provision, and the adoption of 'professional' management and marketing techniques to increase fundraising activities (Taylor-Gooby 1994; Leat 1995a). However, these changes have been criticized as short-term responses rather than longer-term strategies. Economic uncertainty could therefore affect the level of demand for particular types of charitable activity and the capacity of individuals, organizations, and government that could provide support for them.

The overall health of the national economy can also be influenced by the economic performance of international markets, as demonstrated in the global economic slowdown in the late 1990s and since early 2008. The fall in the stock market had impacted not only on the organizations (funders/ corporate donors) holding the investments, but equally on those receiving grants from investment holders (charities and voluntary organizations). One source of income for charities is internally generated income, which includes bank interests and investment earnings from property (see Table 3.4 further in this chapter).

NCVO (2004a) highlighted the potential current and future threats to voluntary income and internally generated income of charities that arose from changes in the economic conditions in the country over the short and medium terms. These included rising personal debt, higher tax burden, and investment risks (e.g., falling equity prices and corporate profits, uncertainty in dividend income, and the property price bubble) that reduce an individual's predisposition to donate. For instance, investment income of general charities amounted to £2.2 billion in 2002, of which two-thirds or £1.4 billion were from dividends and interest (NCVO 2004a). This income, however, fell by nearly 13 per cent from 2000 because of the continued effects of the economic slowdown from the late 1990s and into the new millennium. Although investment returns had increased slightly to £2.5 billion by 2006, they were still well below the levels of the 1990s where this source of income contributed 20 per cent of charities' total income (NCVO 2008). Legacies from wealthy individuals continued to benefit the very large charities (total annual income exceeding £10 million). Seventy per cent of the total legacy income in 2006 was channeled to them, while only 8 per cent of this total was received by smaller charities (NCVO 2008: 36). As a result of the continuing fragile equity prices since 2000, grant-making charities that relied upon investments and legacies as their main sources of income were affected.

Technological Advances

Charitable organizations are affected by changes in technology similarly to how organizations in the wider voluntary and private sectors are. The range of technological advances not only includes information and communication technology, but also innovations in service delivery processes, health and medical technologies, mechanical and engineering developments. Effective use of information and communication technology has been suggested by NCVO (2004a) to enable charities to reach users, beneficiaries, and donors/funders more cost effectively.

The drive to enhance information and communication capabilities in charities and other voluntary organizations stems both from an increasingly discerning public, where access to information is expected, and also from the commitment of the governmental Cross Cutting Review (HM Treasury 2002) to develop the infrastructure capacity of voluntary sector organizations in order to support their public service delivery role. The latter initiative was part of the current Labour Government's wider reform of public services, as were discussed earlier, involving the development of an electronic economy of service delivery (Office of the e-Envoy 2003). This has provided an arguably new opportunity for charitable organizations to secure and strengthen their strategic position within this changing polity (Burt and Taylor 2004; Taylor and Burt 2005).

Information and communication technology capability and capacity are thus expected of charitable and voluntary organizations involved in the delivery of public services that are under contracts from government. For instance, the governmental 2002 Cross Cutting Review had proposed the development for a governmental voluntary sector web-based portal. It aimed to streamline access and performance management requirements relating to government grants and other funding streams into the voluntary sector in the future (HM Treasury 2002). However, research has shown that voluntary and non-profit organizations in the UK, including charities, suffer from a serious deficiency in information and communication technology infrastructure and skills (Taylor and Burt 2005). Wenham, Stephens, and Hardy (2003) found that, whilst many charities in the UK were increasingly adopting web-based (Internet) technology for fundraising, they were not utilizing the technology effectively as part of a strategically integrated marketing plan. Charities therefore continue to face growing tension between the increasing expectations from their various stakeholders to be technologically capable and their internal deficiencies in this capability.

Summary

This section has developed an in-depth understanding of the policy context and external environment in which British charitable organizations operate. In summary, the impact of these key environmental influences on managing charitable organizations in the new millennium has become evident from the major concerns voiced by charity managers (NCVO 1999). These concerns include greater uncertainty and tougher funding opportunities from statutory sources and fundraising from the general public, greater demand and public expectations for services delivered by charities, increase in mutual and self-help, and challenges in managing the changing relationships with organizations in both the public and private sectors, and cross-sectoral partnerships within the voluntary sector itself. The changing policy context and other external environmental influences in the socio-economic and technological landscape have thus continued to put pressure on charitable organizations to manage their operations to effectively satisfy both their short-term survival needs, and their longer-term strategic positioning (Chew 2005, 2006b).

STRATEGIC ORIENTATION IN MANAGING CHARITABLE ORGANIZATIONS

The literature review on strategic positioning in Chapter 2 has identified that much of the theoretical foundations of that concept were based on the commercial (for-profit) organizational context. Therefore, it is important that the discussion on the relevance of contemporary strategic management/marketing models and approaches for charities primarily involve an appreciation of the contextual differences (and similarities) between these organizations and their counterparts in the private sector. An understanding of the differences would enable researchers to ascertain the extent to which charitable organizations require an alternative approach to those adopted by commercial (for-profit) ones in order to effectively manage their organizations (Courtney 2002). This section examines the major differences in terms of their theoretical significance and their implications for the management of charitable organizations compared with organizations in the commercial (for-profit) sector.

Theoretical Differences between Charities and Commercial (For-Profit) Organizations

The extant literature provides numerous ways of organizing the theoretical differences between voluntary and non-profit organizations and commercial (for-profit) organizations depending on the purpose of the comparison. For instance, Harris, Rochester, and Halfpenny (2001) suggest that the policy arguments for a mixed economy of welfare/public service provision were based on claims that voluntary and charitable organizations were different from organizations in the private and public sectors. As highlighted earlier, previous UK government-commissioned committees, such as the Wolfenden (1978), Deakin (1996), and Kemp (1997) Committees had all established that voluntary and charitable organizations possess distinctive positional advantages to delivering public services because of their cost-effectiveness, innovativeness, flexible structures, independence of government, and their ability to reach difficult-to-reach segments of society.

The various attempts made to conceptualize voluntary and non-profit organizations (e.g., Salamon and Anheier 1992a, 1992b; Kendall and Knapp 1996; Osborne 1996a, 1996b, 1998; Hudson 2002) subscribe further to the notion that these organizations are fundamentally different from the public and private sectors. The majority of these authors argue that the distinctive differences between voluntary and charitable organizations and organizations in the public and private sectors require adaptation of contemporary management approaches for the former, or even developing approaches that are unique to the voluntary sector altogether.

However, despite the significance of charities in the voluntary sector, there is a paucity of literature, both conceptual and empirical, that specifically compares the context of charitable organizations with organizations in other sectors, and/or identifies the implications of these differences for charity management. Notable exceptions in the British non-profit management and marketing literature include Octon (1983), Leat (1995a, 1995b), Bovaird and Rubienska (1996), Osborne (1996b), Bruce (1998), Sargeant (1999), Hudson (2002), and Courtney (2002).

This section attempts to synthesize the various literature on this topic by examining the theoretical differences between charitable organizations and commercial (for-profit) organizations under six broad organizational characteristics, namely: organizational purpose/mission, indicators of success, revenue acquisition, accountability, culture and values, and governance. In doing so, it must be acknowledged that there could be other characteristics used for such comparisons. Nevertheless, these six organizational characteristics are selected for this review because they are most frequently cited in both mainstream and non-profit management literature, which could provide the basis for explaining the research findings in this study. A summary of these key differences and their impact on charity management are shown in Table 3.2.

Organizational Purpose/Mission

The charity's purpose/mission has been singled out by several authors as its key differentiating feature (e.g., Leat 1995a; Quarter and Richmond 2001; Courtney 2002). Charitable organizations are legally established for charitable purposes, which were defined by the charity laws. At the same time, charitable purposes must provide some form of social or public benefit as opposed to private benefit, in the majority of commercial (for-profit) organizations.

Another key theoretical difference frequently used as a defense for charitable activity is that they are unconcerned with profits, while private sector organizations are driven by profit maximization (Clarke and Mount 2001). Several authors (e.g., Drucker 1990; Leat 1995a; Courtney 2002) have suggested that the 'profit' argument is not clearly proven for charitable and voluntary organizations. For instance, some charities do set out to generate profits/surplus, for example, through charity shops and selling other charity merchandise/services (Leat 1995a). Also, grant-making charities deliberately seek to raise surpluses in a given year in order to invest these to generate more surplus (ibid.).

Table 3.2 Theoretical Differences between Charitable Organizations and Commercial (For-Profit) Organizations and Implications for Charity Management

Comparative Organizational Features	Key Differences		Impact on Charity Management
	Charitable Organization	*Commercial (For-Profit) Organization*	
Organizational purpose/mission (Charity Acts 1992, 1993, 2006; Leat 1995a; Moore 2000; Clarke and Mount 2001; Quarter and Richmond 2001; Courtney 2002).	• Legally set up for charitable purposes as defined in UK charity laws and updated in Charity Act 2006. • Charity mission often provides a form of 'social' or 'public benefit.' • Non-profit distribution but must be reinvested to further charitable purpose or mission. May earn surpluses from activities if these are performed in pursuance of its purpose.	• Predominance of profit or wealth maximization for shareholders and investors in the mission. • Social benefit may be included in the mission to guide service provision, but is not emphasized as a rule (Quarter and Richmond 2001).	• Charity mission has a strong influence (both distinguishes and constrains) on the strategic choice of primary target audience (users/beneficiaries) and scope of charitable activities. • Mission needs to incorporate measurable goals, rather than vague purposes. • Mission guides social accountability and provides legitimacy for charities (Ebrahim 2003; Moore 2000). • A clear and compelling mission provides direction for the charity's strategies and actions.

Indicators of success (Leat 1995a; Mason 1984; Courtney 2002; Hudson 2002) (Drucker 1990; Sawhill and Williamson 2001).	• Predominance of non-financially orientated performance measures, e.g., usage, service quality, client satisfaction, rather than financially driven ones such as market share, profitability or return on investments. • No or weak direct link between funder and consumer/customer. Predominantly paid for its efforts instead of results (Leat 1995a). • Indicators of success defined or discovered through process of negotiation and participation between internal and external stakeholders.	• Predominance of profit and loss as a measurement of success, i.e., financial bottom line or increased equity value is emphasized (Moore 2000). • Direct link with the consumer/customer who often pays for products and services provided by for-profit organization. Predominantly paid for results (Leat 1995a). • Indicators of success defined by senior management and endorsed by shareholders.	• Measurable goals incorporated in mission statements are important to provide accountability to the charity's external and internal stakeholders. • Different organizational structures and systems are needed to manage dual responsibilities of resource attraction and resource allocation (Mason 1984).
Accountability (Charity Acts 1992, 1993, 2006; Ebrahim 2003; Courtney 2002)	• Legal accountability for UK charity laws to fulfil charitable purpose and to serve users/beneficiaries as primary stakeholder. • Financial accountability to Charity Commission. • Social accountability to wider range of stakeholders in addition to users/beneficiaries, such as donors, funders, government, volunteers, and staff for its actions and decisions.	• Legal accountability to Company Act. • Financial accountability to shareholders and investors.	• Multidimensional and contingent on relationships with diverse internal and external stakeholders (Ebrahim 2003). • Tension between the externally driven accountability and internal generated accountability in charities (Ebrahim 2003). • Charities that deliver public services under contracts from government face incompatible accountability to their principal (funder) and to their users/beneficiaries.

(Continued)

Table 3.2 (Continued)

Comparative Organizational Features	Key Differences		Impact on Charity Management
	Charitable Organization	*Commercial (For-Profit) Organization*	
Revenue Acquisition (NCVO 2004a; Moore 2000; Drucker 1990)	• Different sources of revenues, in particular, donations from individuals and businesses are a key defining difference of charities. • Inherently dependent on various external parties for resources, in particular, revenue for survival (Paton and Cornforth 1992).	• Less diverse sources of revenues. Primary source of revenue is from selling products and services to customers who would pay for these offerings (Moore 2000).	• Different strategies and process of acquiring resources (particularly voluntary donations) are needed in charities (Moore 2000). • Varied approaches needed to manage multiple demands from different stakeholders (Paton and Cornforth 1992).

Culture and Values (Leat 1995a; Moore 2000; Courtney 2002; McGill and Wooten 1975)	• Strong internal values such as participatory and egalitarian, and greater commitment towards equal opportunities. • External orientation tends to be non-competitive and cooperative approaches when carrying activities and partnerships with other organizations. (Courtney 2002).	• Internal values influenced by external orientation to market and interests of shareholders/investors (Moore 2000). • External orientation tends to be predominately competitive (Mason 1984), but this can involve cooperation.	• High degree of conflict and tension between maintaining participative and co-operative goals/values and official strategic initiatives that strive to achieve organizational dominance (Leat 1995a; Wilson 1994).
Organizational Governance (Leat 1995a; Hudson 2002)	• Volunteer board of trustees or management committee legally required to ensuring charity activities adhere to charitable purpose and safe guard financial integrity/trust. • Other volunteers involved in range of activities e.g. fundraising, service delivery, operations and management advisors.	• Paid board of directors appointed by shareholders to ensure financial viability.	• Conservative in managing strategic and financial risks (Leat 1995a). • Highly influential in all strategic decisions of the charities therefore can facilitate or restrict managerial actions.

Moreover, for-profit organizations are also increasingly 'socially responsible' by adopting social objectives in their mission statements that guide their service provision (Leat 1995a), although it is generally not the rule for for-profit organizations to do so (Quarter and Richmond 2001). By law, British charities are allowed to earn surpluses from their trading activities (Charity Commission 2005a). They are, however, not permitted to distribute profits/surpluses to anyone with a beneficial interest in the organization, and therefore should reinvest profits earned to further their charitable purpose/mission. A non-profit organization's purpose/mission hence has a powerful influence on the choice of organizational strategies (Sawhill and Williamson 2001; Hudson 2002). The earlier review suggests that it would be more appropriate to consider the non-profit distributing feature of charitable organizations rather than their profit generation *per se* as a differentiating feature between charities and commercial (for-profit) organizations.

Indicators of Success

The discussion on a lack of profit or financially directed motive in charitable organizations is linked to their indicators of success. Several authors have suggested that the lack of profit as a bottom line deprives charities of any clear basis for performance indicators compared to commercial (for-profit) ones (e.g., Drucker 1990; Bryson 1995). Sawhill and Williamson (2001) argue that it is far more difficult to measure 'success' of a charitable organization that is predominately mission driven using traditional business measures. The literature suggests that charities orientate towards non-financially focused performance measures (e.g., usage of services, service quality, client satisfaction), rather than financially driven ones that are used by for-profit organizations (e.g., market share, profitability or return on investments) (Leat 1995a; Courtney 2002). In other words, charities could compensate their lack of financial bottom line with other indicators of success that measure the impact of their activities and capacity in enabling them to achieve their mission (Sawhill and Williamson 2001).

However, the issue of measuring success in charitable organizations is complicated by a weak link between users/beneficiaries (the party who consumes the services of the charity) and the donor/funder (the party who pays for these services) compared to for-profit organizations. The implications for charity management are significant. For instance, Mason (1984) argues that this weak link would require two separate systems in the charitable organization to manage its relationship between the two parties effectively. Moreover, this crucial difference complicates the management of charities in terms of determining their measures of success and their accountability to different stakeholders (Hudson 2002). This latter point is the focus of the next key difference between charities and commercial (non-profit) organizations.

Accountability

There is no clear definition of the term accountability as it applies to managing non-profit organizations (Ebrahim 2003). Edwards and Hulme (1996: 967) define accountability as 'the means by which individuals and organizations report to a recognized authority(ies) and are held responsible for their actions.' Kearns's (1996) definition suggests accountability to be both socially constructed and relational in nature. In other words, accountability can be externally driven and internally generated depending on the nature of the charity's relationship with its various stakeholders.

In this respect, there are at least three dimensions of accountability when applied to the charitable context. Under existing charity law the board of trustees or management committees of British charities are *legally accountable* to fulfil their organization's charitable purpose and to serve their primary stakeholders, namely, users/beneficiaries. Chisolm (1995: 141) defines legal accountability as 'either an obligation to meet prescribed standards of behaviour or an obligation to disclose information about one's actions even in the absence of a prescribed standard.'

Moreover, registered charities in the UK are *financially accountable* to the Charity Commission, as discussed earlier in this chapter. Charities are also *socially accountable* by virtue of their charitable purpose and the need to demonstrate 'public benefit' to a wider array of stakeholders, such as users/beneficiaries, donors, funders, volunteers, government, contracting partners, and even the wider community or region that are indirectly affected by their activities (Ebrahim 2003). The charity's mission adds an ethical dimension to accountability because it emphasizes the motivation of internal actors and provides a basis for assessing organizational progress and performance (ibid.: 199). Fry (1995, cited in Ebrahim 2003: 199) terms this as 'felt responsibility' compared to externally driven accountability to donors or funders. In an effort to balance the plurality and often conflicting expectations of external and internal stakeholders, some authors have argued that charities that deliver services tend to emphasize accountability for their funders/donors or principals (e.g., government agencies for public service contracts) and have weak accountability for users/beneficiaries (Bruce 1995, 1999; Ebrahim 2003).

Revenue Acquisition

Charitable organizations have developed a variety of ways to generate their revenues. As discussed earlier in this chapter, changes in the policy context and wider external operating environment have exacerbated their search for new and continuing income to ensure their economic survival (also see Tables 3.3 and 3.4). Although charities are increasingly beginning to embark on trading activities to generate earned income, voluntary donations from individuals and businesses have been the traditional and defining source of their income (Moore 2000). Several authors have highlighted that the resource acquisition activities of charities and for-profit organizations differ, and that this difference would make managing charities more challenging that organizations in the private sector (Octon 1983; Mason 1984; Drucker 1990).

Hudson (2002) suggests that the various ways in which charities acquire their income are significantly different in terms of the nature of exchange/transaction compared to those of commercial (for-profit) organizations. As highlighted earlier, this difference is based on the theoretical weak link between the user/beneficiary of the service provided by charities and the donor/funder who pays for it. In commercial (for-profit) transactions there is a trading relationship whereby the 'customer' purchases a product or service from the company and pays the agreed price. The inherent funding dependency of charities on external parties would mean that they are more heavily dependent on donors/funders (voluntary and non-voluntary) to pay for their services provided to users/beneficiaries.

There is therefore an indirect flow of resources from funder to user/beneficiary, through the charitable organization. Moreover, the variety of revenue sources of charities could signal the willingness of different parties (donors, citizens, taxpayers, government, other voluntary and non-profit organizations) to support their activities, thereby providing legitimacy for their cause/mission (Moore 2000).

Culture and Values

Several authors have highlighted that theoretically different internal values exist in charities compared to commercial (for-profit) organizations, such as participatory and egalitarian, and greater commitment towards equal opportunities (McGill and Wooten 1975; Leat 1995a; Courtney 2002). Moreover, the external orientation of charities has been described as non-competitive and cooperative, in contrast to their inherently competitive private sector counterparts (Mason 1984; Wilson 1994). Other authors have argued that these differences are becoming blurred because many commercial (for-profit) organizations are increasingly adopting cooperative and collaborative strategies and focusing on stronger internal organizational cultures, such as teamwork (Leat 1995a; Courtney 2002). Moreover, the notion that charitable organizations are characterized by informal and more participatory managed structures compared to the hierarchical, rational, and goal-defined structures in commercial (for-profit) organizations is debatable. McGill and Wooten (1975) propose that both the informal and formal approaches of doing things in non-profit organizations exist, as do competitive and collaborative strategies (Wilson 1994).

What is perhaps more important as a defining difference of charities compared to private sector organizations is their underlying motive for adopting their organizational values, structures, and strategies. In this respect, the majority of authors are in agreement that a charitable status imposes certain constrains on charities when pursuing competitive strategies (Wilson 1994; Leat 1995a). A high degree of conflict and tension could develop in charitable organizations between maintaining participative/cooperative goals and values that are based on the publics' perceptions of their dedication to public benefit and strategic initiatives, which is to strive to achieve organizational efficiency and effectiveness in increasingly challenging operating environments.

Organizational Governance

A final key theoretical difference between charities and commercial (for-profit) organizations is the charity's volunteer board of trustees or management committee. They perform custodian roles on a voluntary basis as defined by charity law compared to the paid board of directors in private sector organizations (Leat 1995a; Courtney 2002). The charity's governing board is a special category of volunteers with legal obligations, ensuring the activities of the charity adhere to its public benefit purpose and safeguarding its financial integrity. Hudson (2002, 2003) argues that the complexity of the work of the charity's governing board of trustees increases with the growing diversity of its funding sources. Due to the trustees' legal and positional powers in governing the charity, they impose much influence on the charity's strategic direction, culture, and performance.

PROFESSIONALIZATION OF MANAGEMENT PRACTICES IN CHARITABLE ORGANIZATIONS

The external pressures discussed earlier in this chapter have persuaded a growing number of charitable organizations to embark on 'professionalization' of management practices (Chew 2003, 2006a, 2006b). These are designed to help them improve performance, become more efficient and to maintain/raise funds in an increasingly competitive funding environment (Blackmore 2004; Chew 2006a, 2006b).

> There is a feeling that voluntary and community organizations need to move away from well meaning amateurism and become more professional in the ways in which they operate in order to ensure that they are making the best possible use of their limited resources and operating as efficiently as possible in pursuit of their objectives. In itself this is no bad thing. (Blackmore 2004: 33)

The greater dependence on earned income for many charities and the growing complexity in their accountability to the different external stakeholders have increased the momentum for charities, enabling them to make use of their limited resources more effectively in pursuit of their mission/cause. However, the preceding review of the theoretical dissimilarities between charitable organizations and commercial (for-profit) organizations signals key challenges for the management of charities.

Although, as Moore (2000) and Bryson (1995) have argued, there is a common need to have good governance and effective strategies in any organization, as the form of such strategies and the process of developing them would essentially differ in charitable organizations. This variation stems from two important differences in charities: their purpose/mission that needs to demonstrate a social 'raison d'être' and the inherent resource dependency on external parties for financial and other organizational resources to maintain economic survival.

Differing schools of thought on the adoption of mainstream business management/marketing theory and practice by charitable and voluntary organizations persist in the literature. On the one hand, some authors argue that voluntary and charitable organizations are diverse and fundamentally different from commercial (for-profit) organizations. Therefore, it is problematic to transfer generic business theory and practice into these organizations (e.g., Octon 1983; Paton and Cornforth 1992; Guy and Hitchcock 2000; Moore 2000). On the other hand, others have argued for the development of theoretical models and management approaches that are derived from the context of non-profit organizations specifically for use by these organizations rather than looking towards the private sector for answers to their governance/management problems (e.g., NCVO 1994; Clarke and Mount 2001). The Chief Executive of NCVO, Stuart Etherington, suggested that the increasing pressures on charities to be efficient and to focus on performance improvements have resulted in a deluge of performance management tools that were meant for commercially orientated operations being advocated for charities. Etherington argues that the charity sector should develop specific tools that are "developed by us and for us" (NCVO 1994, cited in Blackmore 2004: 33). Guy and Hitchcock (2000: 44) suggest that the 'one size fits all' prescription offered by some business management models have limitations when applied to non-profit organizations because they fail to appreciate the dissimilarities in the cultural and policy constraints non-profit and non-market organizations face. This perception of 'one size does *not* fit all' is shared by McGuire (2003), who argues that generic strategic marketing approaches that are based on oversimplistic presumptions of customer sovereignty, market supply and demand, and the profit bottom line driving organizational strategies have limitations when applied to public services.

Public services have social not just economic value, reflecting welfare or social policy objectives. Sales revenue and profitability are 'bottom line' measures of economic value for private services. Social impact and equity are 'bottom line' indicators of social value for public services.

Demand for public services is derived from public policy processes based on collective political choices. There is currently no place for equity in the service profit chain. (McGuire 2003: 65)

A third school of authors appreciate the dissimilarities between the charitable and for-profit contexts. They suggest adaptation of contemporary business, management, and marketing models when applied to non-profit organizations (e.g., Rees 1998). Andreasen, Goodstein, and Wilson (2005) emphasize the importance of accommodating the non-profit organizational culture, missions, and revenue streams, which could pose barriers to the direct application of marketing techniques and marketing knowledge to non-profit organizations.

Where products or services exist [in non-profit organizations], some marketing techniques, such as organizational branding, are deemed "inappropriate" because such expenditures may be perceived as frivolous or self-aggrandizing while not contributing to the achievement of the organization's mission. This could be a manifestation of a managerial ethos that does not see organizational branding as capacity building. (Andreasen, Goodstein, and Wilson 2005: 63)

Bruce (1998) suggests that for-profit models could provide a starting point for developing adapted approaches that can accommodate the particular context of voluntary and non-profit organizations in general, and charities specifically.

The language of commercial marketing is not attractive in the charity sector but many of the ideas and practices, suitably adapted, work much better than might at first be thought. However, certain important differences between charity and commercial services (e.g. permanent commitment to a particular customer group regardless of loss, the impossibility of hostile takeovers, the legal commitment to the objectives of their cause) require commercial concepts and practices to be adapted. (Bruce 1998: 153)

These differing schools of thought have been featured in the review of the existing literature on strategic positioning in Chapter 2. What is also evident from the literature is that authors who advocated the important role of strategic positioning in non-profit organizations tend to describe the concept of positioning in similar ways to those found in the commercial marketing literature (e.g., Lovelock and Weinberg 1989; Kotler and Andreasen 1996). However, a growing number of charity marketing scholars/researchers have acknowledged the need for adaptation in the types of positioning strategies for charitable organizations (e.g., Wray 1994; Saxton 1996; Bruce 1998). Andreasen, Goodstein, and Wilson (2005) argue that sectoral differences, and in particular, differences in organizational characteristics and culture, between non-profit and commercial (for-profit) organizations could pose potential barriers for the transferal of marketing concepts, including strategic positioning, in their entirety to non-profit organizations. NCVO (2004a) suggests that charities that are increasingly involved in the delivery of public services need to review their strategic positions within the changing political, economic, and social landscape. Against this backdrop, a number of larger charities have embarked on strategic positioning to distinguish themselves from other organizations in their increasingly challenging and competitive environments. The next section explores the key influences that have elevated the importance of strategic positioning for charitable organizations.

KEY DRIVERS FOR STRATEGIC POSITIONING IN CHARITABLE ORGANIZATIONS

Hudson (2002) hints at some early indications of segmentation and differentiation in British charities before the post-industrial era. In the second half of the nineteenth century, and after the introduction of the Poor Law Amendment Act 1834 in Britain, charities began to develop a more strategic approach to managing their activities. In an effort to encourage more self-help and less dependency on state welfare, they started to distinguish the poorest people with no resources, from those less deserving who could rely on workhouses for employment (ibid.: 4). Contemporary charity marketing literature illustrates increasing cases of positioning by large charities (e.g., Wray 1994; Hibbert 1995; Bruce 1998; Kennedy 1998; Maple 2003). These cases perhaps reflect the growing recognition by charities of the important role of positioning in the charity's strategic planning in more challenging and competitive environments. This section highlights four key developments that have elevated the strategic relevance of positioning in charities since the mid-1990s (Chew 2003, 2005).

Impact of Changing External Environment on Competition

An important driver for the utilization of strategic positioning in charitable organizations is the impact of governmental policy developments and other external environmental changes on competitive intensity among charities, and between them and other organizations in the voluntary, private, and public sectors. NCVO (2004b) suggests that the UK government policies that favoured widening participation with citizens and those giving them greater choice in public services have led to an increase in competition between service providers and the various sectors in the country. Additionally, commercial (for-profit) organizations are increasingly forming partnerships with charities in marketing collaborations and cause-related marketing (Abdy and Barclay 2000, 2001).

Further, indirect or 'generic' competition can come from organizations who offer different products/services that provide similar benefits, therefore satisfying some basic needs of users/beneficiaries or donors/funders (Lovelock and Weinberg 1989; Andreasen and Kotler 2003). However, strategic efforts and concerns have not been given due attention by charitable organizations (Taylor-Gooby 1994; Wilson 1994). The challenge for them is to be more strategically oriented, particularly in the context of continued harsh economic, structural, and competitive environments of the future (Drucker 1990; Bryson 1995).

Pressures to Search for New and Continuing Income Sources

The second driver is the increasing pressure on charities to search for new and continuing income and income sources. They face unique pressures in income generation because they inherently depend on external parties for funding. One of the top management priorities cited by charity managers in the new millennium is maintaining funding in an increasingly competitive environment (NCVO 1999). Moreover, the fact that attracting voluntary income in an environment where statutory funding has become more important was cited as a major challenge for charities (CAF/NCVO 2003).

The rapidly increasing number of registered charities each year vying for a slower growing pot of voluntary income in the marketplace has made raising and maintaining income more difficult (Bruce 1998) and achieving long-term financial stability much harder (Frumkin and Kim 2001). Traditionally, registered charities derived their income from voluntary sources, such as legacies and donations from individual and corporations (NCVO 1996). The increasingly competitive environment has forced many charities to either cut back the scope of their activities or to diversify their income sources, for instance, by increasing fee-based activities (including delivering services for government under contracts) and trading (selling products for profits).

Table 3.3 shows the main sources of income of registered general charities in the UK. Table 3.4 compares the changes in the main sources of income in charitable organizations between 1995 and 2005. The number of general charities grew from 120,000 in 1995 to 165,000 in 2005, which was an increase of 37 per cent (NCVO 1996, 2007). Table 3.4 shows that the total income of general charities has increased by 135 per cent during this period to reach £27.7 billion in 2005. Income (grants and contract fees) from the public sector demonstrated the most significant growth in terms of absolute amount and proportion in contribution. Income from private sector corporations remained the lowest both in the absolute amount and proportion of total income compared to contributions from the other sources. During this period, internally generated income, e.g., interest earned from investments, had fallen appreciably by 52 per cent. In part, the impact on charity income demonstrates the effects of the fragile economic condition

Table 3.3 Income Sources and Type of Income of UK Charitable Organizations

Main Sources of Income	Type of Income			
	Earned	*Voluntary*	*Investment*	*Total %*
Individuals/general public	Fees for services provided	Individual donations, legacies, covenants, membership subscriptions.		35.5
Public sector	Central and local government fees and payments for contracted services	Project and core funding grants, grants to charitable intermediaries, grants from the National Lottery* distributors		38.5
Private sector companies	Sponsorship	Corporate grants and gifts		3.9
Voluntary sector	Services provided under contracts (e.g., membership fees).	Grants from charitable trusts and charitable intermediaries.		10.6
Internally generated	Turnover of trading subsidiaries		Dividends, rents from investment property, interest payments from banks and building societies.	11.5
Total %	48.2	44.0	7.8	100.0

Adapted: NCVO (2007: 30–31, Tables 5 and 6) *Reprinted with permission.*
Note: * The National Lottery is an important and significant source of income (grants) for charities. Various distributors among five causes distribute proceeds for the Lottery: charities, sport, the arts and heritage, and the New Opportunities Fund, which covers health, education, and the environment. Funds for charities are distributed entirely by the Community Fund. £1.76 billion of grants were awarded to charities between 1996 and 2000 (NCVO 2002b, 2004a). Refer also to National Lottery Commission website www.natlotcomm.gov.uk; Camelot website www.camelotgroup.co.uk/index.jsp, Institute for Fiscal Studies—Charitable Giving and the National Lottery www.ifs.org.uk/charities/lottery.shtml.

Table 3.4 Comparison of Income of UK General Charities 2005/1995

Main Sources of Income	1995 £ Billion	%	2005 £ Billion	%	Change % 2005/1995
Individuals/general public	4.24	36.0	9.82	35.5	−1
Public sector	3.30	28.0	10.64	38.5	+38
Private sector	0.47	4.0	1.08	3.9	−2
Voluntary sector	1.18	10.0	2.93	10.6	+6
Internally generated	2.59	22.0	3.18	11.5	−52
Total	11.78	100.0	27.65	100.0	+135

Adapted: NCVO (1996: 27, Figure 10; 2007: 31, Table 6) *Reprinted with permission.*

and changes in governmental policies on funding charitable services during these years.

Impact of Resource Dependency

The third driver is the impact of resource dependency other than funding, such as labour and skills dependency, on the positional advantage of charities. Charitable organizations, like other organizations, require physical labour and expertise to create, deliver, and promote their services and programmes. Charities compete for employees working for wages and other employment benefits similar to private and public sector organizations. In addition, many of them rely heavily on volunteers who range from the board of trustees or management committee members to people who carry out the various operational activities. Whilst employees working in the voluntary sector may be concerned with matters beyond financial compensation, such as psychic fellowship, security, and flexible working conditions (Lovelock and Weinberg 1989; Kotler and Andreasen 1996), there is increasing pressure on charities to attract and retain key personnel and skilled volunteers. NCVO (2002b, 2004a) observes that charities face shortages of skills in management, strategic use of information technology, and strategic planning. Moreover, they are at risk of losing their competitive advantage for their traditional flexible working practices as private and public sector counterparts catch up by promoting the work-life balance in their organizations.

Differentiating to Stand Out from the Crowd

The competitive operating environment in the charitable sector has created a greater range of services and products offered by charities. At the same time, uncertainty over the new contracting culture on relationships between charities and the government (central and local) has reinforced the view that notions of partnership and trust, embodied in funding through grants, appeared to have been lost (NCVO 1996). Maintaining voluntary income has therefore remained a key goal for charities in the future (CAF 2004). These concerns have led to a growth in utilization of advertisements and other forms of publicity in different types of media by charitable organizations to promote their cause/offerings to various target audiences. These instances are particularly prevalent in larger charities. Mintel (2001) reported that the top five hundred fundraising British charities have increased their advertising expenditures in national broadcast and press media since the mid-1990s. The two most common promotional objectives were to generate awareness of their charitable causes and to raise funds from donors. Advertising expenditure by the top five hundred charities grew 49 per cent from £31.6 million in 1996 to £47.2 million by 2000 (ibid.: 51).

Charities face increasing pressure to identify their specific target audiences to which they can effectively reach and respond. However, some researchers have observed that many charities lack clearly defined positions, making it hard for them to differentiate their mission/cause and positioning message from other organizations that target similar audiences (Hibbert 1995; Bruce 1998). Positioning is based on the notion of differentiating the organization and its offerings from other providers with similar offerings. Authors have suggested that effective positioning could provide charities with a strategic base upon which to develop clearer communication messages and other tactical marketing efforts to promote the charity's distinctiveness to their target audiences (e.g., Lauffer 1984; Ries and Trout 1986; Lovelock and Weinberg 1989).

Whilst there have been initiatives by the UK government to improve the skills, infrastructure, and performance of charitable and voluntary organizations in public service delivery in the new millennium, such as the ten-year ChangeUp Strategy and Performance Hub,[3] there remains a lack of theoretical models that are able to guide charity managers in understanding and developing their organizations' strategic positions in increasingly competitive external environments.

CONCLUSIONS

This chapter began with a conceptualization of the charitable sector and charitable activities, drawing attention to the difficulty with identifying a single all-encompassing definition that can adequately accommodate the diversity of the charitable entity and activities. The review of the research context has established that British charities are operating in increasingly challenging environments in the new millennium. The evolving policy context and changes in the social-demographic, economic, and technological landscape, in particular from the mid-1990s, have a profound influence on managing charitable organizations. These changes have affected different charities in different ways, reflecting the heterogeneity of organizations within the charitable and voluntary sector.

The suggested theoretical differences between charities and commercial (for-profit) organizations have been explored. It is argued that an understanding of the key theoretical differences could provide a crucial starting point to explore the extent to which contemporary management/marketing approaches can be applied to the charitable context. Although these theoretical differences do not necessarily imply similar differences in charity management in practice, the review nevertheless provides an understanding of the potential challenges in adopting contemporary business management models in their entirety in charitable organizations. Key drivers for the professionalization of management approaches and the emergence of strategic positioning in the charities have also been identified. An understanding of the charitable context in this chapter, coupled with the literature review on the concept of strategic positioning in Chapter 2, provide an important foundation for explaining and discussing the empirical findings in the later chapters of this book. The next chapter begins part two of this book, which describes the research methodology and explains the rationale for its adoption for this study's purpose.

4 Research Methodology

The research upon which this book is based adopts a mixed-methodological approach that recognizes the complementary strengths of both the quantitative and qualitative research meta-frameworks (Denzin 1978a, 1978b; Jick 1979; Bryman 1992; Blaikie 2006). Pluralism in the use of research methods and data sources is appropriate in the theory building process, which involves both inductive and deductive modes (Hammersley 1992; Blaikie 2006). Their contributions are particularly relevant to this study where the research process goes through a number of stages and has different requirements at each stage (Mingers and Brocklesby 1995; Easterby-Smith, Thorpe, and Lowe 2002).

This chapter will outline the methodological approach employed in this study. It will begin by establishing a set of subsidiary questions for each of the two main research objectives established in Chapter 1. This is followed by a classification of charitable organizations and further terminologies utilized in the empirical stages of this study. Next, a methodological path established for this study is described. Methodological issues that underpin the empirical stages of this study and the research tools used in each stage are explained. This chapter will conclude by demonstrating the reliability and validity of the study. However, the larger theoretical arguments behind the choice of methodology and its design are not included here. This wider discussion can be found in Chew (2006a).

RESEARCH QUESTIONS FOR THE STUDY

In the first chapter, two main research objectives were introduced to address the aim of this study. It was further identified in Chapter 2 that there is limited literature and a lack of empirical research exists in the study of organizational-level strategic positioning in charitable and non-profit organizational contexts. This research study is arguably the first study of its kind to examine the strategic positioning activities of charitable organizations within the wider voluntary sector. Due to this situation, it is necessary to begin the research process with a conceptualization stage, which includes a review of the available literature as detailed in Chapter 2. The purpose is to explore and refine the research questions that support the two main objectives in this study (Neuman 2006: 155). These are now presented as follows:

Main Research Objective 1: To What Extent Are Charitable Organizations Undertaking Strategic Positioning Activities?

The objective here is to explore and describe the extent to which British charities undertake strategic positioning activities. The following subsidiary questions have been identified to support this objective.

- To what extent do charitable organizations undertake strategic marketing planning?
- To what extent do charitable organizations undertake positioning strategy activities?
- What are the generic/core positioning strategies pursued by these charities?
- What are the various positioning dimensions used by these charities to differentiate their organizations from other charities/voluntary organizations?
- In what ways are the generic/core positioning strategies and the positioning dimensions of charities similar or distinct from those advocated in contemporary strategy/marketing literature on positioning?

Main Research Objective 2: What Are the Key Factors That Influence a Positioning Strategy in Charitable Organizations?

This objective aimed to identify and explain the key factors that could influence the choice of a positioning strategy in British charities. In order to achieve this second objective the following research questions are identified.

- What are the key factors that influence the positioning strategy of charities?
- How do these key factors affect the positioning strategy components?
- In what ways and why are the key factors similar or distinct from those described in contemporary strategy/marketing literature on positioning?
- How is a positioning strategy developed in charitable organizations?
- In what way and why is this process similar or distinct from those advocated in contemporary strategy/marketing literature?

To summarize, a combination of 'what,' 'why,' and 'how' enquiries are established in order to adequately address the aim of this study. Together, they guide the choice of research strategy and methods that need to be used and the sequence for the implementation of the research process (Blaikie 2006: 61).

CLASSIFICATION OF CHARITABLE
ORGANIZATIONS USED IN THIS STUDY

The conceptualizations of charitable organizations and the charitable sector have been established in Chapter 3. In addition, this study has adopted the CAF's (2003) classification of British charities. The CAF ranks the top five hundred fundraising charities in its annual directory *Charity Trends* (previously named *Dimensions*) in terms of annual voluntary income generated, and classifies voluntary income by broad types of charities, type of causes, and means of giving.

This directory has been used as a sampling frame and as a key source of charity data in previous research on charity management and marketing (e.g., Hibbert 1995; Hibbert and Horne 1996; Kendall and Knapp 1996; Saxton 1996; Balabanis, Stables, and Phillips 1997; Key Note 1997; Bruce 1998; Sargeant 1995, 1999; Abdy and Barclays 2001; Hankinson 2001, 2002; Salamon and Anheier 1994; Mintel 2001; Directory of Social Change 2002; NCVO various years).

This study has also adopted the CAF's (2003) classification of charitable organizations as its sampling frame. Charities here were grouped under ten broad types: medicine/health, general welfare and social care, international aid, religious/missionary work, animal protection, heritage/environment, arts/recreation, youth, education, and other sectors. In utilizing the CAF's classification and ranking of charitable organizations, this study recognizes that charities in the UK have been traditionally classified in different ways as part of the wider voluntary sector. Industry observers, scholars, and researchers in the charitable sector generally acknowledge that there is currently no single best approach that can adequately accommodate the eclectic voluntary and charitable organizations (Kendall and Knapp 1996; NCVO 1996; Mintel 2001). Not all of these classifications accommodated the diversity of charities or the functions they perform in an adequate fashion, such as, the International Classification of Non-Profit Organizations, the National Taxonomy of Exempt Entities, and the Charity Commission's classification, which provided a high-level schema of distinctions between charities that serve different user/beneficiary groups and undertake different functions in various industries (NCVO 1996). It was thus decided that adopting the CAF's classification would be an appropriate sampling framework for this study and would enable the identification of suitable subsectors for in-depth investigation and comparison.

METHODOLOGICAL PATH OF THE RESEARCH PROCESS

This research process consists of three main stages: a conceptualization stage, an exploratory postal survey stage, and a multiple cross-sectional case studies stage. Utilizing different methods with different ontological positions is appropriate and possible at different stages in the research process (Blaikie 2006).

> [T]his practice of combining methods usually involves a time sequence in which the use of one method provides data that can inform the subsequent use of other methods. It matters not whether qualitative methods precede quantitative methods, or the reverse; a range of pragmatic considerations will determine that decision. It is possible that two methods of a different type might be used concurrently, but their role will still be to provide some assistance to the use of other methods, not to provide a more complete unbiased picture of social reality. (Blaikie 2006: 272)

Complementarity of findings from the mixed-methodology approach therefore serve the research purpose, choice of questions, and expected outcomes at different stages in the research process of this study.

The Structure of the Research

Figure 4.1 summarizes the methodological path and the research stages followed in this study. The purpose of these stages will be discussed briefly in the following.

Conceptualization Stage

As highlighted in the preceding section, the conceptualization stage involved defining the research topic, identifying broad research objectives, and refining the research questions to guide the empirical stages of this study. The conceptualization stage included a review of the relevant literature and exploratory discussions with a panel of academic peers who are knowledgeable in the field of voluntary sector and charity management/marketing and from charity practitioners who are responsible for strategic planning and marketing in their organizations. This revealed a notable lack of substantive work in the topic of strategic positioning in the charitable context. Several key themes emerged from this stage that could be explored in this study:

- the ways in which strategic positioning had been perceived by key decision-makers in charitable organizations
- the extent of actual strategic positioning activities by charities that deliver public services
- the motivation for strategic positioning in charities
- the process of strategic positioning within charitable organizations
- the extent to which the alternative theoretical perspectives on positioning could shape a model of influencing factors on positioning strategy in the charitable context

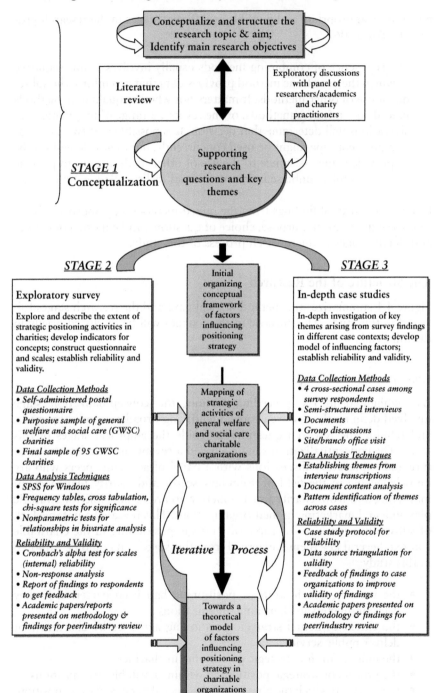

Figure 4.1 Methodological path followed in this study.

An initial organizing conceptual framework of the factors influencing positioning strategy was drawn up. The organizing framework provided a guide for the data collection and analysis at the empirical stages of this study, i.e., the survey and case studies stages.

The Survey Stage

The exploratory postal survey aimed to provide an initial empirical foundation for the research in terms of revealing the extent of strategic positioning activities in charitable organizations. The second stage of the study aimed to achieve the following objectives:

• Map the extent of strategic positioning activities of charitable organizations.
• Identify the components of positioning strategy in charitable organizations and to compare these with the theoretically derived interpretation of these elements.
• Identify the key factors that influence positioning strategy in charitable organizations and to compare these with the theoretically derived understanding of these factors as depicted in the initial organizing conceptual framework drawn up at the conceptualization stage.

However, the survey was exploratory and descriptive in nature and thus limited in its ability to establish deeper understanding of the research issues, particularly from the perspectives of the key actors within charitable organizations, their motivations for positioning, and the process of developing positioning strategy. This led to the third stage of the study, the case studies stage, which built on the findings from the exploratory survey.

The Case Studies Stage

The cross-sectional case studies were designed to overcome the limitations of the survey questionnaire. The case study method's strength is its ability to uncover intimate evidence about a particular phenomenon from the perspectives of different actors; it provides depth in explanation (Yin 2003) and facilitates theory building (Eisenhardt 1989). The case studies in this research were used to investigate the key themes that have emerged from the exploratory survey stage in greater depth. The findings from the case studies stage were then used to refine a theoretical model that integrated the multidimensional factors that could influence the positioning strategy in charities conceived from the exploratory survey stage. Convergent or divergent results that emerged from using a combination of research methods at specific stages in this study could therefore stimulate theoretical development and propose new directions for future research (Blaikie 2006: 275).

The Exploratory Survey

The exploratory survey was intended to encourage an initial picture of the extent of strategic positioning activities in charitable organizations to surface. An inductive research strategy was adopted within a quantitative framework. A postal survey method was used to gather predominately quantitative (with some qualitative) data to answer the research questions established in the conceptualization stage.

Gill and Johnson (1997) and Carson and colleagues (2001) argue that the survey method occupies a variable, intermediate position between ethnography (interpretivist paradigm) and experimental research (positivist paradigm) along the methodological continuum. The choice of survey type would depend on the research objective and questions to be answered. It was decided that a descriptive survey was appropriate at this stage of the study to provide an initial and broad understanding of the topic by exploring the strategic positioning activities in the sample of charities. In contrast to an analytic survey, a descriptive survey is concerned primarily with addressing the particular characteristics of a specific population of subjects, either at a fixed point in time or at varying times for comparative purposes (Gill and Johnson 1997). In this study preliminary findings that emerged from the postal survey were investigated in the cross-sectional case studies to ascertain the extent of strategic positioning activities, constraints, and problems faced by charity managers in more depth.

Sampling Frame and Sample Selection

It was mentioned in the preceding section that the sampling frame adopted in this study was the CAF's *Charity Trends* directory of the top five hundred British charitable organizations (CAF 2003). This directory has been used and referred to in several research studies on charities, and therefore can be considered an authoritative source. The large number of registered charities (over 190,000 charities in December 2006), and the fact that 78 per cent of the total annual income of all registered charities came from only 3 per cent of charities with a total income of £1 million and above (Charity Commission 2006), suggests that it was more practical, feasible, and cost-effective to survey the top registered charities in addressing the research objectives at this exploratory stage of the research. The directory was also a good source of secondary data on charities in the UK. This helped to complement the empirical data that the survey had sought to generate.

The general welfare and social care charitable organizations from among the top five hundred fundraising charities in Britain was adopted as the sample for this study. This purposive sample was selected because of four main reasons: (a) their increasing public profile in delivering social care/ public services, (b) their influence and contribution to policy making in the social care and community development at national and regional levels, (c) their significance in terms of income generated and workforce employed, and (d) their inherent heterogeneity operating in different subsectors that could provide interesting findings about their strategic positioning activities.

The general welfare and social care charities operated in six subsectors: other general welfare, children, benevolent funds, elderly care, service and ex-service, and religious general welfare. Collectively, these subsectors make up a sizable 23.6 per cent of the total number of charitable organizations in the sampling frame and contributed 23 per cent of the total annual income of these organizations in 2002–2003 (CAF 2003). Eighty-nine per cent of the sample received £1 million or more of total annual income in this period. General welfare and social care charities also generated the highest voluntary income among the top five hundred fundraising charities. However, they were also receiving substantial statutory income from delivering services under contract to both central and local governments. Thirty per cent of their total income in 2002–2003 came from government contracts and fees, making this proportion the highest among all the subsectors in the top five hundred fundraising charities (CAF 2004).

Postal Questionnaire

A self-administered postal questionnaire was utilized to gather data from a purposive sample of general welfare and social care charities. The use of a postal questionnaire at this exploratory stage of the research provided several advantages, such as generating interesting variables, enabling coverage of a large sample, and being relatively efficient (DeVaus 1996; Gill and Johnson 1997). A purposive sample is commonly used in exploratory research where the main aim is to select a sample with a particular purpose in mind rather than to produce statistical generalizations of the findings (Remenyi et al. 1998; Saunders, Lewis, and Thornhill 2000). Additionally, the exploratory survey served as a basis for a further in-depth investigation using case studies in stage three of this research process (Stake 1995, 2000).

The survey questionnaire was designed to produce data about the way key decision-makers who were knowledgeable in the planning and/or the implementation of corporate strategy, marketing, or positioning activities in charitable organizations perceived the extent to which strategic positioning activities in their organizations had been undertaken, the type of generic positioning strategy that they had adopted, the degree of competitive intensity for resources in their sector/subsector, the possible factors that have influenced their positioning strategy, and whether positioning strategy decisions were embedded in their strategic planning process.

Two Likert-style summated rating scales were developed for the purpose of this study to measure the extent of positioning strategy and strategic marketing planning and activities that could be undertaken by charities. The literature review in Chapter 2 revealed that a positioning strategy had been depicted in the extant marketing literature as a key outcome of the strategy development phase of the strategic marketing planning process in commercial (for-profit) organizations (Hooley, Saunders, and Piercy 1998), and that it plays a crucial role in marketing planning in non-profit organizations (Lovelock and Weinberg 1989; Kotler and Andreasen 1996; Andreasen and Kotler 2003). Therefore, it was necessary to include the exploration of strategic marketing planning in this study, and to investigate the extent to which positioning strategy activities were undertaken as part of the overall marketing planning in the sample organizations.

The lack of similar existing measures in the extant literature and empirical studies in the charity context meant that the measurements of strategic marketing planning and positioning strategy had to be constructed specifically for this study. These activities and the terminology developed in the questionnaire were drawn from the non-profit strategic marketing and positioning literatures (e.g., Lovelock and Weinberg 1989; Kotler and Andreasen 1996; Sargeant 1999; Andreasen and Kotler 2003) and subsequently adapted for the charity context in this study. The exploratory discussions conducted during the conceptualization stage had also helped in this adaptation process, especially in refining the type of strategy/positioning activities, the appropriateness of language used, and the structure of the questionnaire.

The strategic marketing planning scale was a composite of thirteen items (activities) of key marketing planning activities at the strategic level, while the positioning strategy scale comprised of six items (activities) depicting the key positioning strategy activities for this study. Each item denoted an activity on the scale, which was measured using a ten-point response format ranging from 1 (small extent) to 10 (large extent). Andrews (1984) suggests that the construct validity of rating data improves as the number of categories in the scale increases, while Matell and Jacoby (1972) found that the percentage of uncertain responses goes down as the number of categories in a scale goes up. Therefore, the two scales comprising of greater response categories in this study were aimed at enhancing the quality of the data generated.

The questionnaire design and launch was carried out in six steps in 2004. Literature on survey methodology and design was extensively consulted (e.g., Dillman 1978; Foddy 1993; Robson 1993; Fink 1995a, 1995b; Bruner and Hensel 1996; DeVaus 1996; Gill and Johnson 1997; Saunders, Lewis, and Thornhill 2000) to ensure that the questionnaire was designed with the charitable context in mind and to enhance construct reliability. The questionnaire was pretested on a panel comprised of academic experts in non-profit marketing, charity practitioners, and researchers who were involved in voluntary sector management studies. This helped to improve its contents and layout and to establish content validity (Mitchell 1996).

The pretested questionnaire was piloted on a small sample of charities in both the general welfare and social care subsectors and among the CAF (2003) sampling frame. A telephone script was used to ensure consistency in communication with potential respondents. In addition, pilot test respondents were asked to complete a short feedback form (Bell 1999), which aimed to provide feedback on the clarity and layout of the questionnaire and the covering letter, and highlight difficulties faced in completing the questionnaire. The pilot study, therefore, aimed to enhance construct or face validity of the survey instrument, namely, the questionnaire. The final version of the questionnaire was posted to ninety-five general welfare and social care charities in the sampling frame, together with a covering letter and a freepost reply envelope. Copies of the questionnaire are available from the author upon request.

Respondents were from the six general welfare and social care subsectors as shown in Figure 4.2. The effective response rate achieved was 54 per cent, which was a good response rate when compared to the rates in other postal questionnaire surveys conducted on the top five hundred charities in the UK (e.g., Sargeant 1995; Balabanis, Stables, and Phillips 1997; Hankinson 2002).

The information from the survey was analyzed in three ways. First, the Likert-type scales of positioning strategy and strategic marketing planning activities were used to map the type and extent of these activities engaged in by charitable organizations. The internal reliability of these scales was measured using Cronbach's alpha coefficient test. Basic distributional statistical

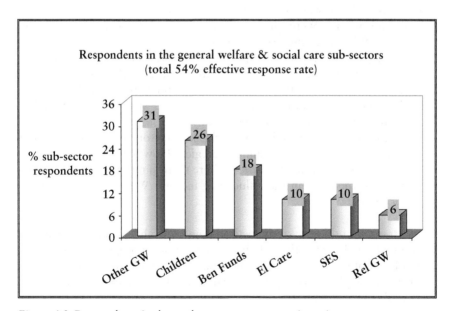

Figure 4.2 Respondents in the exploratory survey questionnaire.

Note: Other GW = other general welfare charities, Ben Funds = benevolent funds, El Care = elderly care charities, SES = service and ex-service charities, Rel GW = religious general welfare charities.

analyses in the type of generic or core positioning strategies, positioning dimensions, and possible factors that influenced the positioning activities of charities as perceived by the charity's key decision-makers were undertaken.

Second, the descriptive organizational statistics were further analyzed using chi-squared tests to explore possible relationships and their significance between charities that adopted different generic or core positioning strategies and their organizational characteristics. Third, bivariate statistical analyses (both parametric and nonparametric tests) were carried out to ascertain the strength of competitive intensity in the subsectors and any correlation between the positioning strategy and strategic marketing planning activities. The results of the data analyses were organized and presented using frequency tables, cross tabulations, and appropriate charts. These findings will be reported in detail in Chapter 5.

The Case Studies

A descriptive survey, in isolation, is limited in its ability to establish causality and reveal processual and explanatory aspects of a phenomenon. In recognition of these limitations, the survey stage was complemented with multiple cross-sectional case studies. The case studies aimed to investigate three key themes that have emerged from the exploratory survey:

- *Process:* How was positioning strategy developed in the case study organizations? Were there similarities or differences between the cases? What were the reasons for these?
- *Strategy:* What were the components of positioning strategy in the case organizations, and why were these adopted? Were there similarities or differences between the cases? What were the reasons for these? Have the strategic positions of charities changed since inception? What prompted or caused this change, if any?
- *Influencing Factors:* What were the key factors that influenced the case organizations' positioning strategies? How have they affected the organization's strategic position? Were there similarities or differences between the cases in the influencing factors? What were the reasons for these?

A key strength of the case study methodology is its ability to provide understanding through evaluation of the phenomenon or population within a particular context. Yin (2003) argues that case studies are more effective in answering explanatory types of research questions in addition to exploratory and descriptive ones.

> [C]ase studies have a distinctive place in evaluation research. . . . The most important is to explain the presumed causal links in real-life interventions that are too complex for the survey or experimental strategies.

A second application is to describe an intervention and the real-life context in which it occurred. Third, case studies can illustrate certain topics within an evaluation, again in a descriptive mode. Fourth, the case study strategy may be used to explore those situations in which the intervention being evaluated has no clear, single set of outcomes. (Yin 2003: 15)

An inductive research strategy was used to gather qualitative and quantitative data in the case studies in this research. However, an element of deduction was evident because of the use of prior theory, the initial organizing conceptual framework established during the conceptualization stage, and key themes that had emerged from the survey stage to guide data collection and analysis in the case studies. In summary, the case studies aimed to gather rich data from within the case organizational contexts to obtain a more holistic view of the extent of strategic positioning activities of charities, to identify both general conclusions and discrepancies from an analysis of data across cases, and to provide methodological and data triangulations to enhance the overall reliability and validity of this study (Denzin 1978b; Jick 1979; Patton 1987).

A recurring issue facing case study research is the problem of generalizing and theorizing from case study findings, in particular, using single case design. This problem could be overcome by employing multiple cases, where the evidence is regarded as more 'compelling and the overall study is therefore regarded as being more robust' (Yin 2003: 46). Therefore, multiple cases were used in this study to adequately investigate the three key themes introduced earlier.

Selection of Case Studies

Four cross-sectional case studies were selected. The cases were identified from a short list of twelve respondents in the survey stage. After a careful review of the respondent's profile, the decision to select the four cases was also based on their organizational characteristics and partly on their responses to the questions in the survey questionnaire, such as contrasting perception of competitive intensity, generic or core position, and positioning dimensions cited.

Due to the qualitative nature of research at this stage, the selection of these case studies was not based on statistical sampling but purposive sampling (Yin 2003; Stake 1995). The cases were considered instrumental because they aimed to provide insights into the issues under investigation and to redraw some preliminary conclusions or generalizations (Stake 1995). A multiple case studies methodology has also been used in other empirical studies on voluntary and charitable organizations that provide different types of public services (e.g., Alcock, Brannelly, and Ross 2004; Osborne 1998). Table 4.1 shows the data sources employed in the case studies to explore the research themes and answer related research questions for each theme.

Two organizational criteria were used to guide the initial selection of the four case studies: total annual income (income bands according to *Charity Trends*, CAF 2003) and proportion of statutory income compared to voluntary income. For the first criterion, two of the four cases were selected from the high-income band (above £10 million) and two cases from the middle-income band (£1 million to £10 million). These two income bands

Table 4.1 Research Themes, Questions, and Multiple Sources of Data Employed in the Cross-Sectional Case Studies

Research Themes	Supporting Research Questions	Data Sources in the Case Studies
Process		
Process of developing positioning strategy	Was there a formal process of developing the positioning strategy? If so, was it part of the strategic marketing planning process or other forms of planning?	27 semi-structured interviews with organizational leaders, strategy planners, key decision-makers, marketing/fundraising managers. Organizational documents.
Strategy		
Components of the current positioning strategy	What was distinctive about the strategic position of the charity? What was the generic or core positioning of the charity? What were the positioning dimensions?	27 semi-structured interviews with organizational leaders, strategy planners, key decision-makers, marketing/fundraising managers, and regional/branch staff. 4 group discussions with operational staff/volunteers.
Changes to positioning strategy/ strategic position	Had the current positioning strategy changed from inception? What prompted/ caused that change, if any?	Organizational documents.
Influencing Factors		
Key factors that influence the choice of positioning strategy	What were the major and minor factors that influenced the core positioning, and in what ways? What were the major and minor factors that influenced the positioning dimensions and in what ways?	27 semi-structured interviews with organizational leaders, strategy planners, key decision-makers, marketing managers, and regional/branch staff. Organizational documents.

were considered significant for this sample as 89 per cent fell into these two income bands in 2002, showing an increase of 33 per cent and 6 per cent respectively from 1997 (CAF 2000, 2003). At the same time, 88 per cent of this study's survey respondents had a total annual income of above £1 million (CAF 2003), which reflected a close approximation to the sampling frame in this study.

Within the first criterion, two cases with a relatively higher proportion of statutory income (and consequently lower proportion of voluntary income) and two cases with a relatively lower proportion of statutory income (and consequently higher proportion of voluntary income) were chosen using the second organizational criterion. This criterion aimed to examine in greater depth to what extent resource dependency had influenced external stakeholders, in particular statutory funding, on the choice of positioning strategy. Overall, the selection criteria employed in the case studies allowed the findings between the different case organizational contexts to be compared, while offering a degree of generalizability of the findings in the charity sector in which they operated.

The Case Study Organizations

In order to ensure anonymity and confidentiality of the case organizations in this study, the pseudonyms Charity A, Charity B, Charity C, and Charity D are used to denote the four cases. Chapter 6 will provide further description of organizational characteristics of the four case organizations. They are introduced briefly here.

Charity A was a national charity that was established twenty-two years ago to provide support and accommodation through its seven fully furnished houses to families of seriously ill children seeking treatment at paediatric hospitals around Britain. It was the smallest charity in terms of its total annual income and size of paid workforce in comparison to the other case study organizations. It depended fully on voluntary income to run its operations.

Charity B was the youngest charity from among the four case studies. It was established sixteen years ago as a grant-giving organization serving the northeast region of England. It was different from the other three case organizations because it did not deliver services direct to consumers/users, but encouraged giving, primarily from local voluntary sources (companies, legacies, families, and individuals) in order to generate funds, and by getting government contracts/grant schemes to support local communities. These funds were then distributed to voluntary and community groups/projects that provide a wide range of community services specifically in the northeast of the country. Voluntary income had declined since 2000, but one key area of income growth had been from programmes managed for government agencies. Thirty per cent of the charity's total annual income came from managing government grants in 2002–2003. This proportion had increased to 49 per cent in 2003–2004, and comprised of grants from a number of local and regional funds.

Charity C was a national charity delivering emergency sea search-and-rescue services to the public for over 180 years. Voluntary income had been and remained the largest proportion of its total annual income. This proportion was over 90 per cent in 2003. Since 2000, it had begun to expand its core service by delivering rescue services on beaches under contracts to local authorities in the southeast of England. However, the proportion of statutory income was relatively small at less than 1 per cent of its total income.

Charity D was set up thirty-seven years ago as a voluntary association of parents who provided drug treatment services to adult misusers. Over the years, its core service had expanded to include alcohol treatment services, which reflected increasing public concerns on alcohol misuse and government policies directed at tackling this social problem in the country. Since the late 1990s, it has been delivering these public services mainly under contracts to local and central government funders. It relied heavily on statutory sources of income in 2003, which amounted to over 95 per cent of its total income.

Process of Case Study Data Collection and Analysis

An important part of the case study methodology is the collection and analysis of data. An iterative process of case study data collection and analysis was utilized for the multiple case studies in this research. A case study protocol was followed in order to guide the data collection in sufficient consistency between the various sources of methods used within each case (Yin 1994, 2003). It included guidelines on pre-interview communication with participants, using pro formas for semi-structured interviews, and adhering to interview schedules to ensure consistency in structuring of interviews and data collection (Osborne 1998).

A pretest was conducted on the twelve case study candidates to test the case study interview guidelines and ascertain that the final four cases were the most appropriate to fulfil the case study objectives. Next, the data collection stage was developed in iterative progression, moving from one case to the other three cases. The use of multiple sources of data enabled a more holistic interpretation of the key themes and research questions; by facilitating triangulation of data, multiple sources of data were collected within each case (Gilmore and Carson 1996; Yin 2003). This study has utilized the following multiple sources of data:

- Semi-structured interviews with key decision-makers of the charitable organization.
- Group discussions with operational staff to compare their perceptions of the charity's positioning activities with the perceptions of senior management.

- Site visits to branch or regional offices to ascertain similarities or discrepancies in the perceptions between staff outside the head office and those at the head office.
- Organizational documentation to be used in a supporting role to corroborate the evidence emerging from the interviews.

An interpretive and iterative approach was adopted in analyzing data gathered from the case studies. This involved coding the data along key themes that have emerged from the semi-structured interviews in one case, then re-analyzed and interpreted as further data was gathered in the other cases (Carson et al. 2001). This approach is appropriate for exploratory type of case studies where depth understanding and theory building are more important than specific measurements (ibid.: 66).

Descriptive data illustrating the process of strategic positioning, the components of a positioning strategy, and influencing factors in positioning strategy within each case were collected and analyzed according to the key themes/research questions as shown earlier in Table 4.1. The first phase of the data analysis helped to develop the experiential knowledge of the researcher in the case study process. The process continued in iterative progression into the second phase by focusing on specific themes from Charity A, but was open to new ideas/themes in the next three cases.

An analytic comparison was then employed to analyze sets of data according to the key themes across the cases (Neuman 2006: 471). At the same time, relevant organizational documents, such as corporate strategies, annual reports, planning processes, promotional and communications materials were analyzed for corroborating or contradicting evidence. For each key theme and corresponding questions, salient points from the findings in each case were drawn out and particular areas of similarities and differences between the cases were highlighted. This method of cross-case data analysis emphasized the effects of particular sets of conditions in the case contexts, and considered complex outcomes across cases that have qualitative differences (Neuman 2006).

> The real strength of analytic comparison is that it helps researchers identify the combination of factors often measured at the nominal level, that is associated with an outcome among a small number of cases. [E]xplanation in analytic comparison tends to be interpretive or structural rather than nomothetic. (Neuman 2006: 472)

Display matrices and word tables were created to display the findings along the key themes and research questions from individual cases according to a uniform framework (Miles and Huberman 1994; Yin 2003). This technique was extended to display the findings for the cross-case comparison. The findings were then interpreted in light of similarities or discrepancies in the patterns that emerged from the data analyzed across cases.

RELIABILITY AND VALIDITY IN THIS STUDY

The Survey Stage

Reliability in social research is concerned with whether the results of a study are repeatable. For quantitative methods such as survey questionnaire, reliability is often about whether the measures used to represent concepts or constructs are consistent (Bryman 2001). Validity is concerned with the integrity of the results or conclusions that are generated from a research study. It comprises of measurement or construct validity, internal validity, and external validity (ibid.: 30). Efforts to enhance reliability and validity in the survey stage were carried out in four ways.

First, the internal reliability of the two Likert-type scales for strategic marketing planning and positioning strategy were measured by correlating responses to each question in the questionnaire with those of other questions in the questionnaire (Mitchell 1996). In the survey questionnaire design, internal reliability was also enhanced by developing multiple-item indictors for operationalizing the constructs in the two scales (Andrews 1984; DeVaus 1996). In addition, each scale incorporated a filter score of zero to indicate non-activity for an activity (item). The order of the questions allowed respondents to look over the whole range of activities (items) in the questionnaire sections before responding.

Second, the internal reliability of these two scales was tested by Cronbach's alpha coefficient. This test is one of the most commonly accepted indicators of the internal consistency of a quantitative scale (Cronbach 1951; Pallant 2001). Cronbach's alpha coefficients of both scales were good at 0.8430 and 0.8082 respectively (see also Chapter 5). The resultant alpha values of both the scales exceeded 0.7, which meant that the scales were considered reliable with the sample. Third, construct or face validity was enhanced by eliciting feedback from different parties (academic experts, charity practitioners, survey participants) during conceptualization stage, pretesting, and piloting of the questionnaire. Fourth, external validity is concerned with whether the results of the survey could be generalized beyond the specific research context. Although the sample for this study was a purposive one (that is, focused on the general welfare and social care subsectors), the survey findings and preliminary conclusions were communicated to other charity subsectors and to academic peers in addition to the survey respondents in order to gather feedback and ascertain their applicability to the wider voluntary sector.

The Case Studies Stage

Case studies present particular challenges to the researcher in establishing the validity and reliability of the research design. Reliability in case studies is proven when the data collection procedures can be repeated with similar results (Yin 2003: 159). Validity in case studies comprises of construct validity, internal validity, and external validity. However, unlike quantitative methods, such as survey questionnaires, tests of validity require alternative approaches to evaluate this quality criteria (Bryman 2001). Yin (2003) suggests adopting multiple tactics during data collection and analysis in order to improve the overall quality of the case study design.

Three procedures were included to enhance reliability and validity in the case studies. First, a case study protocol was used to provide consistent conduct for the interviews and for data collection in each case and across cases, thereby enhancing reliability in the interview technique. Initial agreement on the case study objectives, provisional time plan for each case, and access to data collection sources were also secured with the case study organizations. A key contact person in each case study coordinated the interview schedule and liaised with the relevant parties for the data collection within the organization. This ensured that the data collection procedures were consistently followed across the case studies. Second, identifying and matching patterns during the case study data analysis along the three key themes that had emerged from the survey findings aimed to establish a degree of consistency and internal validity. Third, the use of multiple cases had helped to improve the generalizability of results from the case studies to the wider population. Yin (2003: 33) suggests the use of analytical generalization for generalizing the results in case studies. If two or more cases are shown to support the same theory/outcome, replication may be claimed. Moreover, feedback was sought from the case study participants on the key findings in order to check for accuracy and interpretation, thereby enhancing construct validity and external validity of the results.

Triangulation in the Study

In addition to the techniques described in the preceding, used to demonstrate reliability and validity in the survey and case studies stages, the multi-methodology approach adopted for this study had benefitted from methodological and data triangulation. Denzin (1978b: 291) defines triangulation as 'the combination of methodologies in the study of the same phenomenon.' Importantly, methodological triangulation could improve the external validity of the research results by utilizing dissimilar methods to study the same dimension of a research problem (Jick 1983).

> [T]he effectiveness of triangulation rests on the assumption that the methods or measurements used will not share the same biases. . . . their assets will be exploited and their liabilities neutralized. (Jick 1983:138)

In this study, findings and emerging themes from the survey method were cross-validated with findings from the multiple case studies. This type of triangulation enables cross validation of results from different methods, and if these findings are found to be congruent and provide comparable results, external validity of the study is enhanced.

Moreover, data source triangulation occurred in both the survey and case studies stages. In the survey questionnaire, different items were included to operationalize the positioning strategy and strategic marketing planning constructs in the measurement scales. The case studies stage utilized multiple sources of data to cross-check for internal consistency and reliability. Data gathered along key themes from the semi-structured interviews with different key informants were compared with data gathered from document analysis and group discussions. It was recognized that information from a single source might be biased. Gathering evidence from a variety of sources was thus aimed at validating differing perceptions and also increasing internal consistency within the cases (Yin 1994). Therefore, confidence in the theory that was emerging or being developed from these findings during the study was arguably increased (Jick 1979).

CONCLUSIONS

This chapter has described and justified the three-stage research methodological approach utilized for this study. Explicit links between the three stages in the research methodological path have been highlighted. It has also demonstrated reliability and validity at each stage of the research process and in the overall study in order to provide a degree of generalizability of the results, whilst recognizing the particular charitable context. Due to the lack of both theoretical and empirical studies of the strategic positioning of charitable organizations, it was necessary to draw upon the strengths of a mixed-methodological framework.

From a methodological perspective, combining data and emerging findings from the quantitative survey and qualitative case studies had the effect of achieving breadth and depth in this study. Consequently, the methodological and data triangulations increased the validity and confidence of the research results (Jick 1979; Gill and Johnson 1997; Blaikie 2006). The structured use of this research process aimed to produce a more comprehensive picture of the strategic positioning activities of charities and enhanced the quality of research outputs, while facilitating theory development.

5 Mapping the Positioning Activities of Charitable Organizations

This chapter is the first of two chapters that present the empirical findings of data gathered in this study. It provides descriptive data that was gathered during the exploratory survey stage. As it was established in Chapter 4 on methodology, the survey stage was the second in a three-stage methodology employed in this study. The purpose of this chapter is to answer two sets of questions that have been established in the previous chapter. The first set explores and describes the extent of positioning activities, the type of positioning strategies adopted in charities in the general welfare and social care subsectors, and their organizational characteristics. The second set identifies the possible factors that influence the charities' positioning strategy. Due to the lack of empirical evidence in these areas an inductive research strategy was adopted for this exploratory survey stage. A self-administered postal questionnaire was used to collect quantitative and qualitative evidence to answer the research questions established for this research stage. As discussed in the previous chapter on methodology, this exploratory stage was an essential first step to a deeper understanding of the strategic positioning activities of charitable organizations, but not sufficient for its full understanding. Emerging themes from the survey stage will be identified and subsequently investigated in greater depth at the next stage of the study, that is, the case studies stage.

CHARACTERISTICS OF THE SURVEY SAMPLE AND RESPONDENTS

Chapter 4 has explained that the sample used in this study was the general welfare and social care charities from among the CAF's top five hundred fundraising charities in Britain. Before the final version of the postal questionnaire was launched, pre-notification calls were made by telephone to all 113 registered general welfare and social care charities classified in the CAF *Charity Trends* directory of top five hundred fundraising charities in the UK (CAF 2003). The aim was to establish initial contact with potential respondents and to verify mailing addresses. During the pre-notification calls, eighteen charities (eight benevolent funds, two religious general welfare, two elderly care, three other general welfare, and three children) declined to participate without viewing the contents of the questionnaire. The main reasons given were: the charity's policy was not to participate in surveys, they had no time for surveys, and that the charity staff were mainly personnel delivering services and were not able to competently complete the questionnaire on management matters.

After the questionnaire was launched, conscious efforts were made to follow up actively on non-respondents in order to increase the effective response rate and to reduce non-response bias. Telephone calls were made at four occasions over a six-week period to remind non-respondents the importance of their participation and to encourage them to complete the questionnaire. It was also reported in Chapter 4 that the effective final response rate for the postal questionnaire employed in the survey was 54 per cent or fifty-one usable responses out of ninety-five final mailed questionnaires. Reasons for non-responses were analyzed and did not pose significant non-response bias (Hoinville et al. 1978).

The characteristics of the respondents as a group will now be described. These characteristics include their annual income, voluntary income, statutory income, years in existence, and number of paid staff. Respondents were asked to indicate the average annual income of their organizations over the past three years (2001 to 2003). Table 5.1 shows the total annual income of the respondents in three income bands. These income bands followed those used in the CAF's *Charity Trends* 2003 directory. It can be seen from Table 5.1 that 88 per cent of the respondents generated an average annual total income of £1 million and over during those three years. This proportion closely matched that of the total sample frame, that is, 89 per cent, as highlighted in the previous methodology chapter.

Table 5.2 presents the voluntary income of respondents as a proportion of total annual income in 2002–2003. Over 50 per cent of the total income of 68 per cent of respondents came from voluntary sources. Respondents as a group generated £507 million in voluntary income, which was 66 per cent of the voluntary income generated by the general welfare and social care sample, and 23 per cent of the top five hundred fundraising charities in 2002–2003 (CAF 2003). Table 5.3 presents the statutory income of respondents as a proportion of their total annual income in 2002–2003. As it can be seen from Table 5.3, all respondents received government funding in varying proportions. CAF (2003) reports that 14 per cent of them received more than 50 per cent of their total income from statutory sources. Respondents as a group received £383 million of non-voluntary income in 2002–2003. This income comprised of (among other sources) government grants and contract fees. The amount accounted for a sizable 61 per cent of non-voluntary income from the general welfare and social care sample, and 23 per cent of the top five hundred fundraising charities in 2002–2003 (ibid.). The proportions of voluntary and statutory incomes of the respondents were

Table 5.1 Total Annual Income of Survey Respondents

	General Welfare and Social Care Respondents (2001–2003)						
Total Income	Other Gen Wef (n=16)	Children (n=13)	Ben Funds (n=9)	Elderly Care (n=5)	Service/Ex-Service (n=5)	Rel Gen Wef (n=3)	Total No. (%) (N=51)
Below £1 m	3 (19%)	2 (12%)	1 (11%)	—	—	—	6 (12%)
£ 1–10m	9 (56%)	8 (64%)	6 (67%)	2 (40%)	1 (20%)	—	26 (51%)
Over £10 m	4 (26%)	3 (24%)	2 (22%)	3 (60%)	4 (80%)	3 (100%)	19 (37%)
Total	16 (100%)	13 (100%)	9 (100%)	5 (100%)	5 (100%)	3 (100%)	51 (100%)

Note: Cells with no figures indicate no respondent in that subsector selected that particular category.

Table 5.2 Voluntary Income of Survey Respondents

% Voluntary Income	General Welfare and Social Care Respondents in 2002–2003						
	Other Gen Wef (n=16)	Children (n=13)	Ben Funds (n=9)	Elderly Care (n=5)	Service/Ex-Service (n=5)	Rel Gen Wef (n=3)	Total No. (%) (N=51)
Below 25	6 (39%)	—	2 (22%)	2 (40%)	—	1 (33%)	11 (22%)
Above 25–50	1 (6%)	1 (8%)	—	1 (20%)	2 (40%)	—	5 (10%)
Above 50–75	4 (25%)	4 (28%)	1 (11%)	2 (40%)	1 (20%)	1 (33%)	13 (25%)
Above 75–100	5 (30%)	8 (64%)	6 (67%)	—	2 (40%)	1 (34%)	22 (43%)
Total	16 (100%)	13 (100%)	9 (100%)	5 (100%)	5 (100%)	3 (100%)	51 (100%)

Note: Cells with no figures indicate no respondent in that subsector selected that particular category.

Table 5.3 Statutory Income of Survey Respondents

% Statutory Income	General Welfare and Social Care Respondents in 2002–2003						
	Other Gen Wef (n=16)	Children (n=13)	Ben Funds (n=9)	Elderly Care (n=5)	Service/Ex-Service (n=5)	Rel Gen Wef (n=3)	Total No. (%) (N=51)
Below 25	7 (42%)	11 (84%)	8 (89%)	5 (100%)	4 (80%)	2 (67%)	37 (72%)
Above 25–50	4 (26%)	2 (16%)	—	—	1 (20%)	—	7 (14%)
Above 50–75	3 (19%)	—	1 (11%)	—	—	—	4 (8%)
Above 75–100	2 (13%)	—	—	—	—	1 (33%)	3 (6%)
Total	16 (100%)	13 (100%)	9 (100%)	5 (100%)	5 (100%)	3 (100%)	51 (100%)

Note: Cells with no figures indicate no respondent in that subsector selected that particular category.

Table 5.4 Number of Total Paid Staff of Survey Respondents

Number of Paid Staff	General Welfare and Social Care Respondents						
	Other Gen Wef (n=16)	Children (n=13)	Ben Funds (n=9)	Elderly Care (n=5)	Service/Ex-Service (n=5)	Rel Gen Wef (n=3)	Total Paid No. (%) (N=51)
Below 50	7 (44%)	8 (62%)	4 (45%)	—	2 (40%)	—	21 (41%)
Above 50–100	2 (12%)	2 (15%)	2 (22%)	—	—	—	6 (11%)
Above 100–500	3 (19%)	1 (8%)	1 (11%)	4 (80%)	1 (20%)	1 (33%)	11 (22%)
Above 500–1000	2 (12%)	—	1 (11%)	1 (20%)	2 (40%)	1 (33%)	7 (14%)
Above 1000	2 (13%)	2 (15%)	1 (11%)	—	—	1 (34%)	6 (12%)
Total	16 (100%)	13 (100%)	9 (100%)	5 (100%)	5 (100%)	3 (100%)	51 (100%)

Note: Cells with no figures indicate no respondent in that subsector selected that particular category.

consistent with that of the total sample of general welfare and social care subsectors to the sampling frame.

Nearly all respondents had been in existence for more than ten years at the time of the survey. However, two respondents were exceptions. One of these began its existence six years ago, while another had established itself less than five years ago as a result of a merger between two charities in different general welfare and social care subsectors. Table 5.4 shows the total paid staff employed by respondents. Paid staff in the organization included full- and part-time staff. Forty-one per cent of respondents had less than fifty paid staff, while 26 per cent of respondents had above five hundred paid staff in their organizations at the time of the survey.

Overall, the profiling of the respondents as a group shows them broadly representative of the total sample population in terms of the key organizational characteristics.

CHARITIES' PERCEPTION OF COMPETITION

In Chapter 3 it had been established that the operating environment of charitable organizations is becoming increasingly competitive in terms of raising revenue and vying for other organizational resources. This part of the survey aimed to find out how charities perceived the level of competitive intensity currently experienced in the sector/subsector they were operating in, and if that competition could drive charities to adopt strategic management, marketing, and positioning activities to differentiate themselves from other providers of similar services and to preserve their distinctive cause/mission (Chew 2003, 2006b).

This study defines competitive intensity as the degree to which organizations have to compete with other organizations for financial and other organizational resources in the sector within which they operate (Chew 2006a). As a reference point, the number of registered charities in England and Wales had increased 50 per cent from 120,000 in 1975 to over 190,000 at the end of 2006 (Charity Commission 2006). A high level of competitive intensity would suggest that the charitable organization has to compete with a relatively greater number of other charities vying for these resources within its subsector or providing similar services. Conversely, a low level of competitive intensity means a relatively smaller number of organizations are competing for these resources. Table 5.5 shows that 61 per cent of respondents perceived a high level of competitive intensity, while only 9 per cent of respondents perceived a low level of competitive intensity for financial and other organizational resources in their sector/subsector.

These findings also suggest that the intensity of competition perceived by respondents could be subsectoral specific. For instance, the larger proportion of respondents in the subsectors of elderly care (100 per cent), children (80 per cent), and other general welfare (51 per cent) viewed a high level

Table 5.5 Competitive Intensity Perceived by Survey Respondents

Level of Competitive Intensity	General Welfare and Social Care Respondents						Total No. (%) (N=51)
	Other Gen Wef (n=16)	Children (n=13)	Ben Funds (n=9)	Elderly Care (n=5)	Service/Ex-Service (n=5)	Rel Gen Wef (n=3)	
Low	1 (6%)	2 (12%)	2 (22%)	—	—	—	5 (9%)
Moderate	6 (39%)	1 (8%)	3 (33%)	—	3 (60%)	2 (67%)	15 (29%)
High	9 (51%)	10 (80%)	5 (45%)	5 (100%)	2 (40%)	1 (33%)	31 (61%)
Total	16 (100%)	13 (100%)	9 (100%)	5 (100%)	5 (100%)	3 (100%)	51 (100%)

Note: Cells with no figures indicate no respondent in that subsector selected that particular category.

of competitive intensity in their operating environment. In contrast, low competitive intensity was cited by a proportionately higher percentage of respondents in the benevolent funds subsector (22 per cent) compared to the other subsectors in this study.

CHANGE IN COMPETITIVE INTENSITY

Respondents were also asked about the likelihood of change in the current level of competitive intensity for financial and other organizational resources over five years (2005–2010). Table 5.6 shows 82 per cent of respondents felt that the competitive intensity could experience a moderate to high increase over this period, while 18 per cent felt there was no potential change in current competitive intensity over the next five years. No respondent cited a decrease in current competitive intensity in the future. The findings suggest that the future operating environment of general welfare and social care charities in specific, and of the charity sector generally, is likely to become more competitive, where it is possible that the number of organizations competing for financial and other organizational resources could increase in the future.

RELATIONSHIP BETWEEN CURRENT COMPETITIVE INTENSITY AND CHANGE IN COMPETITIVE INTENSITY

There were significant correlations between the perceived current level of competitive intensity and the change in that level in the future. Due to the purposive nature and the small size of the sample, nonparametric analysis was conducted in addition to parametric analysis in order to reinforce the findings (Pallant 2001). Tables 5.7 (a and b) show Pearson's correlation and Spearman's Rho for nonparametric correlation were both significant at the 0.01 level. In other words, the findings suggest that respondents who perceived the current level of competitive intensity to be high or moderate also perceived a high or moderate increase in the competitive intensity in their subsectors over the next five years.

MAIN COMPETITORS

When asked about their main competitors for financial and other organizational resources, 71.2 per cent of respondents cited other charities that provide similar services as their major rivals. 19.2 per cent of respondents cited private sector organizations as providing similar services, while 11.5 per cent of respondents cited voluntary organizations other than charities as their main competitors. A small minority perceived central government

Table 5.6 Change in Competitive Intensity over Five Years (2005–2010) Perceived by Survey Respondents

Change in Competitive Intensity	General Welfare and Social Care Respondents						Total No. (%) (N=51)
	Other Gen Wef (n=16)	Children (n=13)	Ben Funds (n=9)	Elderly Care (n=5)	Service/Ex-Service (n=5)	Rel Gen Wef (n=3)	
No change	3 (19%)	2 (15%)	2 (22%)	—	2 (40%)	—	9 (18%)
Moderate increase	9 (56%)	8 (62%)	5 (56%)	5 (100%)	3 (60%)	3 (100%)	33 (64%)
High increase	4 (25%)	3 (23%)	2 (22%)	—	—	—	9 (18%)
Total	16 (100%)	13 (100%)	9 (100%)	5 (100%)	5 (100%)	3 (100%)	51 (100%)

Note: Cells with no figures indicate no respondent in that subsector selected that particular category.

Table 5.7a Bivariate Correlation between Competitive Intensity and Change in Competitive Intensity over Five Years (2005–2010)

Correlation between Level of Competitive Intensity and Change in Competitive Intensity for Financial and Other Resources over Five Years		*Competitive Intensity in the Charity Sector/ Subsector for Financial and Other Resources*	*Change in Competitive Intensity over 5 Years*
Competitive intensity in the charity sector/ sub-sector for financial and other resources	Pearson correlation	1	.445 **
	Sig. (2-tailed)	.	.001
	N	51	51
Change in competitive intensity over 5 years	Pearson correlation	.445 **	1
	Sig. (2-tailed)	.001	.
	N	51	51

Note: ** Correlations are significant at the 0.01 level (2-tailed).

Table 5.7b Nonparametric Correlation between Competitive Intensity and Change in Competitive Intensity over Five Years (2005–2010)

Nonparametric Correlation between Level of Competitive Intensity and Change in Competitive Intensity over Five Years			*Competitive Intensity in the Charity Sector/ Subsector for Financial and Other Resources*	*Change in Competitive Intensity over 5 Years*
Spearman's Rho	Competitive intensity in the charity sector for financial and other resources	Correlation coefficient	1.000	.435 **
		Sig. (2-tailed)	.	.001
		N	51	51
	Change in competitive intensity over 5 years	Correlation coefficient	.435**	1.000
		Sig. (2-tailed)	.001	.
		N	51	51

Note: ** Correlations are significant at the 0.01 level (2-tailed).

agencies (5.9 per cent) and local government agencies (1.9 per cent) as their main competitors despite receiving funding from these sources. Other competitors cited by respondents were local charities, professional associations, the national lottery, and trade unions.

MAPPING THE POSITIONING ACTIVITIES OF CHARITIES

The Extent of Strategic Marketing Planning Activities

As it was explained in Chapter 4 on methodology, the lack of existing scales measuring strategic marketing planning activities in charitable organizations in existing literature had necessitated the development of a scale specifically for the purpose of this study. The thirteen strategic marketing planning activities are indicated as SMP1 to SMP13 in Figure 5.1, the order following the items listed in the survey questionnaire. The internal reliability of the strategic marketing planning scale was analyzed using Cronbach's coefficient alpha (Cronbach 1951). Each response to an item, which denoted an activity on the strategic marketing planning scale, was correlated with responses to other items in that scale. The test aimed to measure the consistency of responses across all items used in the scale (Mitchell 1996). As it is shown in Figure 5.1, the overall correlation (Cronbach's coefficient alpha) for the thirteen items was good at 0.8430 as it exceeded the recommended guide of 0.7 for good internal reliability (Pallant 2001). In addition, as demonstrated in Chapter 4, various other efforts were undertaken to enhance the reliability and validity of the survey process and the scales at this stage of the study.

Respondents were asked to select a number from 1 (small extent) to 10 (large extent) to indicate to what extent each of the thirteen activities (items) in the strategic marketing planning scale was undertaken by their organization. A filter score of zero was included to indicate non-activity for an activity (item). As it was established in Chapter 4, the purpose was to strengthen overall reliability of the scale (Andrews 1984). Figure 5.2 shows the total mean scores (highest to lowest) and corresponding standard deviation for the thirteen strategic marketing planning activities of respondents as a group. The findings indicate that strategic marketing activities were undertaken by charities to varying extents.

Four interesting points can be derived from Figures 5.1 and 5.2. First, this study is focused on strategic positioning and marketing planning at the organizational level rather than at the tactical level, such as product/service or promotional planning. The total mean score of the thirteen items (activities) in the strategic marketing planning scale was 6.38 out of a maximum score of 10. This suggests that respondents, as a group, undertook strategic marketing planning activities moderately. However, the type and range of these activities undertaken by charities in this study meant that they had begun to undertake marketing planning at a strategic level, rather than at

	Item-Total Statistics				
	Scale Mean if Item Deleted	*Scale Variance if Item Deleted*	*Corrected Item-Total Correlation*	*Squared Multiple Correlation*	*Alpha if Item Deleted*
SMP1	76.8235	276.3882	.7024	.5944	.8176
SMP2	78.2549	286.5937	.5770	.5681	.8265
SMP3	77.7059	295.3318	.3681	.4565	.8421
SMP4	77.3922	287.4431	.4690	.5938	.8343
SMP5	76.4706	292.9741	.5329	.4435	.8298
SMP6	76.0000	289.2800	.6071	.5384	.8254
SMP7	75.5686	322.6502	.1726	.2926	.8494
SMP8	75.9608	310.4784	.2964	.5365	.8441
SMP9	77.1373	284.5608	.5175	.3793	.8305
SMP10	75.7255	287.8831	.5786	.6354	.8266
SMP11	75.8039	292.1208	.4301	.4117	.8370
SMP12	76.4118	280.9271	.5790	.6256	.8258
SMP13	76.5098	284.3349	.6126	.5825	.8241

Reliability coefficients 13 items
Cronbach's coefficient alpha = 0.8430
Standardized item alpha = 0.8426

Figure 5.1 Reliability analysis of strategic marketing planning scale.

a tactical level, as discovered in earlier studies in the 1990s. For instance, Cousins (1990) found that while marketing planning was being adopted by voluntary and non-profit organizations in the UK, the type of marketing plans were focused more on tactical marketing activities, and had more of a 'marketing mix bias' (ibid.: 30), such as product, promotional, and distribution planning, compared to counterparts in the private and public sector sectors.

Second, 'Segmentation of Donors/Funders' activity had the highest mean score of 7.41. This suggests that while 'Developing Fundraising Plans and Actions' had the third highest mean score of 7.18 in the strategic marketing planning scale, charities increased their efforts in profiling their donors and fund providers in order to support their fundraising programmes. This

Strategic Marketing Planning Activities	Mean Score	Standard Deviation
• Segmentation of donors/funders	7.41	1.88
• Developing communication plans and actions	7.25	2.28
• Developing fundraising plans and actions	7.18	2.63
• Segmentation of user/clients/beneficiaries	7.02	2.17
• Setting marketing objectives in line with mission and goals of the organization	6.98	2.13
• Allocating marketing and other resources to support and implement marketing plans and objectives	6.56	2.59
• Internal organizational and resources analysis	6.51	2.19
• Monitoring marketing performance vs. plans	6.47	2.33
• External environmental analysis	6.16	2.39
• Identifying charity's positioning dimensions	5.84	2.65
• Market research and analysis on users/clients	5.59	2.71
• Market research and analysis on donor/funders	5.27	2.76
• Competitor monitoring and analysis	4.72	2.34

Strategic marketing planning scale 13-items: Scale mean= 6.38
Scale standard deviation = 2.39 Cronbach's coefficient alpha = 0.8430

Figure 5.2 Mean scores (highest to lowest) and standard deviations for strategic marketing planning scale for all survey respondents as a group (N=51).

finding contrasted with some studies conducted in the mid-1990s, which found low levels of adoption and sophistication in the use of market segmentation approaches on donor markets among top British charities (e.g., Sargeant 1995).

Third, 'Competitor Monitoring and Analysis' had the lowest mean score of 4.72 in this study. This finding reinforces previous findings (e.g., Cousins 1990) that voluntary and charitable organizations in the UK paid less attention on competitor monitoring compared to private sector organizations, and that many of them tended to use informal methods of market research to stay in touch with target audiences' needs. For instance, in a study of 143 British charities, Bennett (2003) found that, while the intensity of competition for raising funds from individual donors had increased significantly since the mid-1990s, and while charities appeared to take competitor analysis more seriously compared to the period before 1990, the level of resources dedicated to competitor analysis had remained low. The final point to highlight in Figure 5.2 is the mean score 5.84 for 'Identifying the Charity's Positioning Dimensions,' which was lower than the total mean score for all thirteen activities in the strategic marketing planning scale. The score for this activity provides an early indication of the extent to which respondents undertook that particular positioning activity, which was not as high as other marketing planning activities in their organizations.

The Extent of Positioning Strategy Activities

As with the earlier strategic marketing planning scale, there is a lack of existing scales to measure positioning strategy activities in the charity context. This had necessitated the development of a positioning strategy scale specifically for the purpose of this study. The six positioning strategy activities are identified as PS1 to PS6 in Figure 5.3, and the order follows the items listed in the survey questionnaire. They corresponded closely to the three main components of a positioning strategy as depicted in the initial organizing conceptual framework in Chapter 2. The internal reliability of this scale was tested using Cronbach's coefficient alpha test (Cronbach 1951).

Positioning Strategy Activities as Denoted in the Survey Questionnaire	*Corresponding Component of Positioning Strategy in Initial Conceptual Framework*
PS1 Selection of user/client/beneficiary to serve	Choice of target audience
PS2 Selection of donor/funder to target	Choice of target audience
PS3 Selection of positioning dimensions to use to distinguish the charity from other providers	Choice of positioning dimensions
PS4 Selection of positioning strategy that best differentiates the charity from other providers	Choice of generic or core positioning strategy
PS5 Selection of positioning strategy that can be best supported by the charity's existing resources and capabilities	Choice of positioning dimensions
PS6 Selection of positioning strategy that best fits the charity's mission and culture	Choice of generic or core positioning strategy

Figure 5.3 Positioning strategy components in the survey questionnaire.

118   *Strategic Positioning in Voluntary and Charitable Organizations*

As it is shown in Figure 5.4, the result was found to be good at 0.8082 and exceeded the recommended guide for good internal reliability of a scale at 0.7 (Pallant 2001).

Respondents were asked to select a number from 1 (small extent) to 10 (large extent) for each of the six activities in the positioning strategy scale developed specifically for this study. As with the strategic marketing planning scale, a filter score of zero was included in the positioning strategy scale to indicate non-activity for an activity (item). The intent was to strengthen the reliability of the measurement scale (Andrews 1984). Figure 5.5 shows the total mean scores (highest to lowest) and corresponding standard deviation for the six positioning strategy activities of respondents as a group.

Figure 5.5 reveals four key points about positioning activities in charitable organizations. First, the total mean score of the six positioning activities was 6.64. This suggests that as a group, respondents undertook these activities moderately in order to differentiate themselves from other providers. There appears to be two groups of target audiences for positioning by respondents: (a) the user/client/beneficiary and (b) the donor/funder. 'Selection of Donor/Funder' had the highest total mean score of 7.49, while 'Selection of User/Beneficiary' had the second highest total mean score at 7.06. These scores suggest relatively high emphasis by charities to identify these two distinct target audiences needed for positioning. 'Selecting the Positioning Dimensions to Distinguish the Charity from other Providers' activity had the second lowest total mean score at 6.04. This, together with

Item-Total Statistics				
	Scale Mean if Item Deleted	Scale Variance if Item Deleted	Corrected Item-Total Correlation	Squared Multiple Correlation	Alpha if Item Deleted
PS1	32.8039	93.0808	.4444	.2433	.8099
PS2	32.3725	104.7584	.4315	.2686	.8050
PS3	33.8235	85.0282	.6807	.8467	.7509
PS4	34.0980	84.6902	.6769	.8430	.7517
PS5	33.0588	94.6565	.5629	.4741	.7795
PS6	33.1569	88.8149	.6292	.4978	.7640

Reliability coefficients 6 items
Cronbach's coefficient alpha = 0.8082
Standardized item alpha = 0.8085

Figure 5.4 Reliability analysis of positioning strategy scale.

Positioning Strategy Activities	Mean Score	Standard Deviation
• Selection of donor/funder to target	7.49	2.07
• Selection of user/client/beneficiary to serve	7.06	2.97
• Selection of positioning strategy that can best be supported by the charity's existing resources and capabilities	6.80	2.44
• Selection of positioning strategy that best fits the charity's mission and culture	6.70	2.65
• Selection of positioning dimensions to use to distinguish charity from other providers	6.04	2.76
• Selection of positioning strategy that best differentiates the charity from other providers	5.76	2.80

Positioning strategy scale (6-items) Scale mean = 6.64
Scale standard deviation = 2.61 Cronbach's coefficient alpha = 0.8082

Figure 5.5 Mean scores (highest to lowest) and standard deviations for positioning strategy scale for all survey respondents as a group (N=51).

'Identifying the Charity's Positioning Dimensions' activity, which scored a low total mean of 5.84 in the strategic marketing planning scale (see earlier section), suggests that respondents did not provide a high level of priority for positioning dimensions in their strategic marketing planning compared to other activities in these two scales. Finally, an interesting finding concerns the 'Selection of Positioning Strategy that Best Differentiates the Charity from other Providers' activity, which had the lowest total mean score of 5.76 among the six positioning strategy activities. This finding suggests that, while the respondents had begun to undertake positioning activities, they were devoting the least attention to identifying and deciding the most appropriate positioning strategy for their organization.

THE RELATIONSHIP BETWEEN POSITIONING AND STRATEGIC MARKETING PLANNING

There was a significant correlation between the total mean of strategic marketing planning activities and the total mean of positioning strategy activities. Pearson's Correlation and Spearman's Rho for nonparametric correlation were both significant at the 0.01 levels (see Table 5.8a and Table 5.8b). This suggests that respondents who scored high in the strategic marketing

Table 5.8a Bivariate Correlation between Positioning and Strategic Marketing Planning Activities

Correlation between Total Sum Mean of Strategic Marketing Planning Scale (SMP) and Total Sum Mean of Positioning Strategy (PS) Activities Scale		Total Sum Mean of SMP Scale SMP1 to SMP13	Total Sum Mean of PS Scale PS1 to PS6
Total sum mean of strategic marketing planning scale items SMP1 to SMP13	Pearson Correlation	1	.521 **
	Sig. (2-tailed)	.	.000
	N	51	51
Total sum mean of positioning strategy scale items PS1 to PS6	Pearson Correlation	.521**	1
	Sig. (2-tailed)	.000	.
	N	51	51

Note: ** Correlations are significant at the 0.01 level (2-tailed).

Table 5.8b Nonparametric Correlation between Positioning and Strategic Marketing Planning Activities

Nonparametric Correlation between Total Sum Mean of Strategic Marketing Planning (SMP) Scale and Total Sum Mean of Positioning Strategy (PS) Activities Scale			Total Sum Mean of SMP Scale SMP1 to SMP13	Total Sum Mean of PS Scale PS1 to PS6
Spearman's Rho	Total sum mean of strategic marketing planning scale Items SMP1 to SMP13	Correlation Coefficient	1.000	.455 **
		Sig. (2-tailed)	.	.001
		N	51	51
	Total sum mean of positioning strategy scale Items PS1 to PS6	Correlation Coefficient	.455**	1.000
		Sig. (2-tailed)	.001	.
		N	51	51

Note: ** Correlations are significant at the 0.01 level (2-tailed).

planning scale tended to also score high in the positioning strategy scale. In other words, general welfare and social care charities that undertook strategic marketing planning activities more extensively also tended to carry out positioning activities extensively, and vise versa.

GENERIC OR CORE POSITIONING STRATEGY

The literature review in Chapter 2 discussed Porter's (1980) three generic or core positioning strategic alternatives that organizations could adopt to distinguish themselves in a competitive environment. These are differentiation, focus, and lower-cost leadership positioning strategies. In the survey questionnaire, respondents were asked to indicate which generic positioning strategy best described their positioning of their organizations to appeal to their target audiences. In order to avoid technical jargon in the questionnaire, descriptions were used to denote the three generic positioning approaches, as close as possible to the definitions used by Porter (1980). These are shown in Figure 5.6.

As it was established in Chapter 4, the survey questionnaire and the constructs that needed to be measured were pretested and piloted before being launched in order to enhance construct or face validity of the survey instrument. Table 5.9 presents the generic or core positioning strategies that respondents adopted in their organizations. Sixty-five per cent of respondents cited differentiation positioning and 33 per cent cited focus positioning as their generic or core positioning strategies. Only one respondent used low-cost positioning as its core positioning strategy.

Description Used in the Survey Questionnaire	Conceptual Meaning
• Identifying and communicating the unique ways in which my organization and its services/products meet the needs of clients or donors and are valued by them.	Differentiation positioning
• Identifying and communicating the ways in which my organization can serve a particular group of users (clients, beneficiaries), or in a particular geographical area or by providing a particular type of service better than other organizations.	Focus (or niche) positioning
• Identifying and communicating my organization's ability to provide competitively low priced services/products due to our cost-efficient operations and accessibility to low-cost resources.	Low-cost leadership positioning

Figure 5.6 Description of generic or core positioning strategies used in the survey questionnaire.

Table 5.9 Generic or Core Positioning Strategies Adopted by Survey Respondents

Type of Generic or Core Positioning Strategy	General Welfare and Social Care Respondents						
	Other Gen Wef (n=16)	Children (n=13)	Ben Funds (n=9)	Elderly Care (n=5)	Service/Ex-Service (n=5)	Rel Gen Wef (n=3)	Total No. (%) (N=51)
Low-cost	—	1 (8%)	—	—	—	—	1 (2%)
Focus	5 (32%)	3 (24%)	7 (78%)	1 (20%)	1 (20%)	—	17 (33%)
Differentiation	11 (68%)	9 (68%)	2 (22%)	4 (80%)	4 (80%)	3 (100%)	33 (65%)
Total	16 (100%)	13 (100%)	9 (100%)	5 (100%)	5 (100%)	3 (100%)	51 (100%)

Note: Cells with no figures indicate no respondent in that subsector selected that particular category.

Table 5.9 also identifies the generic positioning strategy adopted by respondents in different general welfare and social care subsectors at the time of the survey. A key point arising from this mapping was the relatively high proportion (78 per cent) of respondents in the benevolent funds subsector that have adopted focus positioning as their generic or core positioning strategy. This contrasted with respondents in other subsectors where the majority (68 per cent and above) adopted differentiation positioning as their preferred core positioning strategy. This finding provides empirical support to the common notion that many benevolent funds, as part of the wider voluntary sector in the UK, were founded to serve the needs of particular groups of users/clients/beneficiaries in particular trades or industries. Focus positioning could be a perceived strength of benevolent funds that seek to be very selective in their choice of both target users/clients/beneficiaries and donors/funders. On the other hand, their narrow target audiences/markets could also be perceived as a weakness during times of rapidly changing operating environments in the trade/industry or geographic location in which they operate.

DISTINGUISHING CHARITIES ADOPTING DIFFERENT GENERIC POSITIONING STRATEGIES

The characteristics of respondents that adopted different generic or core positioning strategies were further examined using nonparametric chi-square test for independence between groups. This test describes the relationship between two categorical variables and indicates the strength of that relationship (Pallant 2001). There was only one respondent that cited low-cost positioning as its generic positioning strategy, meaning that in order to fulfil the general assumptions of the chi-square statistical test, the decision was made to test the relationships between respondents adopting differentiation positioning and focus positioning only. Tables 5.10 to 5.14 show the test results for key characteristics of these two groups of respondents. These

Table 5.10 Total Annual Income of Survey Respondents Using Differentiation and Focus Positioning Strategies

Total Annual Income over 3 Years (2001–2003)	Differentiation Positioning $n = 33$	Focus Positioning $n = 17$	Total $N = 50$
£10 mil and below	17 (51%)	14 (82%)	31 (62%)
Above £10 mil	16 (49%)	3 (18%)	19 (38%)
Total	33 (100%)	17 (100%)	50 (100%)

Note: Chi-square value (with continuity correction for 2 x 2 matrix) = 3.314; 0.069 > p > .05.

124   *Strategic Positioning in Voluntary and Charitable Organizations*

Table 5.11 Proportion of Total Income from Voluntary Income in Survey Respondents Using Differentiation and Focus Positioning Strategies

Proportion of Voluntary Income (2002–2003)	Differentiation Positioning n = 33	Focus Positioning n = 17	Total N = 50
50% and below	9 (27%)	7 (41%)	16 (32%)
Above 50%	24 (73%)	10 (59%)	34 (68%)
Total	33 (100%)	17 (100%)	50 (100%)

Note: Chi-square value (with continuity correction for 2 × 2 matrix) = 0.460; 0.498 > p > 0.05.

Table 5.12 Proportion of Total Income from Statutory Funding in Survey Respondents Using Differentiation and Focus Positioning Strategies

Proportion of Statutory Income (2002–2003)	Differentiation Positioning n = 33	Focus Positioning n = 17	Total N = 50
25% and below	25 (76%)	12 (71%)	37 (74%)
Above 25%	8 (24%)	5 (29%)	13 (26%)
Total	33 (100%)	17 (100%)	50 (100%)

Note: Chi-square value (with continuity correction for 2 × 2 matrix) = 0.003; 0.957 > p > 0.05.

Table 5.13 Number of Paid Staff in Survey Respondents Using Differentiation and Focus Positioning Strategies

Number of Total Paid Staff (2003)	Differentiation Positioning n = 33	Focus Positioning n = 17	Total N = 50
100 and below	15 (46%)	11 (65%)	26 (52%)
Above 100	18 (54%)	6 (35%)	24 (48%)
Total	33 (100%)	17 (100%)	50 (100%)

Note: Chi-square value (with continuity correction for 2 × 2 matrix) = 0.984; 0.321 > p > 0.05.

Table 5.14 Perception of Current Level of Competitive Intensity in Survey
Respondents Using Differentiation and Focus Positioning Strategies

Level of Competitive Intensity	Differentiation Positioning n = 33	Focus Positioning n = 17	Total N = 50
Low to moderate	14 (42%)	6 (35%)	20 (40%)
High	19 (58%)	11 (65%)	30 (60%)
Total	33 (100%)	17 (100%)	50 (100%)

Note: Chi-square value (with continuity correction for 2 × 2 matrix) = 0.033; 0.855 > p > 0.05.

characteristics are, respectively: total annual income, the proportion of total income from voluntary income, the proportion of total income from statutory funding, the number of paid staff, and the perception of competitive intensity.

As it can be seen from Tables 5.10 to 5.14, little statistical evidence was found to significantly distinguish these two groups of respondents along organizational characteristics. However, the data from these tables suggest that respondents adopting focus positioning as their generic or core positioning strategy tended to be smaller organizations in terms of total annual income and number of paid staff. A smaller proportion of their total annual income was derived from voluntary income (59 per cent) compared to those respondents that had adopted differentiation positioning (73 per cent). Furthermore, a slightly higher relative percentage of respondents adopting focus positioning (65 per cent) perceived a high level of competition for financial and other organizational resources in their sector/subsector compared to respondents adopting differentiation positioning (58 per cent).

POSITIONING DIMENSIONS

Respondents supported their generic or core positioning strategy with a variety of positioning dimensions. As it was established in Chapter 2, positioning dimensions are identified in this study as key differentiators, based on the major organizational strengths (assets and competencies) of the organization, which can provide long-term strategic advantages (Hooley, Broderick, and Moller 1998; Hooley et al. 2001; Chew 2003). There were different dimensions that survey respondents had utilized as appropriate bases to support their differentiation or focus positioning strategies. Table 5.15 presents a breakdown of the positioning dimensions cited by respondents in descending order of use. It is evident from Table 5.15 that the charity's mission was the most frequently cited (63 per cent), while a minority of

Table 5.15 Positioning Dimensions Used by Survey Respondents

Positioning Dimensions (Ways in Which Respondents Distinguish Their Organization) (In Descending Order of Usage)	Responses from General Welfare and Social Care Respondents						
	Other Gen Wef (n=16)	Children (n=13)	Ben Funds (n=9)	Elderly Care (n=5)	Service/Ex-Service (n=5)	Rel Gen Wef (n=3)	Total No. (%) (N=51)
We are different based on our organization's mission	11 (35%)	8 (25%)	5 (16%)	3 (9%)	2 (6%)	3 (9%)	32 (63%)
We specialize in serving the needs of particular user/client segments or in particular geographic segments	9 (32%)	6 (21%)	7 (25%)	2 (7%)	1 (4%)	3 (11%)	28 (55%)
We specialize in providing particular types of services/products to our customers (user/client/beneficiary)	8 (35%)	7 (30%)	2 (9%)	3 (13%)	1 (4%)	2 (9%)	23 (45%)
We are different based on the quality in which we deliver our services	8 (35%)	7 (30%)	4 (17%)	1 (4%)	2 (8%)	1 (2%)	23 (45%)
We are different based on the quality of the services/products offered	7 (39%)	6 (33%)	2 (11%)	3 (17%)	—	—	18 (35%)

We are different based on the wide range of services/product available	7 (47%)	3 (20%)	2 (13%)	1 (7%)	1 (7%)	1 (7%)	15 (30%)
We are different based on the degree of support/ancillary services that we provide	5 (46%)	3 (27%)	1 (9%)	—	2 (18%)	—	11 (22%)
We are different based on our network of branch offices	1 (14%)	1 (14%)	1 (14%)	—	3 (43%)	1 (14%)	7 (14%)
We are different based on our unique relationship with central and/or local government agency/branch	2 (29%)	1 (13%)	—	2 (29%)	2 (29%)	—	7 (14%)
We are different based on our low cost of operations	2 (40%)	3 (60%)	—	—	—	—	5 (10%)
We are different based on our competitively low priced services/products	2 (100%)	—	—	—	—	—	2 (4%)

Note: Totals do not add up to 100% because respondents in each subsector could choose more than one positioning dimension, but not necessarily all of them. A cell with no figure indicates that no respondent in that subsector selected the particular dimension.

respondents cited low cost of operations (10 per cent) and competitive low prices of services/products (4 per cent) as their positioning differentiators. Additionally, 14 per cent of respondents cited their unique relationship with government agencies (central and local) as a positioning differentiator.

Overall, charitable organizations used a range of positioning dimensions within their generic or core positioning strategies to distinguish themselves from other charities/providers offering similar services. However, the dimensions cited by respondents did not appear to be subsectoral specific. Moreover, some of the dimensions cited appeared to be similar to those advocated in the extant literature, such as quality service, superior service/product benefits, specialist services, low cost, and specialization (e.g., Lovelock and Weinberg 1989; McLeish 1995; Kotler and Andreasen 1996; Hooley, Saunders, and Piercy 1998). On the other hand, other dimensions cited, such as the charity's mission, unique relationships with government, and support/ancillary services, seemed to apply specifically to the charitable context.

KEY FACTORS THAT INFLUENCE A POSITIONING STRATEGY

This section presents the key factors that respondents perceived to be most influential in their choice of positioning strategy. Respondents were asked to select the five most important factors from a list of twelve factors provided. At the same time, they were asked to rank the five factors selected in order of their perceived importance from numbers 1 to 5 (1 denoting highest importance). Table 5.16 presents the key factors most frequently cited by respondents.

Overall, the findings suggest that the choice of positioning strategy was influenced by factors external and internal to their organizations. The charity's mission was a particular influential factor cited by a majority of respondents in all subsectors. It played a crucial role in the organization's positioning, both as a primary influence in the choice of positioning strategy (82 per cent cited) and a major strategic positioning differentiator (63 per cent cited), as established in the previous section.

The choice of positioning strategy was also influenced by both the needs of users/clients/beneficiaries (78 per cent cited) and the needs of donors/funders (53 per cent cited) as two key external stakeholders. External environmental factors, such as shifts or changes in socio-demographic, economic, political, regulatory, and technology environments, and internal organizational factors, such as availability of organizational resources, were cited by 67 per cent of respondents. Trustees/board members were perceived to be influential internal influencers. Thirty-eight per cent of respondents cited preferences of this internal group of decision-makers as a factor in the choice of their positioning strategy. Another internal factor was organizational culture, which was cited by 31 per cent of respondents.

Table 5.16 Key Factors Influencing Choice of a Positioning Strategy in the Survey Respondents

Most Influential Factors on Choice of Positioning Strategy (In Descending Order of Importance)	Responses from General Welfare and Social Care Respondents						
	Other Gen Wef (n=16)	Children (n=13)	Ben Funds (n=9)	Elderly Care (n=5)	Service/Ex-Service (n=5)	Rel Gen Wef (n=3)	Total No. (%) (N=51)
My organization's mission	11 (69%)	11 (85%)	8 (89%)	4 (80%)	5 (100%)	3 (100%)	42 (82%)
The needs of various groups of target users/clients/beneficiaries targeted	14 (88%)	9 (76%)	8 (89%)	5 (100%)	2 (40%)	2 (67%)	40 (78%)
My organization's available resources (financial, human, physical)	12 (75%)	10 (77%)	6 (67%)	1 (20%)·	4 (80%)	2 (67%)	35 (69%)
External environmental factors (political, regulatory, economic, social, technology, demographics)	11 (69%)	9 (69%)	6 (67%)	4 (80%)	3 (60%)	1 (33%)	34 (67%)
The needs of various groups of target donors/funders	9 (56%)	9 (69%)	4 (44%)	2 (40%)	2 (40%)	1 (33%)	27 (53%)
Preference of trustees/board members	4 (25%)	6 (46%)	6 (67%)	1 (20%)	—	2 (67%)	19 (38%)

(Continued)

Table 5.16 (Continued)

Most Influential Factors on Choice of Positioning Strategy (In Descending Order of Importance)	Responses from General Welfare and Social Care Respondents						
	Other Gen Wef (n=16)	Children (n=13)	Ben Funds (n=9)	Elderly Care (n=5)	Service/Ex-Service (n=5)	Rel Gen Wef (n=3)	Total No. (%) (N=51)
My organization's culture	4 (25%)	5 (38%)	2 (22%)	2 (40%)	2 (40%)	1 (33%)	16 (31%)
Actions of other charitable organizations in the same sector/subsector	5 (31%)	1 (8%)	3 (33%)	2 (40%)	2 (40%)	2 (67%)	15 (29%)
Government (central or local) funding agency	5 (31%)	1 (8%)	1 (11%)	—	—	1 (33%)	8 (16%)
The needs of various other groups of volunteers	2 (12%)	1 (8%)	—	1 (20%)	1 (20%)	—	5 (10%)
Actions of voluntary organizations other than charities	1 (6%)	3 (23%)	—	—	—	—	4 (8%)
One or more dominant non-government funding organization(s)	2 (12%)	—	—	1 (20%)	1 (20%)	—	4 (8%)

Note: Totals do not add up to 100% because respondents select five factors that they think are most important in influencing their choice of positioning strategy and dimensions. A cell with no figure indicates that no respondent in that subsector selected the particular factor.

As mentioned earlier, respondents perceived increasingly competitive intensity for resources in their sector/subsectors. They were also asked the sources of competition that had influenced their choice of positioning strategy. Twenty-nine per cent of respondents cited actions of other charities in the same sector/subsector and 8 per cent cited actions of voluntary and non-profit organizations other than charities as important external influencing factors.

Another area of interest in this study was how respondents perceived the influence of funders/donors and volunteers. Government (central and local) funding agencies were perceived to have an external influence on positioning strategy by 16 per cent of respondents. A further examination of the profile of these respondents revealed that they had derived at least 30 per cent of their annual income from government funding, with two-thirds receiving above 65 per cent of their funding from statutory sources (CAF 2003). In addition, one or more dominant non-government funding organization(s) was perceived by 8 per cent of respondents to influence their positioning strategy. However, when it came to volunteers, only 10 per cent of respondents perceived the needs of other volunteers (besides the board of trustees) as a factor that could influence the choice of their organization's positioning. A closer examination of the profile of these respondents revealed that they relied heavily on voluntary income for at least 90 per cent of their total annual income (CAF 2003).

SUMMARY OF KEY FINDINGS FROM THE SURVEY STAGE

This chapter has been concerned with mapping the extent of positioning activities of charitable organizations and surfacing an initial picture of the key factors that influenced their positioning strategy. This section summarizes and discusses the key findings that have been presented in this chapter with a view dedicated to answering the research questions posed for this stage of the study.

The first concern was to explore the extent to which charitable organizations undertook strategic marketing planning activities in their organizations, as explained in Chapter 4. It was also necessary to uncover whether positioning was part of their strategic marketing planning activities as prescribed in contemporary marketing literature. The extent of strategic marketing planning activities was measured for the first time for this study using a thirteen-item Likert-style summated rating scale. The total mean score of 6.38 for the thirteen activities suggests that general welfare and social care charities had begun to undertake strategic marketing planning fairly extensively in their organizations. This finding proposes that marketing planning was undertaken at a more strategic level rather than at a tactical level, as concluded in earlier studies in the 1990s.

Charities also undertook strategic marketing planning activities to varying extents. Activities such as 'Segmentation of Donors/Funders,' 'Developing

Fundraising Plans and Actions,' and 'Developing Communications Plans and Actions' occupied the top three places in the list of strategic marketing planning activities found in the study.

Evidence from this stage of the study also revealed that charities acknowledged the presence of intensifying competition for financial and other crucial organizational resources. This finding supports previous reports and studies (e.g., Sargeant 1995; NCVO 2004a, 2004b) that commented on the increasing competition for funding and other organizational resources evident among charities. However, 'Competitor Analysis' and 'Market Research' on donors and users were the least extensively performed by charities in this study.

There was also evidence to suggest that some form of positioning activity was undertaken as part of the overall strategic marketing planning activities, but this was performed less extensively than other strategic marketing planning activities. As revealed earlier, the mean score for 'Identifying the Charity's Positioning Dimensions' was 5.84, which was below the total mean score of all thirteen strategic marketing planning activities.

In terms of revealing the extent of positioning strategy activities undertaken by charitable organizations, the survey had specifically developed a six-item Likert-style summated rating scale to measure this activity for the first time. The total mean score of 6.64 for the six positioning strategy activities suggests that general welfare and social care charities undertook these activities fairly extensively in their organizations.

However, these charities gave lower priority to identifying/selecting the positioning dimensions that distinguished their organization from other providers. Positioning dimensions are critical components of a positioning strategy. They reflect the key strengths (distinctive competences) of the organization, which need to be supported by organizational resources and capabilities in order to be sustainable over a period of time (Hooley, Broderick, and Moller 1998; Hooley et al. 2001). The implication for strategic positioning in charitable organizations is to understand how different positioning dimensions can serve as strategic bases upon which their positioning strategy draws its advantage.

We now turn to the type of generic or core positioning strategy pursued and positioning dimensions utilized by charitable organizations, and in what ways these are similar or distinct from those proposed in the extant marketing/strategy literatures. The majority of respondents adopted differentiation positioning and focus positioning as their preferred generic or core positioning strategy. This finding supports the assertion by some authors that differentiation positioning and focus positioning are more appropriate for voluntary and non-profit organizations (e.g., McLeish 1995; Saxton 1996; Bruce 1998). Charities that have adopted focus positioning tended to be smaller in size in terms of total annual income and number of paid staff, and derived a smaller proportion of their total income from voluntary income compared to those adopting differentiation positioning. Low-cost positioning was pursued by only one respondent in the study. Bruce (1998) suggests that low-cost positioning is difficult to apply to the charitable context as it requires a charitable organization to be a dominant player or occupy a monopoly position in the sector/subsector that it operates. At the same time, the inherent resource dependency of many charities on external resource providers suggests that sustaining a low-cost leadership position is often difficult, if not impossible, over the long term (Chew 2003).

Charities in this study utilized a variety of dimensions to distinguish themselves from other providers and to support their generic or core positioning strategy. Some of these positioning dimensions were similar to those advocated in the strategy/marketing literature. However, other dimensions cited by respondents did not appear to be subsectoral specific nor did they conform fully to textbook prescriptions. Mission was the most frequently cited positioning dimension by respondents. Zineldin and Bredenlow (2001) propose that vision, mission (or purpose), and strategic positioning of an organization are interrelated. However, in identifying reasons for the organization's existence and what it does, the mission could either guide or constrain positioning strategy choices. Perhaps the most significant finding is the unique relationships with central or local government agencies, which were also cited as key differentiators by 14 per cent of respondents. Over 40 per cent of them had received at least half of their annual income from government sources of funding. This finding reflects the evolution of the UK government's policy of partnership and contracting of public services delivery over the past decade (NCVO 2003). An impetus for the increasing visibility of the UK voluntary sector since the later part of the 1990s had arguably been the government's encouragement and support in the form of tax concessions and direct financial funding (Strategy Unit 2002). In such a climate, strategic relationships between central and local statutory organizations and voluntary and charitable organizations that deliver key public services could be an increasing trend in the future (Chew 2006a). This has implications for charities in deciding and maintaining their strategic positions in the future.

Finally, what are the key factors external and internal to charitable organizations that influence their positioning strategy, and in what ways are these factors similar or distinct from those proposed in contemporary strategy/marketing literature? The most important influencing factors perceived by charities comprised of a combination of external environmental and internal organizational factors, some of which are not commonly cited in the extant literature. External factors cited (e.g., shifts or changes in socio-demographic, economic, political, regulatory and technological environments, and competition) and organizational factors (e.g., availability of organizational resources and organizational culture) appeared to be similar to those mentioned in the marketing literature on positioning. However, other factors cited by respondents appeared to be unique to the charitable context. These included the charity's mission, the needs of two distinct groups of key external stakeholders (users/clients/beneficiaries and donors/ funders), preferences of the charity's board of trustees, needs of volunteers, and influence from government funding agencies.

The charity's mission, in particular, was cited as the most influential factor in the organization's positioning strategy. However, it is less clear from this exploratory survey why the charity's mission and other factors were selected and how they had/could have influenced the charity's positioning strategy. These factors would have major implications on the strategic directions and priorities of organizations in the charitable context.

CONCLUSIONS AND EMERGING THEMES

The findings presented in this chapter provide empirical evidence that charities had begun to undertake positioning activities at the strategic planning level. These activities, however, were performed to varying extents. There was also evidence suggesting that the major components of a positioning strategy, such as generic or core positioning strategies and positioning dimensions, were apparent in the survey respondents.

In addition, it was also found that while some of the strategic marketing planning activities, positioning strategy activities, and key factors conformed to those advocated in the literature, others did not. As highlighted in Chapter 4, the lack of adequate existing research into the strategic positioning of charitable organizations had necessitated the use of this survey stage to explore the positioning activities of these organizations. The exploratory survey has provided empirical evidence that illuminates the extent of positioning activities undertaken by charities. However, the evidence was descriptive in nature and cannot provide adequate explanations for the phenomenon under investigation. Therefore, in order to fully understand the extent of strategic positioning in charities and the factors that influence their choice of positioning strategy, it was necessary to examine the phenomenon in more depth. In summary, three emerging themes became evident from the key survey findings that required further investigation at the next stage of the study, namely, the case studies stage. These themes and related research questions are outlined in the following.

- *Process of strategic positioning*—How was positioning strategy developed? In order to gain a better understanding of the relationships between various external and internal factors on positioning strategy choices and the impact of the factors' influences, it is necessary to examine the process of strategic positioning in the charitable context in greater depth.
- *Anatomy of positioning strategy*—What were the components of the current positioning strategy of charities? How and why has the charity's strategic position changed since the organization's inception? The

survey findings had provided a snap-shot view of the key components of a positioning strategy in the sample charities. They did not, however, explain why a particular generic or core positioning strategy or a particular positioning dimension was adopted by the organization. It is therefore necessary to go beyond the surface and examine the components of the organization's current positioning strategy and explore the rationale behind the choice of those components in more detail.

- *Influencing factors*—What factors were more important in the charitable context? Why and how have they influenced the positioning strategy components? Evidence from the exploratory survey suggested that a complex combination of external environmental factors, organizational factors, and key stakeholders influenced the choice of the charity's positioning strategy. Additionally, some factors appeared to conform to propositions made in the extant literature, while others did not. However, the exploratory nature of the findings would not be able to explain why some factors were perceived as more influential than others, and how these factors had influenced/could have influenced the organization's positioning strategy. An in-depth investigation into the emerging themes in the charitable context was therefore required to adequately answer these additional research questions.

Finally, it is important to be clear about what has been identified in this chapter. The findings from the exploratory survey stage are largely descriptive in nature. Whilst they illuminated broadly what charities do in their positioning activities, they did not tell us how and why. It is therefore necessary to examine the themes emerging from the survey findings in greater intensity at the third stage of the study. This will involve the use of cross-sectional case studies in order to provide causal explanations of the emerging themes from the survey and to address this study's research objectives more comprehensively. The next chapter will present the findings from the case studies.

6   Process, Anatomy of Positioning Strategy, and Influencing Factors

In Chapter 5, evidence from the postal survey stage was presented and discussed. This chapter presents evidence gathered during the case studies stage, that is, the third stage of the three-stage methodology used in this study. The main purpose of the case studies was to investigate in greater depth the extent of strategic positioning activities according to the three main themes, which have emerged from the exploratory survey stage as explained at the end of the previous chapter. The case organizations are first profiled in this chapter, which includes their responses to the exploratory survey questionnaire. This initial pool of data from the case organizations provided an important base upon which findings from the case studies would be complemented, compared, and validated. The results of the intra-case and inter-case investigations along the three main themes are next detailed. The intent here is to identify commonalities and differences between the four cases along the main themes guiding the investigation. In order to adequately answer the research questions for this stage of the study, the findings presented in the case studies are a combination of descriptive and explanatory evidence.

PROFILES OF THE CASE STUDY ORGANIZATIONS

In Chapter 4, the four case study organizations and their selection criteria were briefly introduced. This section profiles the case organizations further and explains the selection criteria in more detail. The four cases were selected from twelve survey organizations that had agreed to participate in the case studies. The four case study organizations were assured of anonymity, therefore pseudonyms Charity A, Charity B, Charity C, and Charity D are used to ensure confidentiality of their identities. As it was explained in Chapter 4, the selection of the four case studies was based on a combination of organizational characteristics and their responses in the survey questionnaire.

Figure 6.1 shows that these criteria produced four organizations, which relatively contrasted to each other. Charity A and Charity B were relatively

Over £10 million	£1 to £10 million
Charity C 1% statutory income 90% voluntary income	**Charity A** 0% statutory income 100% voluntary Income
Charity D 95% statutory income 1% voluntary income	**Charity B** 49% statutory income 41% voluntary income

Figure 6.1 Four cross-sectional cases based on different bands of total income, proportion of statutory versus voluntary incomes in 2003–2004.

smaller organizations in terms of their total annual income (within the income band of £1 million to £10 million) compared to Charity C and Charity D (above £10 million). Three of the four cases, i.e., Charity A, Charity C, and Charity D, had relatively higher proportions of statutory income compared to voluntary income. For instance, voluntary income was the predominant source of income for Charity A (100 per cent) and Charity C (90 per cent), while Charity D depended on 95 per cent of its total income from statutory income. On the other hand, nearly half of the total annual income in Charity B was derived from statutory sources at the time of this study. Whilst voluntary income remained the most important source of income for this organization since 2001, it had taken on an increasing number of local government contracts, resulting in a growth of statutory income for that charity. The different funding patterns in the four cases were useful in providing cross-case comparisons on the influence of external sources of funding on the charity's positioning strategy under different funding situations.

Within the initial organizational criteria, other characteristics in the four case studies were utilized as additional selection criteria. These were: the age of the organization in terms of the number of years since it was founded, number of paid staff, number of volunteers to support the activities of the charity, and the types of services provided in the organizations' respective subsectors. The combination of criteria employed would therefore allow for a comparison of findings between the case organizational contexts, while offering a degree of generalizability in the findings in the subsector that they operate in.

Charity A was the smallest of the four cases in terms of total annual income and number of paid staff at the time of this study. The charity operated in the 'children' subsector of the general welfare and social care charities in the UK. It was ranked in the 388th position amongst the top five hundred British charities based on voluntary income in 2002 (CAF 2003). It was set up twenty-two years ago with a mission to provide high quality 'homes from home' accommodation for families of sick children who were receiving treatment at paediatric hospitals, regardless of the type of illness. The concept of 'homes from home' was established by the charity's management to guide its strategies and operations, ensuring that families (parents, guardians, relatives) of seriously sick children could remain close to them while receiving treatment at the hospital.

Ever since December 2004, the charity had been operating seven 'homes from home' accommodations in various parts of the country. Each accommodation was acquired or built by the charity after successfully gaining a contract with a nearby publicly funded hospital to refer families of sick children to use its accommodation services. Together they provided accommodation support to 3,600 families in 2004. The charity's total income was derived mainly from voluntary sources, such as corporate and individual donations, legacies, charitable trusts, hospital donations, and other fundraising activities. At the time of this study, Charity A received no financial support from statutory sources, nor did it actively use volunteers, although some volunteers helped with fundraising events.

Charity B was the 'youngest' charity among the four case studies in terms of years in operation since its inception. It was founded seventeen years ago as a regional grant-making charity serving the northeastern part of England. It operated in the 'other general welfare' subsector of the general welfare and social care charities. It was ranked in the 102nd position amongst the top five hundred British charities based on voluntary income in 2002 (CAF 2003). The charity's business model for grant making had originated from the US and was shaped after the 'community foundation' concept, in order to channel local giving more effectively.[1] Its mission was to help build stronger communities by promoting local giving for the benefit of local community needs/causes. Since its inception, the charity has grown rapidly to become the largest community foundation in terms of the amount of its endowed assets that had been accrued in the UK and Europe by 2004.[2]

Charity B generated funds by encouraging local giving primarily from voluntary sources (companies, legacies, wealthy families, and individuals) and distributing these to voluntary and community groups/projects that provide a wide range of services specifically in the northeast region of the country. Since 2000, the charity had managed an increasing volume of government grant schemes/programmes to support local communities. Thirty per cent of the charity's total annual income came from managing government grants in 2002–2003. This proportion had increased to 49 per cent in 2003–2004, and comprised of grants from the Community Chests, Included Community Fund,[3] and the Local Network Fund[4] on behalf of the Government Office, One NorthEast, and in partnership with local development agencies. Sixty per cent of its total grants given out in 2003–2004 were from government-funded programmes/projects.

Charity C was the largest of the four case studies in terms of its total annual income and number of its paid staff. It operated in the 'other general welfare' subsector of the general welfare and social care charities. It was ranked in the 4th position amongst the top five hundred British charities based on voluntary income in 2002 (CAF 2003). Since its inception 180 years ago, Charity C's mission has been to save lives at sea through its emergency lifeboat service. From 2000 it had begun to expand this core service into beach lifeguarding services delivered under contracts to local authorities. Since 2004, the charity provided rescue services from 233 lifeboat stations located across the coastlines of the UK and the Republic of Ireland [5] and fifty-seven beach lifeguard units on behalf of seven local authorities in the southwest of England.

Voluntary income was the largest proportion of Charity C's total annual income, which was over 90 per cent in 2004. The proportion of statutory income was relatively small at less than 1 per cent of total income, which was sourced from local government contracts for beach lifeguarding service. This charity was the only organization among the four case studies that relied heavily on volunteers to deliver its core services, i.e., to operate the lifeboat stations and in fundraising at its three hundred regional branches and guilds across the country. The charity utilized over forty-three thousand[6] volunteers to support its core and supporting services.

More than 95 per cent of the charity's forty-five hundred lifeboat crew were volunteers; while its beach lifeguards were mainly paid staff.[7] Besides service delivery, it had increased its range of preventative activities, such as education/training on sea safety. In April 2004, its flagship training centre was opened at a cost of £19.7 million to provide training for its volunteer lifeboat crew and other educational purposes on sea safety to support its operations.

Charity D was set up thirty-seven years ago as a voluntary membership association aiming to provide drug treatment services to adult misusers. The charity operated in the 'other general welfare' subsector of the general welfare and social care charities. It was ranked in the 341st position amongst the top five hundred British charities based on voluntary income in 2002 (CAF 2003). The charity's mission was to reduce both the use of, and the harm caused by, drug and alcohol misuse. By April 2005 it operated seventy treatment services in England and Scotland and provided services to twenty-three thousand people yearly with a range of support in the form of community-based services, day and residential programmes, criminal justice and prison-based services, young people services, alcohol services, helplines, and education.

The proportion of income from statutory sources had increased substantially during the past decade, in particular since 1998, which was when the Labour Government's ten-year National Drug Strategy began. This strategy was the first cross-cutting strategy introduced by the government to tackle illegal drug misuse in the country in an integrated way (Home Office 2005b). A key part of this strategy was an increase in treatment services for misusers, as the government had increased its financial commitment to drug treatment, which would reach £478 million by 2008 (Home Office 2005a). Consequently, a key area of income growth since then had been from statutory grants and programmes managed for central/local government funding agencies.

Moreover, Charity D's core service of drug treatment expanded into alcohol treatment from 2003 at the same time as the government's introduction of its Alcohol Strategy to tackle the growing social problem of alcohol addiction in the country. Annual income had grown nearly sixfold from £3.4 million in 1997–1998 to £16.8 million in 2003–2004 (Charity Commission 2005c). The charity's heavy dependency on statutory sources of income (fees and contract income) had increased since the mid-1990s and amounted to over 95 per cent of its total income in 2004. These non-voluntary funding sources included local Drug Action Teams and Health Authorities, Local Authorities, Home Office (Police Service, Probation Service, and Prison Service), Community Fund, and the European Social Fund in 2004. In contrast, income from voluntary sources has declined over the years. This amounted to below 1 per cent of this charity's total income in 2004. Corporate donations/sponsorships constituted the largest proportion of voluntary income.

Besides its core treatment services, Charity D undertook research into drug and alcohol issues to influence central government and local commissioning agencies on the design and implementation of drug and alcohol policies and to identify good practice in delivering services to its clients. Whilst volunteers were at the heart of this charity's activities during its founding years, their involvement had diminished over the years. At the time of this study, it operated two volunteer schemes and an apprentice scheme involving fifty to sixty volunteers. These schemes recruited former substance misusers and trained them to become drug and alcohol workers with the organization.[8] However, the size of these schemes and other volunteer involvement in the charity had remained limited because of funding constraints.

Table 6.1 summarizes the key features of the four case studies at the time of this study. It illustrates that the four cases contrasted in their organizational characteristics and the nature of services they provided. Charity C was the most established among the four case study organizations in terms of age and the largest in terms of their total annual income and size of paid staff. It was ranked the highest in the top five hundred fundraising charities among the four charitable organizations (CAF 2003). On the other hand, Charity A was the smallest of the four charities along the same organizational characteristics.

Although the four case organizations were involved in the delivery of different types of public services, their dependency on voluntary income

Table 6.1 Key Features of the Case Study Organizations

Key Features	Charity A	Charity B	Charity C	Charity D
Charity subsector	Children	Other general welfare	Other general welfare	Other general welfare
Years in existence from inception to 2004	22	16	180	37
Scope of core services	Accommodation for families of sick children receiving treatment in hospitals in England	Grant-making community foundation in northeast England	Emergency sea and beach rescue in England and Republic of Ireland	Drug and alcohol treatment to misusers in England and Scotland
Paid staff in 2004	22	26	1234	704
Volunteers involvement (& estimated number of volunteers)	Trustees, Fundraisers (20–30)	Trustees (15)	Trustees, lifeboat crew, lifeboat stations helpers, fundraisers (45,000)	Trustees, volunteer scheme-drug treatment workers (50–80)
Voluntary income (% of total income in 2004)	100%	41%	90%	Less than 1%
Statutory income (% of total income in 2004)	0%	49%	Less than 1%	95%
Total income (2004)	£1 million	£9 million	£125 million	£17 million
CAF top 500 ranking based on total annual voluntary income in 2002	388th position	102nd position	4th position	341th position

Source: Data extracted from case organizations' annual reports, other organizational documents, semi-structured interviews with key respondents at head/branch offices, and Charities Aid Foundation's 2003 ranking of top five hundred charitable organizations.

142 Strategic Positioning in Voluntary and Charitable Organizations

compared to statutory income varied. An interesting point was the degree to which the charities depended on volunteers in their organizations. Charity C was also the most dependent on volunteers among the four charities. Besides contributing as trustees, volunteers played other crucial roles in this charity by delivering its rescue services, operating the lifeboat stations, and managing the fundraising branches and guilds across the country.

RESPONSES MADE BY THE CASE ORGANIZATIONS IN THE SURVEY QUESTIONNAIRE

In addition to the organizational characteristics identified in each of the four cases, the case study organizations' responses to selective questions in the survey questionnaire gathered at the exploratory survey stage of this study are presented here. Two main purposes for this are intended here. First, the information was intended to provide an important source of data to complement the findings from the case studies, thereby building a more complete picture of each case organization. A second aim was to compare them to the case studies findings, where appropriate, thereby facilitating methodological triangulation in this study (Jick 1979; Osborne 1998). Table 6.2 reviews and compares the answers of the case studies' respondents to selective questions at the exploratory survey stage of this study.

Table 6.2 shows the mean score, indicating the extent of strategic marketing planning in the four case organizations as a group was 6.83. This was slightly higher than the mean score for the total survey respondents, which was 6.38 (also see Chapter 5). In terms of the extent to which the case study organizations undertook positioning strategy activities, the mean score for them collectively was 6.35. This was slightly lower than that for the total survey respondents, which was 6.64 (also see Chapter 5). These findings suggest that the four case organizations undertook both strategic marketing planning and positioning strategy activities moderately as a group, and the extent of their activities was not significantly different from the total survey sample respondents.

However, when the individual case organization's scores were taken into consideration, they revealed that Charity D was the only organization out of the four case studies that had a mean score below the collective mean scores of the four cases and the total survey respondents, for both strategic marketing planning and positioning strategy activities. The other difference was Charity C's mean score for positioning strategy activities, which was below that of the four case studies as a group. The variance could be explained when comparing its organizational context, history, and different funding pattern with the other three case organizations (also see Table 6.1 and Figure 6.1).

Table 6.2 Comparison of Case Study Organizations' Responses in the Survey Questionnaire

Survey Question	Charity A	Charity B	Charity C	Charity D	Four Case Studies n=4	Survey Respondents N=51
Extent of strategic marketing planning activities (*Mean score for 13 items on scale of 0–10*)	7.16	7.69	7.69	4.77	6.83	6.38
Extent of positioning strategy activities (*Mean score of 6 items on scale of 0–10*)	6.50	8.70	5.70	4.50	6.35	6.64
Perception of current competitive intensity for funding and other resources in subsector	Moderate	Moderate	Low	High		
Change in competitive intensity over next five years in subsector	High increase	Moderate increase	Moderate increase	High increase		
Main competitor(s) for funding and other resources in subsector/sector	Other charities providing similar service	Other charities & private sector firms providing similar service	Private sector providers of similar service	Other charities providing similar service		
Responsibility for marketing activities in the organization	Marketing & PR* manager	Marketing & Comm* manager	Head of central FR/Comm*	Head of external affairs		

*Note: Abbreviations used in table PR = public relations, FR = fundraising, Comm = communications.

There were also variations in the level of competitive intensity for funding and other organizational resources in the four cases. Only Charity C perceived a low level of competition, while the other three charities perceived moderate to high levels of competition. All four cases felt that there would be further increase in the current level of competition. This finding was consistent with the perceptions of the survey respondents as a group (also see Chapter 5).

Overall, the case organizations' responses in the survey questionnaire discussed earlier were intended to highlight similarities and variances for in-depth investigation in the case study analysis.

KEY FINDINGS FROM THE CASE STUDIES

Following the introduction of the four cases' organizational contexts in the preceding section, this section presents the findings from the case studies that have been analyzed according to the three main themes that were presented at the end of Chapter 5, namely, (a) the process of developing a positioning strategy, (b) the key components of a positioning strategy and changes to the charity's strategic position, and (c) the key factors that have influenced the choice of a positioning strategy in the charitable context.

The evidence was gathered from a total of twenty-seven semi-structured interviews with key organizational decision-makers at the charities' head offices, four group discussions with operational/branch office staff, and organizational documents relating to the charities' corporate/strategy plans, annual reports, and marketing communication materials. The use of multiple sources of data provided data triangulation and aimed to enhance the validity of the findings from the case studies (Denzin 1978b; Jick 1979). A case study protocol was utilized to guide the data collection in each case study to provide consistency in the various data sources used, thereby enhancing reliability (Yin 2003).

An iterative process of data collection and analysis was adopted. This involved coding the data along key themes that emerged from the semi-structured interviews in one case, and then re-analyzing and interpreting them as further data that was gathered in the other cases (Carson et al. 2001). Analytic comparison of the themes was then employed to unveil similarities and differences in the influencing factors across cases (Neuman 2006). It considers the particular environmental and organizational contexts of each case and highlights effects across cases that have qualitative differences. Relevant organizational documents, such as the charities' corporate/strategic plans, annual reports, planning processes, promotional and communications materials, were also analyzed for corroborating or contradicting evidence.

PROCESS OF STRATEGIC POSITIONING

This first theme explored the process of identifying the charitable organization's strategic position and developing its positioning strategy. The findings from all four case studies suggest that there was evidence of a formal process to developing their corporate strategy. However, this formalized process had evolved over time as the organizations grew and became more established in their particular areas of service provision. Table 6.3 compares the process of identifying the strategic position and developing a positioning strategy in the four case studies, and summarizes the key emerging findings.

In all the four case organizations the process of identifying their strategic positions and developing their positioning strategies had only begun recently. Moreover, the charities' strategic positions had emerged from their corporate strategy planning process, rather than being developed separately or as part of a conscious and deliberate strategic marketing planning process as advocated by several authors in the marketing positioning literature (Lovelock and Weinberg 1989; Kotler and Andreasen 1996; Hooley, Saunders, and Piercy 1998).

> The positioning direction and positioning statement of the charity were developed within the corporate strategy planning process, which are reflected in the mission statement and in the strategic focus of the organization today. (Chief Executive, Charity A)

> Our new five-year corporate plan reinforced the organization's core positioning and was developed to ensure the organization, people, and resources are focused in that direction without straying too much into government funding and statutory services. (Grants Manager, Charity B)

Although the case study organizations had dedicated marketing functions, these played an operational role in the strategic positioning activities rather than taking the lead in the process itself, namely, by communicating the charity's positioning messages to various audiences once these messages had been defined by the senior management team and the board of trustees. The supporting role of marketing in the charities' strategy development process is summarized by one case study interviewee:

> Marketing has positive contributions to the changes in the organization, especially in developing consistent external communications, rebranding, and fundraising to support corporate developments. But these can be better, for example, we need to be clearer about the role of marketing for the organization and in our positioning activities. (Development Director, Charity D)

Table 6.3 Cross-Case Analysis and Comparison—Process of Strategic Positioning in the Case Study Organizations

Research Questions	Charity A	Charity B	Charity C	Charity D
Was there a conscious preplanned process of strategic positioning in the charity?	No conscious preplanning prior to 2001. Emergent process, evolved unconsciously, adapting to changes in external environment.	No conscious preplanned prior to 1998. Emergent process with adaption to evolving external environment.	No conscious preplanning prior to 1999. Emergent process with periods of learning from trial and error.	No conscious preplanning prior to 1998. Emergent process from various decisions and actions taken over time.
Was the process part of the organization-wide corporate planning process or part of the strategic marketing planning process?	Current strategic positioning had emerged from the new five-year corporate strategic plan developed since 2001 (see Figure 6.2).	Current strategic positioning had emerged since 1998 and reinforced when developing first five-year corporate plan in 2004 (see Figure 6.3).	Current strategic positioning had emerged from strategic review of mission, vision and values in 1999/2000 and reinforced in concept of operations in its 20 years long-range strategic plan 2004–2024 (see Figure 6.4).	Current strategic positioning had emerged from changes in corporate direction from 1998, and reinforced in new corporate plan since 2003 (see Figure 6.5).
Who/What prompted formal organizational-level strategic planning or initiated strategic positioning?	• Appointment of new chairman and new general manager from 1999/2000. • Changes in external environment/increase competition for voluntary funds.	• Declining legacy and investment income. • Changes in external environment/increase in government grants for local community development in northeast England.	• Appointment of new chief executive from 1999. • Changes in external environment, decline in legacy income, increase competition for voluntary income.	• Changes in external environment, government policies affecting its core services, increase in competition for service contracts.

Furthermore, conscious efforts to develop more formalized longer-term strategic plans and positions had been prompted by certain critical 'trigger events' that could happen unexpectedly, which the charity's management had little or no control over. These included a sudden change of organizational leadership, such as the arrival of a new chairman of the board of trustees or a new chief executive, who brought strategic management thinking into their organization's planning approaches and led the positioning reviews. In addition, the aforementioned changes in governmental policy on the provision of public services and other specific external environmental changes, as explained in Chapter 3, had resulted in an increase in competition among these charities for voluntary income and statutory funding, and in the changing relationships with their various key stakeholders. As the charities became more established, a conscious process of reviewing their strategic positions was deemed necessary. A more proactive, deliberate approach to their strategic planning and management was consequently pursued. Interviewees were in agreement that the emergent corporate planning and organizational positioning were part of a learning process for them.

> I think it would be around the time that our current Chief Executive arrived that a more conscious process of reviewing our corporate position began. The planning process has happened mostly organically for us and I think for most other charities. The growth period for us was fast and quite unplanned. When we get to a certain size and developmental stage, we need to consolidate and review our positioning. So, it has sort of emerged for us. (Head of Fundraising, Charity D)

> The main motivation behind the charity's long-term strategic plan and positioning was the then Board of Trustees's realization that the future environment is becoming more uncertain and the past ten to fifteen years of unprecedented growth of the charity will not repeat itself in the future. At that time, the charity's free reserves levels were high and the management considered various new initiatives to develop for the future. There is an emerging process of strategic planning and positioning—where there were processes in place previously; some worked, some did not. The organization learned as it grew and improved on those that worked, and removed those that did not. (Information and Research Manager, Charity C)

Figures 6.2 to 6.5 illustrate the schematics that trace the process stages of developing the corporate strategy and identification of their positioning strategy components in the four case organizations. The use of diagrammatic representation here is intended to clarify and rationalize what could in reality be a halting and uneven process of strategy development. It is therefore acknowledged that a degree of post hoc rationalization was inherent in the case study interviewees' depictions of this process.

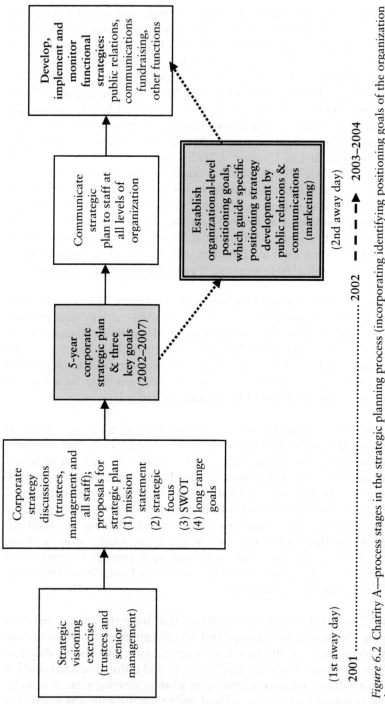

Figure 6.2 Charity A—process stages in the strategic planning process (incorporating identifying positioning goals of the organization from 2001). Source: The charity's five-year corporate strategic plan 2002–2007; strategy development process framework from the chief executive (September 2004/April 2005); branding strategy and fundraising strategy 2004; interviews with the head of the public relations/communications and the head of fundraising (September 2004).

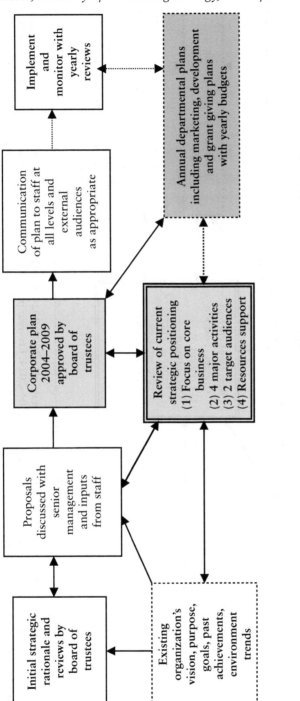

Figure 6.3 Charity B—process stages of developing corporate plan 2004–2009 (incorporating reviewing the strategic position of the organization). Source: The charity's five-year vision and strategic plan 2004–2009; interviews on strategy development process with the chief executive, the marketing and public relations manager, and the grants team manager (November 2004).

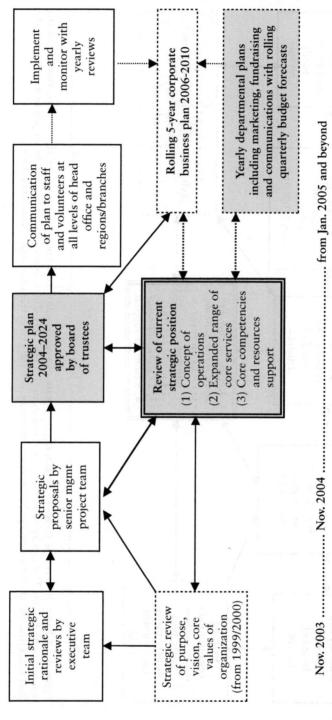

Figure 6.4 Charity C—process stages of developing corporate plan 2004–2024 (incorporating reviewing strategic position of the organization). Source: The charity's corporate strategic plan 2004–2024; five-year business plan 2004–2008; interviews on strategy development process with the corporate planning manager, the information and research manager, the beach lifeguarding officer (March 2005); interview with the regional manager (June 2005).

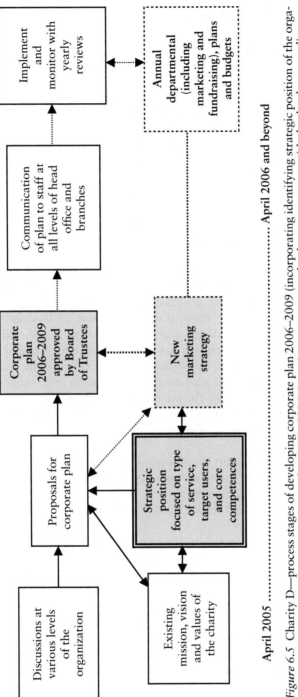

Figure 6.5 Charity D—process stages of developing corporate plan 2006–2009 (incorporating identifying strategic position of the organization). Source: The charity's corporate plan 2003–2006; interviews on strategy development process with the development director, the branch service officer, and the head of fundraising (March 2005).

ANATOMY OF A POSITIONING STRATEGY

The second theme examined two sub-themes: the components of the case organizations' positioning strategies and changes to their strategic positions over time. As it was established in Chapters 2 and 4, a positioning strategy has been operationalized in this study as comprising of three interrelated components: (a) the generic or core positioning strategy, (b) the key target audiences, and (c) the positioning dimensions developed to distinguish the charity from other providers/charities (Chew 2003, 2006a, 2006b). These indicators were used to compare the components of the positioning strategy in the four case organizations.

Table 6.4 summarizes and compares the components of the positioning strategy in the four cases' organizations.

Distinctiveness of Strategic Position

In all four cases, the charity's stated mission or purpose identified the key distinctiveness of each case study organization and the primary target audience it served. Despite their contrasting histories and features, the case organizations had a strong sense of mission, vision, and values that were communicated openly to external and internal audiences. The charity's mission provided the main direction for the organization's strategic position (i.e., how to be distinctive) and guidance on developing the positioning dimensions (i.e., how to differentiate the organization from other charities/providers of similar services). The interviewees in some of the case organizations suggested variations in the use or value of their strategic positions, as illustrated in the quotations following.

> We provide high quality 'homes from home' accommodation for families whose children are receiving hospital treatment for serious illness. In carrying out this mission we will ensure that the highest standards of services are applied throughout. (Fundraising Manager, Charity A)

> Our strategic position reflects the charity's purpose. It is the main selling proposition—people are attached to the charity because of this single emotive purpose. (Head of Central Fundraising and Communications, Charity C)

> Our core position is to remain focused on our mission (purpose) but also to be flexible about the approaches in treatment services to meet changing needs of drug misusers and concerns of the wider society. (Branch Manager, Charity D)

The strategic positions of Charity A and Charity D were used primarily to manage their service provision, albeit with an accent on flexibility. In

Table 6.4 Cross-Case Analysis and Comparison—Current Positioning Strategy Components in the Case Study Organizations

Research Questions	Charity A	Charity B	Charity C	Charity D
What was the generic or core positioning strategy of the charity?	**Focus positioning** A niche service delivered direct to specific users in selected locations in England.	**Focus positioning** A particular type of service aimed at a particular geographic location in England.	**Differentiation positioning** A valued service with capital-intensive operations needed to provide nation-wide coverage in the UK and Republic of Ireland.	**Focus positioning** A niche service working with network of statutory and other partner organizations to deliver services to particular clients across England and Scotland.
Who were the key target audiences for the positioning strategy in the charity?	**Primary audience** —families of sick children receiving care at hospitals —sick children in hospitals **Secondary audience** —partner hospitals —voluntary donors	**Primary audience** —local donors/local govt funders providing grants —local voluntary and community groups receiving grants **Secondary audience** —local and regional statutory funders and agencies	**Primary audience** —sea and beach users receiving potential life-saving services **Secondary audience** —voluntary donors —local authorities for beach rescue —govt coast guards —partner organizations for sea and beach rescue	**Primary audience** —drug and alcohol misusers receiving services —children and families of drug and alcohol misusers who are at risk **Secondary audience** —statutory funders —voluntary donors —partner organizations

(Continued)

Table 6.4 (Continued)

Research Questions	Charity A	Charity B	Charity C	Charity D
What were the key positioning dimensions that supported the core positioning strategy of the charity?	• Specialize in unique service to particular target users • High quality standards of service delivery to users • Close working partnership with NHS hospitals in selected locations in the England	• Largest community foundation within a particular geographic region in northeast England • High quality of service delivery to grant donors/funders and grant applicants • Focused mission	• Leader (size, capital-intensive hardware and technology, specialized expertise) in providing a unique service to potential users • Largest network of branches/lifeboat stations providing joint-up service with govt/other maritime organizations across the coasts of UK and Republic of Ireland • High quality of service delivery • Strong volunteer ethos • Focused mission	• Expertise provider in particular service to particular users in England and Scotland • High quality of service delivery • Strong government funding and working relationships with statutory, health, social and other voluntary organizations • Focused mission

Charity C's case, the emphasis placed by the interviewee was on communication and functionality.

Generic or Core Positioning Strategy

The generic or core positioning strategy provides the broad positioning stance of the organization and isolates the core business of the organization (Porter 1980). In the case studies, focus positioning appeared to be the core positioning strategy of three out of the four case organizations, while differentiation positioning was adopted by the fourth case. However, there were significant differences in the use or value of the core positioning strategy in the four case organizations. Charity B was the only community foundation in the UK that served a specific geographic location in the northeast of England, while Charity A and Charity D were specialized in providing particular services that catered for a focused group of users/beneficiaries.

> We have a very good unique niche position as a local grant-maker in the northeast that provides mainly small grants to local voluntary and community groups. We are a community foundation with quite specific geographic boundaries for its operations with little competition in that market. (Chief Executive, Charity B)

> We are specialized in serving a niche market. We want to be recognized as a leader in providing quality 'homes from home' accommodation, and a benchmark for other providers to follow. (Chief Executive, Charity A)

> The organization is a leading UK charity working solely in the drugs and alcohol treatment service. (Charity D's corporate statement about the organization in the charity's website, April 2005)

The importance of serving 'niche' markets in Charity A and Charity B underscores the charities' commitment to developing their current competences in serving a specific target group of beneficiary better than other providers. In the same vein, the emphasis placed on the key term 'solely' by Charity D highlights an apparent determination to maintain focus on the core competence as its distinguishing feature.

In contrast, Charity C had adopted differentiation positioning as its core positioning strategy. Being ranked among the top five largest fundraising charities in the country since 1978 (CAF 2004), Charity C claimed to be the leading independent emergency sea search-and-rescue service in the UK and Republic of Ireland at the time of this study. It has grown to be the largest independent provider of sea rescue services and with a mostly volunteer-manned service. It provided an integrated joined-up emergency service with the government coast guards and other sea and beach rescue agencies to a wide spectrum of sea/beach users.

> We are the leader in providing lifeboat rescue services in terms of being the biggest and the best in providing that service. We are maintaining that position to save lives at sea across the coastal areas and to ensure that this service meets the needs or satisfies the demands for this service in the future. (Head of Central Fundraising and Communications, Charity C)

Here, Charity C's differentiation positioning emphasized providing its services to anyone who could be at risk at sea, and not focused on a particular geographic area or group of potential beneficiaries.

Key Target Audiences

There were two such audiences for the case organizations. The primary audience was users who benefitted directly from their services such as the sick children and their families who used the accommodation provided by Charity A, voluntary and community groups who received grants distributed by Charity B, people at risk at sea for Charity C, and people who received drug treatment in Charity D.

> Our clients, which are drug misusers and their families, are the most important target audience. They are also our key external stakeholders and as a client-focused organization, our strategies and services do really revolve very strongly around them. (Head of Fundraising, Charity D)

The secondary audience comprised of a number of parties, such as external stakeholders who provided supporting services for the case study organizations (such as the NHS, Criminal Justice agencies, and the Maritime and Coastguards Agency) and those who provided funds (such as local authorities and commissioners). What was specifically emphasized by interviewees was governmental agencies (local and regional), who were regarded as important external stakeholders in their role as funder, provider of community grants/projects, and legitimizer for their work. This latter perspective was shared by two case study interviewees:

> We have been involved and referred to by government bodies for our services and for our viewpoints. I think that has certainly helped us professionally—it would be nice to be part of an organization that has a certain amount of respect and credibility amongst professional and statutory bodies and communities in general. (Branch Manager, Charity D)

The government is a key stakeholder in the sense they provide grants to local community and voluntary groups and we manage an increasing number of projects on their behalf. The amount of government grants that we distribute amounted to 52 per cent in 2002, which has increased to nearly 59 per cent by 2004. Therefore, we rely on them a lot. (Marketing and Communications Manager, Charity B)

Moreover, interviewees in all four cases stressed the importance of communicating to their primary and secondary external stakeholders effectively and building close relationships with them. In this regard, the charities had developed various marketing approaches to communicate the charity's strategic position to both groups of key target audiences over time, which is well summarized by an interviewee.

There has been a positive change in the way the organization communicates to external parties and volunteers about its plans, strategies and gives clearer guidelines for volunteers to work with. Over the past two years since 2003, the Fundraising and Communications department has produced a standard guideline for external communications, that is, to guide staff and volunteers to communicate consistent messages about the charity's mission, vision, values, its core services, and results achieved. These are essentially to communicate to the charity's key position and its core competences to various external audiences. (Regional Manager, Charity C)

Positioning Dimensions

In Chapters 2 and 5, positioning dimensions have been operationalized as key differentiators based on major organizational strengths that are distinctive of the charity, and that provide long-term strategic advantages (Chew 2003, 2005). Differentiators are the specific instruments through which the organization distinguishes itself from other providers. However, they require appropriate supporting resources if they are to sustain the core positioning strategy over time (Hooley, Broderick, and Moller 1998; Hooley et al. 2001).

Whilst each case organization had its own particular combination of positioning dimensions, two of these dimensions appeared to be the most frequently cited across all the four case studies. These were the high quality of service provided to service users and strong expertise developed in that particular service, which are highlighted in the following quotation:

Our leadership position guarantees a certain level of expertise and professionalism, which enables staff to deliver services to various specifications. National standards and quality of services are consistently adhered to but we also have the flexibility and ability to tailor our services to meet local needs of clients. (Development Director, Charity D)

A possible explanation for the emphasis on expertise and quality of service is that the four charities were involved in direct delivery of services to users/clients as part of their core positioning (as reflected in their mission/purpose) rather than in providing indirect services such as advocacy or campaigning activities (Handy 1990; Bruce 1998). A service of high quality was therefore considered by interviewees as an important strength to develop and maintain. Moreover, demonstrating evidence of these key strengths had helped the organizations in attracting funds and other crucial resources from statutory and voluntary sources. As one interviewee in Charity A put it:

> We are already delivering the charity's ideal positioning, for example, we are providing quality homes with unique services very successfully. These could be referred to as benchmarks for others to follow. We receive feedback from house users and donors that we are delivering our services and support very well to families at our homes. (Marketing and Public Relations Manager, Charity A)

Interviewees had also perceived some unique dimensions in each case organization. These dimensions had helped to strengthen the distinctiveness of the particular charity. For instance, Charity A had developed unique partnerships with different NHS hospitals with paediatric care for children in certain locations in England, while Charity D considered its strong government funding and close working relationship with statutory and other partner organizations as legitimacy for its service expertise. On the other hand, interviewees in Charity C cited its strong volunteer ethos and its ability to provide the largest independent all-year emergency rescue service at sea and beaches as its unique positioning dimensions. Charity B considered itself as the only community foundation in the northeast of England and had been successful in becoming the largest community foundation in the UK in terms of endowed assets.

CHANGES TO STRATEGIC POSITION

This sub-theme in Theme 2 examined the changes to the strategic position of the case organizations since they were founded. The intent was to uncover underlying reasons for these changes and the impact of these changes on the organization. Interviewees in all four case studies were in agreement that their organizations' strategic positions, which reflected their mission/purpose, had remained largely unchanged since its inception. For instance, Charity A had remained committed to providing free accommodation to families of sick children who were receiving treatment in nearby hospitals.

Charity B's focused mission ensured that it continued to attract funding from within the northeast region to fund activities of small voluntary and community groups in that region. Similarly, Charity C remained committed to providing emergency lifeboat rescue service to anyone who was at risk at sea, whilst Charity D had continued to provide drug treatment service to substance misusers.

However, interviewees were in agreement that their organizations had changed structurally and operationally over time to support their core mission/purpose. Table 6.5 compares the changes in the positioning strategies of the four case organizations and the reasons that prompted those changes.

For all four charities, structural and operational changes were necessitated due to the combination of external environmental pressures and internal organizational development. These changes ranged from transformation of the organization's form and structure, as in the case of Charity D, to more subtle reviews of their services to be offered to existing or new users/beneficiaries as in the cases of Charity B and Charity C. They reflect adjustments to the charities' positioning dimensions that were based on reviews of their key strengths and distinctive competences over time. Moreover, changes in government policy context and increased competitive intensity for financial and other organizational resources appeared to have triggered more conscious strategic reviews and formalized strategic planning by their senior management.

IMPACT OF CHANGES IN STRATEGIC POSITION

While structural and operational changes were arguably necessary from the case organizations' perspective to adapt to changing external environmental pressures over time, these changes had begun to create tensions between the charities' long-term economic survival and their established core values. These tensions had affected the case organizations in different ways. Three major impacts of these changes have emerged from the findings, which are explained in the following.

Erosion of Volunteer Ethos

In an effort to be strategically effective and efficient, Charity D had embarked on strategies that eroded its volunteer ethos to some degree. By realigning its strategic position over time, it had become highly professional with an increasing number of paid staff, and to quote one interviewee, '[we] are a business now, but a non-profit making one.' Furthermore, the high dependency on statutory contracts and governmental funding had created much uncertainty about the future strategic direction of the organization, in particular, after the government's ten-year Drug Strategy ends in 2008.

Table 6.5 Cross-Case Analysis and Comparison—Changes to Strategy Positions in the Case Study Organizations

Research Questions	Charity A	Charity B	Charity C	Charity D
Were there changes to the current positioning strategy compared to the past?	No change to its strategic position, which was guided by the charity's mission. Since 2003, there was realignment in its structure/resources and in communicating its strategic position to a wider target audience. These changes coincided with the appointment of a marketing and public relations manager.	No change to its mission and its geographic position. Since 2002, there were changes in its core business from focusing on donors or fundholders in the early years to providing services to grant applicants, increasing funding from government funded grants, and communicating its strategic position to a wider target audience.	No change to its strategic position, which was guided by the charity's mission. Since 2000, there were changes in its core services—expanding its sea rescue services to include beach lifeguarding, and in communicating its strategic position to a wider target audience.	No change to its mission as a service delivery charity. Since 1998, there was further restructuring in the organizational form/structure and funding pattern—from a membership association of parents funded by voluntary income to a highly structured organization with paid staff delivering mainly government funded contracts.
Who/What prompted strategic planning initiatives and changes to its strategic position?	• Appointment of new chairman and chief executive from 1999/2000. • Changes in external environment and increased competition for voluntary funds.	• Declining legacy and investment income. • Changes in external environment and increased government grants for local community development.	• Appointment of new chief executive in 1999. • Changes in external environment, declining legacy income and increased competition for voluntary funds.	• Chief executive instrument in leading strategic change. • Changes in external environment and government policies affecting its core services and resources • Increased competition for voluntary income and service contracts.

Interviewees felt that future changes in the charity's funding mix could affect its ability to raise funds from voluntary sources.

> After 2008 when the Drugs Strategy ends, funding may not be there to enable the charity to provide more of the services which reflects its mission, that is, to provide treatment for any adult, child, and their families that come to us for treatment. Then it will affect the charity's mission, and consequently our core position. (Head of Fundraising, Charity D)

In Charity C's case, its beach lifeguarding services were delivered using mostly paid staff under contract to local authorities. For some interviewees, this strategic initiative conflicted directly with the core value of the charity, namely, to remain funded by voluntary sources of income, and had created tension in preserving its strong volunteer ethos. This concern is reflected in the comment by an interviewee:

> The pure volunteer ethos in the charity's core values has been challenged somewhat over the years because of the increasing use of paid lifeboat crews, and has been eroded by the recruitment of beach lifeguards who are mostly paid staff. (Beach Lifeguarding Officer, Charity C)

Managing Relationships

Tensions have arisen in Charity B between maintaining good working relationships with government funding agencies/local authorities and competing with them for the delivery of services in the northeast region of the country. At the same time, managing government grants required dedicated resources (staffing and grants selection/awarding and monitoring systems) that were distinctive from those required for the charity's general grant-making activities. The board of trustees and chief executive had recognized the need to be cautious about the over-reliance on short-term government funding on the longer-term sustainability of the organization's business.

> One of the things that has happened to the organization since the late 1990s is that it has taken on a lot of grant-making contracts with the government into its core business. Governmental contracts has become a significant growth area and account for about half of the charity's annual income in 2004. However, governmental contracts required us to have a different language, different performance reporting—much more scrutiny. We are beginning to change into the kind of organization that does not suggest that our real work is about finding more donors and doing more voluntary work. We must not deviate from our core donor activities because these provide endowment funds that will stay with us for years and years. (Chief Executive, Charity B)

Limiting Operational Choices

Although Charity A was dependent on voluntary sources of income for its activities, it also relied heavily on publicly funded hospitals with paediatric care for the majority of its accommodation users. Contractual relationships with these partners had limited the charity's choices to work with different partners and in other parts of the country. Tension was developing within the organization between adhering to its focused mission and its senior management's desire to grow the organization in different ways. Interviewees were concerned about the charity's vulnerability in the future if its role became less relevant. For instance, changes in societal needs and government policies, in particular those affecting the NHS and ancillary health-care services. The charity's positioning dimensions would then be challenged and would need to be reviewed in light of these external pressures. This concern of the charity's future is accentuated by its chairman:

> If the government decided it would, as part of the wider public services, finance and support the concept of 'homes from home' within the NHS, then our charity's role could cease to exist. (Chairman, Board of Trustees, Charity A)

KEY FACTORS INFLUENCING A POSITIONING STRATEGY

The third research theme examined the factors that influenced the positioning strategy in the four case organizations. Table 6.6 summarizes the factors influencing the charity's core positioning strategy and positioning dimensions as cited by interviewees in the four case studies. Major factors were categorized as those cited by 50 per cent or more interviewees, while minor factors were cited by less than 50 per cent of them. For the purpose of clarity in reporting, the influence of a major or minor factor on the charity's core positioning strategy was assigned 'X' or 'x' respectively in Table 6.6. The influence of a major or minor factor on a positioning dimension was assigned 'Y' or 'y' respectively. The utilization of major and minor factors in this study was to highlight the degree of concurrence among the interviewees for each factor. However, they do not necessarily imply that major factors were more or less important than minor ones in this study.

Table 6.6 shows several factors that had influenced the core positioning strategy and positioning dimensions in varying degrees. Collectively, they implied strength of agreement or common perception of interviewees across the four cases. Several of these factors were commonly cited in all the four case studies. Factors that were cited as having affected the choice of the charity's generic or core positioning strategy were governmental influence, environmental factors (other than government), the charity's mission, and the needs of users/beneficiaries. Factors that have influenced the development

Table 6.6 Key Factors Influencing a Positioning Strategy in the Case Study Organizations

Key Factors Influencing Positioning Strategy in the Case Study Organizations	Charity A n=7	Charity B n=8	Charity C n=8	Charity D n=4	Mean Frequency of Responses from Total of 27 Interviewees on Factors Cited in the Cases
Governmental influence (*funder, policy maker, and legitimizer*)	xY	XY	Y	XY	85%
External environmental factors (*other than government/political, e.g., shifts in socio-demography, economic, technology, international developments, media influence*)	Y	XY	XY	Xy	59%
Needs of users/ beneficiaries	XY	X	X	X	41%
Mission of the organization	XY	X	X	X	38%
Organizational resources (*include availability of funds, skills, and capabilities*)	XY	Y	Y	XY	68%
Competition (*other than statutory*)	Y	Y	Y	Y	60%
Trustees/Chief Executive of the charity	Y	X	Y	y	40%
Organization size (*size and number of branch offices, number of staff, total income, and assets*)	y	—	Y	y	(a)
Needs of donors (*non-statutory*)	y	X	X	—	(a)
Needs of volunteers	—	—	X	—	(b)
Organizational culture	—	—	—	X	(b)

Note:
(a) Factors particular to some of the case study organizations.
(b) Factors particular to one case study organization only.

of positioning dimensions were: the availability of organizational resources, intensity of competition (other than from statutory sources), and the influence of the charity's board of trustees and its chief executive. These factors and their effects on the case organizations are explained in the following.

Governmental Influence as Policy Maker, Funder, and Legitimizer

The most frequently cited influencing factor in all four case organizations was governmental influence. The type and extent of influence depended on the perceived role that government played in the case organization's sub-sector and in their particular operations. In all the cases, the predominant influence was from government's role as a major policy maker in social care and community welfare in the particular service area that the charity operated in. These policies took the form of national strategies or major funding commitments, which had affected the case organizations in different ways. The charities have responded in their particular ways to the evolving policy context.

For instance, each of Charity A's accommodation houses was strategically partnered with a nearby NHS hospital. The hospitals provided important sources of referrals for potential families to use the charity's accommodation services. The links with hospitals and the NHS legitimized the continued pursuance of the charity's mission and its activities. Although the charity had provided an important public service funded entirely by voluntary income, government policies and funding priorities on the type of health services that the NHS should or should not provide could influence the charity's strategic positioning in the future. Any change in health policies or regulations would impact on the charity's current distinctive competences, which in turn could affect the way it positions itself when based on these strengths.

In Charity D's case, all its interviewees cited government as the major influence on its core positioning strategy and its positioning dimensions. As the major policy maker in substance misuse in the UK, government had provided an enabling policy context where the eradication of substance misuse had become an important public service target. It had also become a dominant contractor for the charity's services. This increasing emphasis on statutory projects and income had subsequently directly influenced the range of services that the organization delivered and the nature of its workforce. However, these changes had not altered the charity's mission. Rather, governmental policies and statutory funding commitment in drug treatment had reinforced its mission, while enlarging the scope of the charity's activities.

> The government's direction and strategies for substance misuse, such as what do they plan to do and what services do they want to develop as good standards of practice, will be linked to what gets funded. Their strategies will affect our charity's current leadership position. For example, the Home Office and Criminal Justice have much work out there,

which has been given increased funding. These developments have affected the type of services that the charity provides—we focus on treatment of drug misuse rather than preventative measures. Government holds the key to the 'safe.' They decide where and how money in those areas are going to be spent. These have a waterfall effect on us. (Development Director, Charity D)

Uncertainty in future government policies including funding commitments could also impact the methods of delivery of services and type of services offered in the future. Moreover, the government's role was also perceived to be an important legitimizer of charitable work in the area of social care and community welfare.

Local authorities are important to us because they are legitimizers for our charity's work with the local communities as a grant giver, and as a funder because the charity does a lot of work funded by the local authority grants. All of these schemes are part of the government's strategy to reduce poverty, and to build stronger relationships within the community. They don't do this through private foundations but prefer to give these to us. (Marketing and Communications Manager, Charity B)

However, a majority of interviewees raised concerns about the potential impact of the government's influence on their organization's operational autonomy.

Local authorities as our funder are major stakeholders for beach lifeguarding because of the lifeguarding contracts that the charity is funded to deliver. They can also influence what the charity says to the media in the local areas under the lifeguarding contracts, and what are reported to council members. (Beach Lifeguarding Officer, Charity C)

External Environmental Factors (Other Than Government)

Other external environmental influences were cited by an average of 59 per cent of interviewees in the four cases. The nature and degree of influence differed depending on the type of service provided and consequently the major sources of funding. For example, Charity A and Charity C depended heavily on voluntary income from individuals and corporations rather than on government funding. Eighty-three per cent and 67 per cent of interviewees in Charity A and Charity C, respectively, considered shifts in societal economic and socio-demographic factors as most influential on their charity's core positioning strategy and its resource base.

Economic situation and demographic changes affect the different ways of getting the income that the organization needs to run its operations.

We are too dependent on the older social-demographic segments of the population for support, and we are too dependent on legacy income. We are finding it difficult to attract a younger volunteer and fundraising population. We have been grappling with this environmental issue over the past several years. The outcome has been the expansion of our services to beach lifeguarding. The charity needs to also get more aggressive with direct marketing, which could have some negative impact on the charity's core values and positioning. (Regional Manager, Charity C)

On the other hand, a third of interviewees in Charity D cited public attitudes in the UK towards drug addiction and the influence of media coverage on government policies on substance misuse as affecting the charity's core positioning over time. This is accentuated in the comment by an interviewee:

The media is very influential in reinforcing or changing the public's perceptions about the charity and what it is doing or should be doing. They can also sway the general public's or society's beliefs and attitudes toward substance misuse or providing free treatment for people with substance problems. Media therefore has an influence both on the charity's core positioning direction and its positioning dimensions to support any change in its position over time. (Head of Fundraising, Charity D)

Charity's Mission

Over a third of interviewees in the four charities cited the charity's mission as a major influence in guiding the choice of and the change in their charity's strategic position over time. As discussed earlier in Theme 2, the case study interviewees cited the charity's mission as the foundation of their organization's strategic position. Mission has also been identified as a key positioning dimension of the charity's positioning strategy, which had enabled the organization to distinguish itself from other charities operating in the same subsector/sector. The quotation that follows from one interviewee highlights the crucial role of the charity's mission in directing the organization's overall strategic direction and positioning.

We are very focused in what we do and the type of services we provide. This is guided by our mission. What we don't do is to go into other people's territory, that is, do other things that are not within our mission's scope of activities. We are sometimes asked to do things that other organizations undertake, such as employee volunteering. That's not the business for us. We are clear that our role is a local grant-maker and that voluntary money from donors is at the heart of this role. (Chief Executive, Charity B)

Needs of Users/Beneficiaries

An average of 41 per cent of interviewees in the case studies cited this as a factor that has influenced their choice of core positioning strategy. However, two-thirds of interviewees in Charity D felt that the needs of their users/beneficiaries were instrumental in affecting its focus positioning strategy. Shifts in the needs of users determined the type and range of treatment regimes that the charity has developed and the resources available to support the delivery of these regimes. On the other hand, a third of interviewees in Charity B and Charity C cited the needs of their primary target audience (local community/voluntary groups and sea users) as influencing its strategic position. The contrast in response could be explained by the differential funding patterns in these charities, which has been explained earlier in this chapter.

Availability of Organizational Resources

The most frequently cited factor that had affected the positioning dimensions of the four charities was the availability of adequate resources, including funding, skilled workforce, and technical competences. An average of 68 per cent of interviewees felt that the appropriate type of organizational resources were crucial in sustaining the key strengths and distinctive competences of the organization in order to support its core positioning strategy. Managing the cost of delivering services effectively ensured quality service standards within the amount of funding available for their services.

> We require financial, human, and technical resources to support the charity's core differentiation positioning strategy. £120 million needs to be raised each year to maintain the lifeboats, lifeboat stations, and the overall charity's operations. These are capital-intensive operations and running costs are also very high. Technical innovation and competence are also needed to run the fleet of boats and ensure lifeguarding services are delivered professionally. (Information and Research Manager, Charity C)

Competition (Other Than from Statutory Sources)

This was the third most cited influencing factor. However, its influence lay in the charity's choice of positioning dimensions, rather than its core positioning strategy or its choice of primary target audience. Interviewees in all four case studies were in general agreement that competitive intensity in their sector/subsector had increased since the 1990s. Moreover, they perceived further increase in the current level of competitive intensity over the next five years. However, the sources of competition in the four charities varied. The differences reflected the nature of services provided by each charity and their historical orientations. For instance, interviewees in Charity D cited high competition for financial and other organizational resources to have influenced the standards of services to its clients and the increase in operating costs in pursuit of higher quality standards. Competitive intensity was perceived by this charity to be high for both government service contracts and funding.

> Competition has enabled the charity to reinforce its strong corporate position of providing high quality services that are supported by policies and procedures designed around client-focused services. When we deliver the service, we need to achieve what we are going to achieve because it will affect the well-being of our clients, the perception of the community in terms of the reputation of the charity, and its longer-term security at the end of the day. (Branch Manager, Charity D)

Competitive intensity had also affected the ways in which Charity A and Charity C distinguished themselves in their respective subsectors to attract voluntary funding and for service delivery. As a relatively small provider of free accommodation for families with sick children being treated in paediatric hospitals, Charity A considered other larger charities that offer similar services as competitors in fundraising from voluntary sources. Its focus positioning strategy was therefore aimed at avoiding direct confrontation with their larger competitors.

In contrast, as the largest independent lifeboat rescue service in the country, Charity C did not consider providers who offered similar services as threatening mainly because these other providers were relatively smaller in size. Competition had, however, influenced the need for the charity to adapt to the changing patterns of sea users and for it to remain relevant over time. In the same vein, but for a different reason, interviewees in Charity B perceived low competition from providers of similar services in its locale mainly because of its geographically focused strategic position as the only community foundation grant-maker serving the northeast of England.

> As the only community foundation and a charitable grant-maker in a focused area in the country, we don't find the competition for attracting funds from voluntary sources terribly competitive because we are quite specific in what we do and to whom our services benefit. (Development Director, Charity B)

Board of Trustees/Chief Executive

An average of 40 per cent of interviewees in the four case organizations mentioned that their board of trustees approved major strategic decisions, including changes to the organization's strategic position. The chief executive, in particular, guided the initiation and implementation of their major strategic directions/plans. In all the case study organizations these internal key decision-makers had been instrumental in initiating major strategic reviews to the organization's future directions and positioning over the past six to seven years.

> Since 2001, the board of trustees has been increasingly involved in planning, developing, and reviewing the strategic directions of the charity. A change in that direction could affect the way the charity positions itself. For example, if the corporate strategy decides that the charity begins to provide day accommodation only, this will influence where our competition is, and consequently where our positioning lies. (Chief Executive, Charity A)

> Strong leadership shapes the charity's corporate culture. A leadership change, especially a new Chief Executive, will affect the types of corporate strategies pursued, and could affect the charity's positioning. Our current Chief Executive is very mission-orientated—he is instrumental in directing our efforts to strengthen our charity's position. (Head of Fundraising, Charity D)

FACTORS THAT APPLY IN SOME CASES OR ONE CASE ONLY

In addition to the influencing factors that were commonly cited in all four case organizations, there were other factors that were cited in only some or one of the cases. Interviewees in three cases cited two factors only: organizational size and needs of donors. Two other factors were cited in one case organization only: needs of volunteers and organization culture. Table 6.6 shows these additional factors. The variations among the charities stem primarily from the differences in their organizational contexts and their funding mix. These are reviewed in the following.

Size of Organization

This factor was cited by a minority of interviewees in three cases. Less than a sixth of interviewees in Charity C and Charity D perceived that the large size of their organization (in terms of having a wide geographic reach, large numbers of users/beneficiaries, and annual income) had made it increasingly difficult to sustain its mission, and therefore, its core positioning strategy. However, Charity A considered its small organizational size as a major positioning weakness. Its positioning strategy was very focused in order to avoid direct confrontation with larger charities that offered similar services. Therefore, it had worked closely in partnership with specific types of hospitals, namely, government-funded teaching hospitals that provided paediatric care in selected geographic areas in the country.

We lose out to larger charities that have larger marketing and fundraising budgets and are more publicly attractive to corporate donors. We are small and therefore we try to focus on selective projects for cost efficiency. We also don't offer accommodation services at those hospitals that have links with larger providers. (Fundraising Manager, Charity A)

In contrast to the other three charities, interviewees in Charity B did not consider organizational size as a major influence on their charity's core positioning strategy or its positioning dimensions. Due to the fact that as a community foundation serving a particular geographic region in the country, it had developed particular expertise and local knowledge that had enabled it to serve its geographical niche better than other providers. Being efficient and effective in that service was considered by Charity B as more important than size.

Needs of Donors and of Volunteers

This factor was cited by three cases that had relied on voluntary income as their main source of income. Charity A and Charity C depended on voluntary donations for 100 per cent and 90 per cent of their income respectively. Whilst Charity B had taken on an increasing number of local statutory grant projects, it had remained dependent on voluntary sources of funding for half of its total income as of 2004.

In addition to relying heavily on voluntary income, Charity C had also utilized volunteers to carry out over 95 per cent of its sea rescue services. Maintaining its volunteer ethos was one of the six core values of this charity. However, the charity's strategic decision to expand into beach lifeguarding under local government contracts had started to erode its pure volunteer ethos, as the beach lifeguards recruited by the charity were paid staff, which was in accordance to contractual specifications. Interviewees raised concerns about the charity's ability to retain its volunteer base and volunteer ethos in the future, within an increasingly competitive external environment for fundraising and service delivery.

The charity must maintain its strong traditional volunteer ethos and to be free from government funding. Volunteers in the organization want to be involved with it and not because they get paid for the job that they perform for the charity. (Branch fundraising officer, Charity C)

Organization Culture

This factor was cited by Charity D interviewees only as strongly influencing the charity's core positioning strategy. Schein (1992) defines corporate culture as a set of basic assumptions, which are invented, discovered, or developed by a given group as it learns to cope with its problems of external adaptation and internal integration. In terms of strategic positioning, culture has been classified as a source of sustainable competitive advantage in commercial (for-profit) organizations (Amit and Schoemaker 1993).

Culture takes time, skill, and capital to develop (Dierickx and Cool 1989), where these investments are irreversible (Peteraf 1993), and hence difficult to imitate. The chief executive of Charity D was credited with inspirational leadership and guiding the development of its mission-focused organizational strategies. These had helped to shape a strong organizational culture that was results-orientated and competitive in nature and had influenced the organization's ability and competence in adapting to the changing and increasingly competitive external environment.

> The organizational culture is a key factor in influencing the strategic decisions. Its ethos is results-orientated and competitive. We aim to do things well. Management provides an enabling and learning environment with a can-do attitude. We have a passionate workforce with good teamwork, integrity, and openness to change. (Development Director, Charity D)

SUMMARY OF KEY FINDINGS FROM THE CASE STUDIES STAGE

The preceding sections in this chapter have provided a detailed description and a comparison of evidence emerging from the four case studies in three main themes: process of developing a positioning strategy, the components of a positioning strategy, and the key factors that influence the choice of positioning strategy in the charitable context. The consistent use of the same themes in both the intra-case analysis and cross-case analysis aimed to enhance internal reliability in the case study methodology. A summary of the key findings in these three main themes is now presented in order to answer the research questions posed for this stage of the study.

Process of Strategic Positioning

There was strong evidence from the case studies that, despite their contrasting histories and organizational characteristics, charities have indeed begun to undertake strategic marketing planning and positioning strategy activities as defined in this study. However, there was little evidence found to suggest that the positioning strategy of charitable organizations was an outcome of their strategic marketing planning process in a competitive environment, as argued by some authors in mainstream marketing literature (e.g., Lovelock and Weinberg 1989; Hooley, Broderick, and Moller 1998; Andreasen and Kotler 2003). This process was found to be firmly embedded in the corporate planning process, with the marketing function playing a role mainly in communicating this position once it had been agreed by the board of trustees/chief executive.

Moreover, the positioning strategies of charities had not been the result of a deliberate or preplanned process, but rather they had emerged as responses to the organizations' external environmental influences and internal organizational changes. These emergent positioning strategies appeared to have been developed as patterns of past decisions and cumulative experiences (Mintzberg 1978). Mintzberg and Waters (1985) suggest that Porter's (1980) generic positioning strategies could be emergent in nature.

It was apparent that in more established charities in this study, such as Charity C and Charity D, there were extended periods of learning from experimentation and past experiences (Levitt and March 1988; Brodtrick 1998). In relatively younger charities, such as Charity A and Charity B, this process had evolved quite unconsciously mainly in response to the rapidly changing external environment, and with limited preplanning. However, there was little evidence in this present study to suggest that such emergent positioning strategies of charities were more or less effective than deliberate ones to enable the organizations to achieve their positioning goals. Nevertheless, the interviewees in the case study organizations perceived that the process of strategic positioning had provided serendipitous organizational learning, which paved the way for subsequent, more deliberate, strategy development (Mintzberg and Waters 1985).

Positioning Strategy

There was evidence from all four case studies that their positioning strategy comprised of distinct but interrelated components, namely, a generic or core positioning strategy, key target audiences, and positioning dimensions. There was further evidence to demonstrate that these organizations did adopt differentiation positioning and focus positioning as their generic or core positioning strategies (Porter 1980). Three of the four cases adopted focus positioning, while one case (Charity C) had adopted differentiation positioning. The charities that adopted focus positioning tended to be smaller in size (total annual income and paid staff) compared to those that employed differentiation positioning to distinguish themselves from other providers of similar services. This finding was consistent with that uncovered by the exploratory survey data analysis, which was explained in Chapter 5.

It was also evident that two distinct groups of audiences were targeted in the positioning strategies of charitable organizations. The first group comprised of users or beneficiaries of the charities' services, and was denoted as the primary target audience. The secondary target audience comprised of a variety of individuals or groups/institutions that provided funds and other vital organizational resources to support the delivery of services to the primary audience. Some of these groups/institutions were considered to be the charity's key external stakeholders, such as governmental funding agencies, central and local authorities, donors, volunteers, and other partner organizations. These findings supported those revealed in the exploratory survey stage detailed in Chapter 5.

The positioning strategies in the case study organizations were created or pursued for purely competitive motives. The reasons for adopting their strategic positions were multiple and differed from the often singular purpose of gaining competitive advantage that is commonly attributed to commercial (for-profit) organizations (Hamel and Prahalad 1989). One common positioning dimension cited in all the four cases was the close working relationship with statutory, voluntary, and private sector organizations in pursuance of their charitable missions. It suggests that charitable organizations have developed strategic relationships with key external stakeholders, such as funders and partner service providers, by cooperating/collaborating with them, as part of their portfolio of distinctive competences to support their positioning strategy over time.

Despite their contrasting backgrounds and services delivered, there were common positioning dimensions among the four case studies, such as high quality of services delivered to users/beneficiaries, expertise in their particular service, and strong working relationships with statutory, private, and other voluntary sector organizations. Importantly, however, each organization had developed its particular distinctiveness, which became a key distinguishing feature in its strategic position. Although the case study organizations perceived varying degrees of competitive intensity in their subsectors for funding and other resources, they had developed idiosyncratic positioning dimensions that reflected their key strengths.

In all the four case studies, there was evidence that the organizations had changed structurally and operationally whilst maintaining their core positioning strategies. These changes were necessitated because of a combination of external environmental and internal organizational factors. They adapted to external environmental pressures (an evolving policy context, competition for income streams for investible funds, socio-demographic shifts, and technological innovation) by making structural, operational, and resource adjustments. Key triggers to changes in positioning activity included a change of organizational leadership, shift in governmental policy, or changes in other specific external environmental conditions.

The changes most often had adversely impacted the charities' core services and financial resources, such as declining voluntary income and increased competition for service contracts. Therefore, these trigger events were instrumental in initiating more formalized strategic planning and review of the charity's strategic position in all the four case studies. Interestingly, changes in the case studies' strategic positions had, however, begun to create tension between their long-term economic survival and core values. The impact of these changes varied in the four cases organizations, which reflected differences in the nature of services provided, degree of governmental influence, and strategic decisions taken by their organizational leaders. The most common concern of the interviewees was that they had embarked on strategies that had eroded their volunteer ethos in varying degrees. By realigning their strategic positions over time, the charities had become increasingly 'professional' with increasing number of paid staff. Osborne (1998: 16) argues that the defining characteristic of voluntary and non-profit organizations is the 'voluntary value' that they hold. For charities, this means that they should show some form of 'public benefit,' such as participation of volunteers in service delivery, fundraising, or in the charity's management. The erosion of that core value had, in part, made it difficult for charities to attract voluntary donations, especially for those charities that had relied heavily on statutory income.

Influencing Factors on a Positioning Strategy

The components of a charity's positioning strategy were influenced by a combination of external environmental and internal organizational factors. From the inter-case analysis, these factors were further categorized as those influencing the core positioning component of the positioning strategy and those that have influenced the positioning dimensions.

Several factors identified at this stage of the study were consistent with those identified in the exploratory survey stage, as described in Chapter 5. These were the charity's mission, needs of services' users/beneficiaries, needs of donors/funders, availability of organizational resources, external environmental factors, influence of the board of trustees/chief executive, needs of volunteers, and organizational culture. However, the case studies have generated additional factors that were less prominently cited in the exploratory survey stage. These were governmental influence and organizational size. The most frequently cited factors that influenced the core positioning strategy were: governmental influence, other environmental influences, the charity mission, and needs of users/beneficiaries.

Factors that have influenced the positioning dimensions component of the positioning strategy were: availability of organizational resources, presence/ degree of competition (other than from government sources), and the board of trustees/chief executive. Some factors were common across all cases, but others were found to be distinctive of a particular charity. The variations appeared to be the result of differentials in size of the organization, organizational culture, and funding pattern. For instance, government was the most frequently cited factor in influencing both choice of the core positioning strategy and positioning dimensions in the case study organizations. In contrast, a minority of respondents had cited this factor in the exploratory survey stage. The variance could be because in the survey questionnaire the degree of governmental influence was from their role as a funder of the charities' activities. On the other hand, the case studies have revealed other influences of government, such as their policy maker or legitimizer of organizational activity. The degree of governmental influence also depended on the nature of the services provided by the charity and the extent to which the charity's leaders decided to engage with government as a partner or acted to maintain the charity's independence and autonomy.

Additionally, the case studies demonstrated that a charity's mission played a crucial role in its strategic positioning because not only did it act as a positioning differentiator, but it posed a major influence on the charity's strategic position. This finding was consistent with the exploratory survey finding, as reported in Chapter 5.

The case studies have also found that the degree to which competition could affect the positioning strategy in charities varied depending on the nature of services they each provide, their historical orientations, and the organizational leaders' overall perception of competition in the sector/ subsector in which the charity operated. This finding was corroborated by the case organizations' responses in the exploratory survey questionnaire, which showed variations in the perception of competitive intensity across the case studies (see Table 6.2).

Influence of board of trustee/chief executive played an important role in shaping the strategic position and choice of core positioning strategy of charitable organizations. They initiated a more formalized process for positioning activities and led the strategic reviews. Moreover, the case studies suggested that a leadership change, e.g., in the chairman or the chief executive, could trigger a change in positioning activities or in initiating the process of strategic positioning itself.

CONCLUSIONS

The purpose of this chapter was to present an analysis of key evidence from the four cross-sectional case studies. The evidence was presented according to the three main themes that have emerged from the preceding exploratory survey stage. This approach was undertaken in order to address the research objectives and answer the research questions posed by this study more comprehensively. Four case studies from amongst the survey respondents were examined. They were selected based on both organizational criteria and from their responses in the survey questionnaire. The multiple cross-case analysis utilized the method of analytic comparison where similarities and differences in the evidence across the four case studies were drawn out using the three themes to guide the analysis. This method of analytic comparison thus enabled in-depth examination of the themes. In addition, it provided further probing for explanations to answer the research questions, whilst facilitating data triangulation in the case studies and methodological triangulation with the findings from the preceding exploratory survey. Consequently, and more importantly, they have provided a more complete picture of the strategic positioning activities in charities.

Evidence from the case studies presented in this chapter has demonstrated that strategic positioning activities were undertaken by the charities. They have begun to position themselves strategically in their unique ways within their complex and changing operating environments. The evidence also suggests that the process of developing an organizational-level positioning strategy in charitable organizations was a more emergent process rather than a preplanned one. Differentiation and focus core positioning strategies were adopted by charities that target two key audience groups. Charities have also developed a range of positioning dimensions in order to support their core positioning strategy and to distinguish their organizations from other providers of similar services. The choice of different components in the charities' positioning strategies was influenced by a combination of external environmental and internal organizational factors that were unique to them.

The evidence from the case studies presented in this chapter and from the exploratory survey in Chapter 5 collectively form the basis of a theoretical model, which integrates the factors influencing a positioning strategy in the charitable context more aptly. The next chapter discusses further the combined evidence from both the survey and case studies stages, and unveils the theoretical model of influencing factors derived from this study.

7 Towards an Integrating Model
of Influencing Factors

This chapter draws together the major findings from the exploratory survey stage (Chapter 5) and the case studies stage (Chapter 6) presented so far, and reviews them in light of the existing literature. The chapter begins with a summary of the key points that arose in the previous two chapters. The intent is to highlight the conceptual and methodological links between the various stages in the study. It will also discuss a number of key findings and points of convergence and divergence between the empirical data and the existing literature/research. This discussion is guided by the two main research objectives established for this study. Thereafter, a theoretical model that integrates the key factors that could influence the positioning strategy of charities, which had been shaped from the empirical evidence in this study, will be unveiled. Where possible, the emerging factors will be evaluated with those identified in the initial organizing conceptual framework suggested in Chapter 2 and other relevant literature on strategy development in the voluntary and non-profit organizational contexts. This chapter concludes by reviewing and explaining the significance of the four major premises underpinning the theoretical model.

THE STORY SO FAR ...

A driving force behind this research has been the emphasis for voluntary and charitable organizations to be more strategically orientated as they become increasingly propelled into the forefront of public service policy development and delivery in and outside the UK (NCVO 2004b, 2005a; Anheier 2005). The diverse nature of voluntary sector organizations has made it necessary for this study to focus on charitable organizations, in particular those that operated in the general welfare and social care subsectors in the UK. These charities were chosen because a high proportion of them were involved in the delivery of public services.

This story thus began in Chapter 1 by establishing the focus of this research, that is, ascertaining to what extent contemporary strategy/marketing literatures on strategic positioning are applicable to the charitable context.

The public policy context and other external environmental changes in the socio-economic, technological, and competitive landscapes have continued to exert pressures on charitable organizations to manage their operations in order to effectively satisfy both their short-term survival needs and their longer-term strategic positions (Chew 2005, 2006a, 2006b). Charities have responded in various ways, including adopting professional management approaches and marketing techniques to help them adapt their operations and resources in pursuit of their missions/causes. The external environment pressures and internal organizational responses have resulted in the changing relationships between charities and their counterparts in the public and private sectors.

Yet because of the paucity of empirical research in this area, little is known about how charitable organizations have responded in terms of strategically positioning themselves in their changing environments. At the same time, it was noted that the majority of theoretical underpinnings in strategic positioning depicted in the extant literature have been derived from the context of commercial (for-profit) organizations, and that there is a lack of theoretical models/conceptual frameworks to guide positioning research and inform practice in non-profit and non-market contexts. Consequently, two main research objectives were defined to guide this study: to explore and describe the extent to which charitable organizations undertake strategic positioning activities at the organizational level and to identify and explain the key factors that influence the positioning strategy in charitable organizations.

While this study has been primarily focused on the charitable organization's view of its strategic position, it has also recognized the importance of the 'market' view of its position. However, the charity's perspective of its strategic position is an important starting point in shaping the external audience's perspective of its distinctiveness compared to other organizations providing similar services. This chapter has established that organizational-level positioning is distinct from, but provides direction for, positioning at the lower organizational levels (e.g., product or brand positioning). The organization's strategic position explicitly or implicitly identifies the key direction for its core positioning strategy (its distinctiveness) and provides guidance on developing its positioning dimensions (deployment of resources and core competences) to differentiate the organization from other providers.

Following the introductory chapter, the second chapter reviewed the current literature on strategic positioning at the organizational level, both in commercial (for-profit) organizations and non-profit organizations. It was noted that there remains scant literature and empirical studies on positioning in organizations other than for commercial (for-profit) ones. At the same time, positioning research in the charitable context had been largely ignored. Moreover, there is a lack of conceptual clarity and considerable confusion around the concept of positioning, which stems from different theoretical perspectives and from different levels of analysis. Much of the existing strategic management/marketing literature on the concept of positioning for non-profit organizations tended to describe this concept in similar ways, as depicted in the commercial marketing literature. From the literature review, three perspectives were evaluated for the purpose of identifying contrasting arguments on the forces that could shape the components of a positioning strategy: (a) the competitive industry forces/market-orientation perspective, (b) the resource-based view on positional advantage, and (c) the stakeholder-orientation/resource dependence perspective. This review led to an initial organizing conceptual framework that depicted the components of a positioning strategy and the possible factors that could influence the choice of a positioning strategy in the charitable context. The use of a multidimensional approach to the literature review had facilitated theory development in complex organizational contexts, such as in the charitable context (Thomas and McGee 1986).

Chapter 3 reviewed the voluntary and non-profit management literatures on the adoption of strategic management and marketing in the charitable context. It was focused on understanding the context of British charitable organizations in light of their changing policy and regulatory and other external environmental conditions. The purpose was to identify the drivers for and relevance of strategic positioning in the charitable context. Key differences between the context of charities and that of commercial (for-profit) organizations were explored. The analysis revealed a lack of theoretical and conceptual models that could adequately accommodate the complexities of developing and managing strategic positioning in the charitable context. This analysis supported the calls for more research into examining the appropriateness and applicability of contemporary strategy/marketing concepts to the context of voluntary and charitable organizations. Therefore, a principal output of this study was a new theoretical model, shaped from empirical evidence findings, which integrates the factors that influence a positioning strategy in the charitable context.

The fourth chapter began the empirical stage of this study and outlined the three-stage methodology employed for the investigation. Due to the limited existing literature and a lack of previous empirical research on positioning activities in the charitable context, an inductive research strategy was adopted to answer the research questions established for this study and to facilitate theory development (Bryman 2001). Specifically, this chapter began with an outline of the conceptualization stage that had resulted in an initial organizing conceptual framework of influencing factors on positioning strategy in charities. This framework was developed from the literature review in Chapter 2 and through exploratory discussions with a panel of academic experts and practising managers who were knowledgeable in strategic planning/marketing in charities.

A mixed methodology for data collection and analysis was employed. An exploratory postal survey was used to map the extent of positioning strategy activities in a sample of general welfare and social care charities. This was followed by four cross-sectional case studies investigating the emerging themes from the survey in greater depth. Comparing the findings derived from a combination of research methods had the advantage of stimulating theoretical development and guiding new directions for research (Blaikie 2006). This chapter had considered reliability and validity in the research, and had emphasized the need to use both data source and methodological triangulations (Denzin 1978b; Jick 1979; Osborne 1998) to establish these conditions.

Chapter 5 presented the findings from the second stage of this study, that is, from the exploratory postal survey of positioning activities in the general welfare and social care charities. The aim at this stage was to provide an initial and broad mapping of the strategic positioning activities of charities. The survey findings were therefore mainly descriptive and were not aimed at establishing causality. Due to the role of strategic marketing planning in the development of a positioning strategy as suggested in the marketing literature, it was necessary to examine the extent of strategic marketing planning activities and the relationship between these activities and positioning strategy on charities. However, the lack of existing scales to measure strategic marketing planning and positioning strategy in the charitable context had necessitated the development of two 'new' scales specifically for this study. Therefore, these measurement scales have contributed to methodology development in positioning research in charitable organizations.

The findings highlighted that charitable organizations considered their operating environment for funding and other organizational resources to be increasingly competitive in their sector and subsectors. They had begun to undertake strategic positioning activities extensively within their changing environment. Charities that undertook strategic marketing planning more extensively also tended to carry out positioning activities extensively, and vise versa. Despite this apparent relationship, there were variations in the extent to which the different marketing planning and positioning activities were pursued by charities. A notable finding was that charities did not provide a high level of priority in their strategic planning on competitor monitoring and in identifying their positioning dimensions (key strengths and distinctive competences) that differentiated their organizations from other providers. It was also apparent that charities adopted generic or core positioning strategies, in particular 'differentiation' and 'focus' or niche positioning strategies (Porter 1980). Further analysis revealed that charities that had adopted focus positioning tended to be smaller in size (total annual income and number of paid staff) and a smaller proportion of their income was derived from voluntary income compared to charities that adopted differentiation positioning. Moreover, a range of positioning dimensions was utilized by charities to support their core positioning strategy. The choice of core positioning strategy and positioning dimensions were influenced by external and internal factors. There were dimensions and influencing factors that appeared to be unique to the charitable context. These included the charity's mission, the needs of two groups of target audiences (users/ beneficiaries and donors/funders), the unique relationship between charities and local/central government funding agencies, and the board of trustees/chief executive. The chapter emphasized that the survey findings were mainly descriptive in nature and could not provide in-depth explanations as to the motivations for strategic positioning in charities and the reasons for the variations in positioning dimensions and influencing factors on the choice of positioning strategies. Three broad themes were conceived from this exploration that required further investigation at the third stage of the methodology, namely, the cross-sectional case studies.

Chapter 6 developed the four case studies according to the three themes that had emerged from the exploratory survey stage. It was established earlier in Chapter 4 and reinforced in this chapter that the selection of the case study organizations was aimed at enabling a comparison of findings in the different charitable organizational contexts, whilst providing a degree of generalizability in the findings in the general welfare and social care subsectors. It was argued that the three themes necessitated further investigation into the extent of strategic positioning activities in charities. Specifically, examining the themes has enabled the process of strategic positioning (process theme) in charities to be uncovered, determined the components of a positioning strategy and explored how these have changed over time (strategy theme), and explained the factors that have influenced the choice of positioning strategy (influencing factors theme).

The three themes were evaluated in turn, both from findings within each case organization and from findings across the four cases. There was strong evidence from both the intra-case and cross-case analyses that, despite their contrasting histories and organizational characteristics, charitable organizations were undertaking strategic positioning activities to varying extents. However, there was little evidence of a structured or formulaic process of strategic positioning in the case study organizations. Instead, there was evidence of an emergent process that was embedded in the corporate planning activities. The charity's mission played a dominant role in determining the core positioning strategy and key target audiences. The mission had also guided the development of the charities' positioning dimensions (its key strengths and distinctive competences) to support their positioning strategies over time. The strategic intent or motivation for strategic positioning in charities was found to be more complex compared to the singular purpose of gaining competitive advantage over rivals that has been commonly associated with commercial (for-profit) organizations. Cooperative and collaborative working relationships with other organizations in pursuit of their mission was one determinant of the charities' positioning strategies, whilst key triggers for positioning activities included a change either of organizational leadership or of governmental policies.

The key factors that could influence the choice of positioning strategy in charitable organizations were a complex combination of external environmental and internal organizational influences, some of which were unique to them. One major factor was governmental influence, which did not emerge as a significant factor from the postal survey findings nor was it commonly cited in the extant positioning literature. This chapter had demonstrated that the degree of influence from government varied depending on the perceived role that it played in the relationship with a charity, e.g., as a funder, a policy maker, or legitimizer of its public service/charitable activity. Other factors, such as the influence of volunteers and organizational size were unique to specific charitable organizations. The emerging findings from the case studies challenged the current marketing literature on positioning that advocates a positioning strategy as a key outcome of the strategic marketing planning process, and that the *main* goal of positioning is to create a competitive advantage over the organization's rivals. In addition, some of the influencing factors found in the case studies were not among those commonly cited in the literature on positioning for commercial (for-profit) organizations.

To summarize, the findings from both the exploratory survey stage and the case studies stage provided an arguable first attempt to empirically map the strategic positioning activities of charitable organizations. They revealed that charities were employing significant approaches to strategic positioning and that these approaches offered a distinctive addition to positioning theory and research. In particular, they have reinforced the need to develop theoretical and conceptual models that can better accommodate the specific contexts of non-profit organizations, such as charities.

The following sections in this chapter bring together and discuss in depth the key findings that have been drawn out from the data analyses in the survey stage and the case studies stage. These are evaluated in light of the existing literature. The discussion will be guided by the two main research objectives that were established for this study in Chapter 1 and that have been restated in Chapter 4.

TO WHAT EXTENT ARE CHARITABLE ORGANIZATIONS UNDERTAKING STRATEGIC POSITIONING ACTIVITIES?

Chapter 3 has established that the profound changes taking place in the public policy context coupled with a continued challenging wider external environment within which British charitable organizations operate in recent years have increased the pressure on them to be strategically orientated as they pursue their missions/causes. The combined evidence from both the exploratory survey stage and the case studies stage have demonstrated empirically that charities, in particular those that were involved in public service delivery, have indeed begun to position themselves within the changing operating environments, both at the subsector level and in the wider voluntary sector. The first main research objective will be dealt with in three parts: first, evidence of strategic positioning activities; second, an anatomy of a positioning strategy; and third, the process of strategic positioning in the charitable context.

Evidence of Strategic Positioning Activities

There is strong evidence from both the survey findings and the case studies that charitable organizations have begun to undertake strategic positioning at the organizational level. Earlier positioning research conducted on charities offered different depictions of positioning for charities, such as market positioning (Hibbert 1995), product positioning (Wray 1994), and competitive positioning (Saxton 1996). These studies were focused primarily on positioning of charities to support their fundraising efforts. In their different ways, these earlier studies concluded that charities lacked strong positions that could differentiate the organizations in the eyes of their external audiences, in particular, donors and funders. It is argued in this present study that strategic positioning at the organizational level is distinct from, but provides direction for, positioning at the lower (product/brand) levels (Hooley, Saunders, and Piercy 1998; Fill 2002; Ellson 2004).

While strategic positioning at the organizational level is a long-term process of developing the charity's overall distinctive advantage in the marketplace, positioning at the product/brand level involves identifying how the particular offerings are perceived by consumers relative to other competing products/brands (Hooley, Saunders, and Piercy 1998). The aim is to identify the charity's place (its strategic position) in its environment, which depends on its mission and distinctive competences (Chew 2006b). This present study has provided empirical evidence to support that assertion. In particular, the case studies have revealed that a strong organizational-level strategic position supported certain core values in the charities, which translated into their distinctive range of services/offerings and unique relationships with various stakeholders (such as users/beneficiaries, funders, and other partner organizations). It provided the vehicle through which the charities' key strengths and distinctive competences were communicated in their fundraising and advocacy campaigns. This communication role was undertaken by the marketing function in the case study organizations.

However, it is interesting to note that although the survey findings and the case studies revealed that charitable organizations were undertaking marketing planning activities at a more strategic level than previously concluded (e.g., Cousins 1990; Sargeant 1995), this present study has also revealed that positioning was not given a high level of priority relative to the other strategic marketing planning activities. For instance, the mean score for 'Identifying the Charity's Positioning Dimensions' activity among all survey respondents was below the total mean score for all the thirteen activities in the strategic marketing planning scale. This does not imply that strategic positioning was less important for charities in this study. On the contrary, they were undertaking positioning activities, albeit to varying extents. The six activities in the positioning strategy scale corresponded closely to the three main components of a positioning strategy: (a) generic or core positioning, (b) key target audiences, and (c) positioning dimensions. The case studies provided evidence to reinforce the presence of these interrelated components of a positioning strategy in charitable organizations.

The findings have also revealed that the charity's strategic position explicitly or implicitly identifies the key direction for its core positioning (its distinctiveness) and provides guidance to develop its positioning dimensions (key strengths and distinctive competences) to differentiate it from other providers of similar services. Strategic position embodies the 'strategic intent' or overriding ambition of the organization to reach its desired position (Hamel and Prahalad 1989: 64). Strategic intent for positioning by commercial (for-profit) organizations is often viewed in the extant strategy/ marketing literature as focusing on competitive goals, in particular, to strive for a leadership position by winning over rival providers. However, there has been a lack of research into understanding the strategic intent for positioning in the charitable context.

An integrating theoretical model developed from the empirical findings in this present study was thus aimed at providing an arguable first attempt to understand the motives for strategic positioning in charities, and consequently, to appreciate how strategic positioning at the organizational level is undertaken by them. This theoretical model will be unveiled and discussed fully in a later section in this chapter.

Anatomy of a Positioning Strategy

A crucial starting point in developing the integrating model of influencing factors on a positioning strategy in this study was to firstly identify the components of a positioning strategy in the charitable context. Maggard (1986) suggests that a positioning strategy could be more constructively understood as a broader organizing concept for various strategic decisions and techniques.

The findings from both the survey and case studies suggest that a positioning strategy for charitable organizations comprised of three interrelated components. They adopted generic or core positioning strategies, which provided the broad positioning stance of the organization. The core positioning strategy directed the choice of target audience(s) and the positioning dimensions of the charities. Moreover, the case studies revealed that a strong organizational-level strategic position created and/or supported certain core values in the charity. This position was then translated into a distinctive range of services/offerings and unique relationships with other stakeholders (users/beneficiaries, donors, statutory funders, and other partner organizations). It also provided the framework for communicating the charity's strengths and competences in its fundraising and advocacy campaigns. A positioning strategy was found to be a means through which the charity's desired strategic position was communicated to its external and internal audiences. Each of the three main components in the charitable context is discussed next with reference to the existing literature.

Generic or Core Positioning Strategy

Porter (1980) advocates 'differentiation positioning,' 'focus positioning,' and 'low-cost leadership' as three generic or core positioning strategies for commercial (for-profit) organizations. These strategies are aimed at achieving the main positioning goal of gaining a competitive advantage over rivals in the sector/subsector in which the organization operates. This study has revealed that charities have adopted generic or core positioning strategies, with differentiation positioning and focus positioning being demonstrably more evident. The survey has revealed that differentiation positioning was used by two-thirds of the respondents, while a third of them adopted focus (or niche) positioning as their core positioning strategy. Three of the four case studies utilized focus positioning while differentiation positioning was adopted by the fourth. These findings therefore support the assertion by some authors that differentiation and focus positioning strategies are more appropriate for charitable organizations (e.g., Wray 1994; McLeish 1995; Saxton 1996; Bruce 1998).

Differentiation positioning in charities entailed establishing some positively distinctive ways in which the charity's offerings met the needs of its target audiences and were valued by them (Porter 1980). Focus or niche positioning was serving a particular group of users/beneficiaries, geographic area, or providing a type of service better than other providers of similar service. As reported in Chapter 5 there was little significant statistical evidence in the survey findings to distinguish between those charities that had adopted differentiation positioning and focus positioning strategies along key organizational characteristics.

However, the findings suggested that charities adopting differentiation positioning tended to be larger in size (in terms of total annual income and paid staff), derived a larger proportion of their income from voluntary sources, and fewer of them perceived high competitive intensity for funding and other organizational resources compared to charities adopting focus positioning. These findings were corroborated with evidence from the case studies. For instance, Charity C was the only charity among the four case study organizations that adopted differentiation positioning as its core positioning strategy. It was the largest and the most established in terms of the number of years from its inception among the four case studies. It derived over 90 per cent of its income from voluntary sources and less than 1 per cent from statutory income.

Additionally, because of the inherent dependency of charitable organizations on external parties for funding and other resources, low-cost positioning, where the organization leads the market with low prices of its services, is arguably less appropriate for charities (Bruce 1998). This argument is supported by findings from both the survey and the case studies in this research. Only one survey respondent cited low-cost positioning as the charity's core positioning strategy. Low-cost positioning required the charity to be a dominant player or to occupy a monopoly position in the sector/subsector in which it operated (Bruce 1998). However, sustaining a low-cost leadership position for this charity would be difficult over the longer term due to its high dependency on external parties for funding and other key resources (Chew 2003).

Key Target Audiences

This study has revealed that charitable organizations recognized the important influence of two key groups of external stakeholders in their positioning activities, compared to a singular 'customer' in commercial (for-profit) firms. Interviewees in the case studies regarded users/beneficiaries of their services as the charity's primary target audience, while their secondary target audience comprised of a number of different parties, such as donors/funders and government agencies that provided essential financial resources or support to enable fulfilment of their mission.

Mason (1984) argues that charities, unlike commercial (for-profit) organizations, require separate organizational structures or processes to manage their resource attraction and resource allocation functions to effectively serve the different needs and expectations of these two target audiences. Bruce (1998: 45) goes further to suggest that charities have to develop consistent positioning strategies that are acceptable not only to users/beneficiaries and donor/funders, but also to a wider range of stakeholders. This study thus found charities striving to communicate a singular strategic position to different groups of target audiences, whilst maintaining focus on their mission.

Positioning Dimensions

Positioning dimensions are the specific ways through which charities differentiate themselves (Porter 1980; Hooley, Saunders, and Piercy 1998). The survey and the case studies found that charitable organizations utilized a range of dimensions to distinguish themselves and to support their core positioning strategy. Some dimensions used by the charities reflected those advocated in the non-profit marketing literature, such as quality of services or the provision of specialist services (Lovelock and Weinberg 1989; McLeish 1995; Andreasen and Kotler 2003).

However, other dimensions were unique to the charitable context, such as the charity's mission, strong relationship with statutory bodies, and network of branches and volunteers. These variations suggest important differentiation in subsectoral/organizational contexts and highlight the limited applicability of existing generic positioning typologies for the diverse charitable and voluntary non-profit sectors.

Different positioning dimensions draw heavily on the resources and capabilities available to the organization in different ways (Porter 1985; Hooley, Broderick, and Moller 1998). The case studies revealed that the positioning dimensions used by charities were not static but could change over time as the organizations adapted to their external and internal environments. For instance, quality of service delivery and expertise in a particular service to users/beneficiaries were the most common strengths cited by interviewees in all the case studies. However, these strengths had to be developed over time in order to support their evolving corporate strategies. The case studies also revealed that different charitable organizations developed different dimensions that have helped them differentiate their organizations from other service providers and to support their core positioning strategies over time. These findings support the resource-based view's argument that resources and capabilities are potential sources of an organization's core or distinctive competences (Prahalad and Hamel 1990).

Process of Developing a Positioning Strategy

It was established in Chapter 2 that the existing positioning literature tends to describe the process of developing a positioning strategy in non-profit organizations in similar ways to commercial (for-profit) organizations. Two key differences, which were identified in Chapter 6, stood out from the evidence about the strategic positioning process in charitable organizations. These are discussed in the following.

First, evidence from the case studies showed that identifying the charity's strategic position was firmly embedded in its corporate strategy planning process. The strategic management literature suggests that strategic positioning is an integral part of the strategic planning and review process (Hudson 2002). It is about matching the organization's strengths and resources to its external operating environment in order to take advantage of opportunities and overcome/circumvent threats (Johnson, Scholes, and Whittington 2006: 43). The marketing perspective, on the other hand, advocates that identifying the organization's strategic position and developing a positioning strategy are conducted within the strategic marketing planning process (Kotler 1994; Lovelock, Vandermerwe, and Lewis 1996; Hooley, Saunders, and Piercy 1998; Hooley et al. 2001). The primary positioning goal for commercial (for-profit) organizations is to create and sustain a competitive advantage that seeks superior financial performance for the firm (Porter 1985). The findings from this study provide some support for the strategic management perspective, but found little evidence to support the marketing perspective. The case study charities have established procedures for their corporate planning process compared to their marketing planning.

The key motivation for positioning by charitable organizations stemmed primarily from their mission/purpose, which was rooted in their core social values and ideology. Johnson, Scholes, and Whittington (2006: 26) argue that the underlying charitable ethos of charities and non-profit organizations plays a central part in the development of their strategic positions.

Second, there was no clear evidence from this study that charities adopted an explicit preplanned and formulaic process of developing a positioning strategy, which has been advocated by the 'design lens' on strategy development. As highlighted in Chapter 2, this perspective on developing a positioning strategy is commonly emphasized in the existing literature for non-profit organizations (e.g., Lovelock and Weinberg 1989; Kotler and Andreasen 1996; Andreasen and Kotler 2003). It portrays the deliberate positioning of the organization through a rational, structured, and directive process (Johnson, Scholes, and Whittington 2006).

In contrast to the 'design lens' perspective on strategy development, this research has revealed that a positioning strategy in the charitable context was more likely to have emerged from actions taken in response to external environmental influences and internal organizational changes. This finding does not imply that charities are unaware of their strategic positions or that the process of identifying their strategic positions is chaotic. On the contrary, the charities in this study had a very strong sense of their strategic positions, which were robustly influenced by their missions. Their experiences support the 'experience lens' perspective to strategy development. Proponents of the 'experience lens' approach, such as Lindblom (1959), Mintzberg (1978, 1987), and Behn (1988), argue that the rational decision-making models on strategy development have limitations when applied in complex organizational situations where strategies are often the outcome of experiences, culture, and 'taken-for-granted assumptions' (Johnson, Scholes, and Whittington 2006: 45).

Moreover, Mintzberg and Waters (1985) argue that an emergent positioning strategy could stimulate organizational learning and pave the way for a more deliberate approach to strategy development. This situation was demonstrated in the case study charities in this research—they have identified their strategic positions and developed unique positioning strategies through serendipitous organizational learning and adaptation to their evolving environments.

Zineldin and Bredenlow (2001) suggest that the process of developing a positioning strategy in voluntary and non-profit organizations is complex and iterative, and requires a deliberate and proactive commitment from the organization's management on resources to deliver its positioning goals. Moreover, they (ibid.) argue that whilst a positioning strategy does evolve over time, the initial choice of the non-profit organization's strategic position will constrain future change in its positioning activities. This present study provides some support for this argument but also offers a new perspective on explaining the phenomenon in the charitable context.

It was highlighted in Chapter 6, that the strategic positions of the case organizations in this study demonstrated resilience to change despite adjustments in their positioning dimensions over time. This was because the missions and core values of the charities have strongly shaped the creation of their strategic positions since their inception. However, they have adapted to opportunities and threats in their external operating environments by realigning their structures, operations, and resource support. From the charities' perspectives, these changes did not represent deviations from their core positioning strategies or their missions. As it will be discussed later in this chapter, the charity's mission is a fundamental influence on the choice of its positioning strategy by explicitly or implicitly determining the choice of its core positioning strategy and its key target users/beneficiaries, but not necessarily constraining the choice of its positioning dimensions.

WHAT ARE THE KEY FACTORS THAT INFLUENCE THE CHOICE OF A POSITIONING STRATEGY IN CHARITABLE ORGANIZATIONS?

The second research objective will be addressed in two parts: identifying the influencing factors that were common in both the survey and the case studies stages, and those factors that were not commonly cited in these two stages. Table 7.1 summarizes the factors that were most frequently cited by respondents in the exploratory postal survey (shown in Table 5.16) and those that have emerged from the case studies (shown in Table 6.6). Some factors were common in both the survey and case studies, whilst others were specific to one or some of the case studies only. This differentiation was crucial in building the theoretical model because it enabled inclusion of those factors that could be generalized across charities, whilst recognizing the possibility of other contingent factors.

Factors Commonly Cited Across the Survey and Case Studies

Table 7.1 shows seven factors that were cited in both the survey and by interviewees in all the four case studies. Viewed together, they could imply strength of concurrence for these factors by charitable organizations in the general welfare and social care sectors. The commonly cited factors were: governmental influence, external environmental factors (other than government/political dimension), needs of users/beneficiaries, the charity's mission, organizational resources, competition, and influence of the board of trustees/chief executive. It must be reminded that factors revealed in the case studies were further differentiated between those that have influenced the core positioning strategy and those that have influenced the positioning dimensions of the strategy. The survey did not make this distinction because it was primarily exploratory in nature and was aimed at providing

Table 7.1 Summary of Key Factors Influencing Positioning Strategy in the General Welfare and Social Care Charitable Organizations

Key Factors Influencing Positioning Strategy	Mean Frequency of Factor Cited by Postal Survey Respondents (N=51)	Mean Frequency of Factor Cited by Interviewees in Case Studies (a) (n=4)
Governmental influence (funder, policy maker, legitimizer)	16% (b)	85%*
External environmental factors (other than government/political, e.g., shifts in social-demography, economic, technology, international developments, media influence)	67% (c)	59%*
Needs of users/beneficiaries	78%	41%*
Mission of the charity	82%	38%*
Organizational resources (include availability of funds, skills, and capabilities)	69%	68%**
Competition (other than statutory)	37% (d)	60%**
Trustees/chief executive of the organization	38%	40%**
Organization size (number of branch offices, number of staff, total income and assets)	NA (e)	(f)
Needs of donors (non-statutory)	53%	(f)
Needs of volunteers	10%	(g)
Organizational culture	31%	(g)
One or more non-governmental funding organization(s)	8%	(h)

Note:
(a) Factors in the case studies were further differentiated between those that influenced the core positioning strategy (cells with *) and those that influenced the positioning dimensions of the strategy (cells with **). The postal survey did not make this distinction.
(b) Governmental influence was cited in the postal survey as from its role as funder only. The case studies identified other influences from government as policy maker and legitimizer of the charities' work and their expertise.
(c) External environmental factors included political dimension in the postal survey.
(d) Competition in the postal survey included other charities, voluntary and private sector organizations.
(e) Organizational size was not cited in the postal survey but cited in three of the four case studies.
(f) Factor particular to some of the case study organizations.
(g) Factor particular to one case study organization only.
(h) Factor not cited in all case study organizations.

only an initial overview of the strategic positioning activities in charitable organizations.

Some of the emerging factors were similar to those depicted in the initial organizing conceptual framework developed in Chapter 2 (Figure 2.2), such as external environmental factors, mission, organizational resources, and competition. Other factors were not as explicitly distinctive, such as needs of users/beneficiaries and donors/funders, and the influence of the board of trustees/chief executive. This apparent difference can be explained conceptually and methodologically. The initial framework had depicted key primary stakeholders as those entities/groups that the charity depend on for their survival (Clarkson 1995), and who possess the power and legitimacy to influence organizational behaviour by virtue of their resource dependent relationships with the charity (Mitchell, Agle, and Wood 1997). Within this definition, key primary stakeholders in the initial framework broadly included external and internal stakeholders, such as dominant funders, volunteers who provided critical resources to the charity, or an influential trustee/chief executive.

In the case studies, certain stakeholders emerged as exerting significant influences on the charity's positioning strategy, and were consequently differentiated as distinct factors in their own right. The factor of particular interest was governmental influence. The government was cited in the survey as emanating from its role as a funder of the charities' activities. The in-depth investigation in the case studies had enabled other influences of government on the charities' positioning dimensions to emerge, such as the charities' policy maker and legitimizer of their public service work and expertise. The other significant influence came from users/beneficiaries, which did not explicitly emerge from the conceptualization stage of this present study.

Factors Not Commonly Cited in the Survey and Case Studies

Four factors are depicted in Table 7.1 that were cited in the postal survey but were only mentioned by interviewees in a single or a few of the case studies. These are: the needs of donors, the needs of volunteers, organizational culture, and the influence of dominant non-governmental funders. In addition, organizational size was mentioned in three of the four case studies but was not uncovered in the survey. It was suggested in Chapter 6 that the possible reason for these variations was the different funding patterns and organizational size of the case study organizations. Further, Chapter 5 highlighted that the 10 per cent of the survey respondents who cited volunteers as an influencing factor on their charity's positioning strategy were from charitable organizations that relied heavily on voluntary income (e.g., at least 90 per cent of their total annual income).

Moreover, these survey respondents had cited the needs of donors as another influencing factor. These findings were corroborated with evidence from the case studies. For instance, Charity C was the largest among the four case study organizations in terms of organizational size and it depended on volunteers to deliver over 95 per cent of its emergency sea rescue services. At the same time, it was also heavily reliant on volunteers to raise 90 per cent of its income from voluntary sources.

In contrast, the other three case study organizations were less reliant on volunteers in either their service delivery or fundraising activities, which were increasingly performed by paid staff. In terms of the influence of donors, Charity D was the only case study organization that was reliant on statutory funding (contracts and grants) for the bulk (95 per cent) of its total income. The varying experiences in different charities reaffirmed the importance of organizational context and the degree of resource dependency of charities on external parties in explaining some of the factors influencing positioning strategy in the charitable context (Pfeffer and Salancik 1978).

In summary, the combined empirical evidence from the exploratory survey and the in-depth case studies have provided a more comprehensive picture of the various factors that influence the positioning strategies of charities from their experiences, compared to those depicted in the initial organizing framework drawn up at the conceptualization stage in this study.

TOWARDS AN INTEGRATING MODEL OF FACTORS INFLUENCING A POSITIONING STRATEGY IN THE CHARITABLE CONTEXT

Figure 7.1 unveils the theoretical model that integrates the multidimensional factors influencing positioning strategy in charities, which had emerged from the combined evidence in the survey and case studies. It identifies three groups of factors: organizational, environmental, and mediating factors. Several of these factors are not commonly cited in the commercial (for-profit) marketing/strategy literature. They include the charity's mission, needs of two distinct groups of stakeholders, influence of the board of trustees/chief executive, needs of volunteers, and governmental influence. The most significant factors and their influence on the components of the charity's positioning strategy are explained in the following.

Organizational Factors

Three organizational influences on positioning strategy are depicted in the model: the charity's mission, organization-wide or corporate plan, and organizational resources.

Mission

Mission is identified in Chapters 2 and 3 as the fundamental purpose of a charity (Hudson 2002). From a strategic management perspective, mission

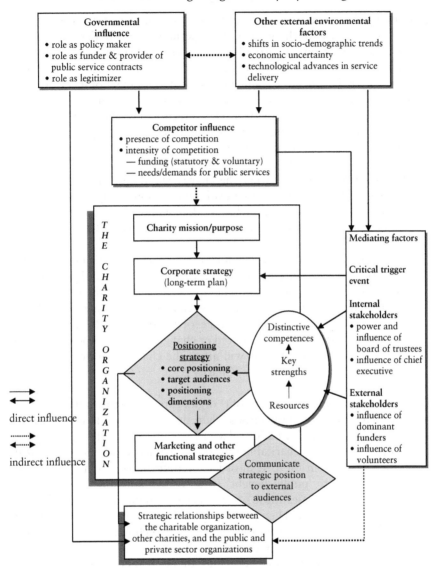

Figure 7.1 Integrating model of factors influencing a positioning strategy in the charitable context. Source: Chew and Osborne (2008b) *Reprinted with permission.*

helps direct organizational efforts and resources to achieve its ideal view of the world: its vision and purpose (Zineldin and Bredenlow 2001). Frumkin and Kim (2001) suggest that positioning around the charity's mission could be a unique way for charitable and non-profit organizations to differentiate themselves in a competitive fundraising environment. This study has found that the charity's mission played a crucial role in determining its positioning direction. Mission could guide or constrain the charity's strategic choices by establishing their strategic intent and by determining the scope of its operations. It provided the central direction for the charity's core positioning strategy (how to be distinctive), identified its primary target audience (users/beneficiaries), and guided the development of its positioning dimensions (resources and core competences) to differentiate the organization from other charities/providers. This directional quality of the charity's mission on its strategic positioning is well articulated by two interviewees who participated in the case studies:

> Our charity's mission—what the charity stands for and what it aims to do—is the lynchpin to its positioning. If somebody asks what our organization stands for and what we do, I will read to them our mission statement. (Marketing and Communications Manager, Charity B)

> Our charity's mission predetermines our focused strategic positioning— the type of service the charity provides, its target users, and partner hospitals, which are limited to teaching paediatric hospitals. In the longer term: Is the charity fulfilling a need when its role no longer exists due to changes in government policies and evolving social needs? The charity's mission would need to be reviewed or changed then in response to those external influences, and this will affect the charity's strategic position. (Chairman, Board of Trustees, Charity A)

In contrast to commercial (for-profit) organizations, charities have a much stronger sense of mission or purpose than their counterparts in the private and public sectors (Hudson 2002). Two explanations are offered to support this proposition. First, charitable purpose is explicitly required by charity laws, such as those in the UK, in order to conform to specified categories and to demonstrate 'public benefit' (Charity Commission 2004, 2005b). This means that charities must serve either the community as a whole or a sufficient section of it. They are legally prohibited from distributing surpluses that are generated from their activities, which must be reinvested in the charity to further their mission or cause.

Second, the missions of some charities are implicit because they are part of the accepted values and ethos of people working in these organizations (Hudson 2002: 100). These two levels of shared values (the charitable sector ethos, which explicitly specifies how charities should behave towards various stakeholders, and the organizational ethos implicit to the individual charity) combine to make the charity's mission a potent influence on its strategic positioning activities as suggested in this study.

Moreover, charitable status requires a substantive and often intangible mission, which is more resistant to change without damaging its purpose and legal status for existence (Hudson 2002; Leat 1995a). The findings from this study support this assertion. In all the case organizations, their core positioning strategies reflected the charities' missions, which remained essentially unchanged over time. However, the charities had adapted to external environmental changes by embarking on changes in their organizational structure, operations, and resources in order to remain relevant to their cause. This relationship of operational change with fixity on basic purpose is well illustrated in the following quotation:

> The strategic position of the charity has not changed—the purpose and core values of the organization today are the same when it was set up over 180 years ago. How the charity provides its services has changed for us to remain relevant to the changing times. (Regional Manager, Charity C)

Organization-Wide Corporate Plan

This study revealed that a charity's positioning strategy often emerged from its organization-wide corporate planning process. It did not typically develop separately or as part of a conscious and deliberate strategic marketing planning process, as advocated for non-profit organizations by, for example, Lovelock and Weinberg (1989), and Kotler and Andreasen (1996). Interestingly, larger charities in this study had dedicated marketing functions but these played mainly a communications role in the strategic positioning process. This contrasted with the marketing perspective that depicts a positioning strategy as a key outcome of the strategic marketing planning process.

Changes to the charity's organization-wide corporate plan could affect its strategic direction, such as its scope of operations, geographic location, or primary target audiences, which would then necessitate a shift in the charity's positioning dimensions. For instance, a change in public policy that supported local community development had provided Charity B with an opportunity to strategically revise its corporate plan to manage the growing number of local government grant projects. Consequently, efforts were made by its senior management to 'professionalize' the charity's approach to delivering community services contracted for government, such as service quality standards, providing customized training for staff, and establishing performance targets.

This phenomenon was also reflected when Charity C decided to expand its core services into beach lifeguarding in an effort to reach new and younger target audiences. The change in its corporate strategic direction had compelled the charity to compete with other charities, voluntary and private sector organizations for local government contracts, and to employ paid lifeguards to deliver this new service. These developments were initially alien to the charity because it had traditionally depended mainly on volunteers to deliver its sea rescue services and in its fundraising activities. These two examples illuminate these charities' desire to realign their resources and distinctive competences in order to support the new strategic direction mandated by the change in their corporate plans.

Organizational Resources

As it was reviewed in Chapter 2, organizational resources are those financial, physical, human assets and capabilities that an organization has acquired or built over time, and that could be developed into the organization's distinctive advantage (Wernerfelt 1984; Fahy 2000). Several authors who advocate the resource-based view of creating a positional advantage (e.g., Barney 1991; Grant 1991; Hall 1993), differentiate between the assets and capabilities of an organization. Together, organizational assets and capabilities provide the foundation for the organization's core competences (Prahalad and Hamel 1990) and from which a positioning strategy draws its strength.

Hooley, Broderick, and Moller (1998) and Hooley and others(2001) suggest that marketing resources and capabilities play key roles in establishing competitive advantage of commercial (for-profit) organizations in the marketplace. However, for charitable organizations that are arguably more dependent on external parties for resources than their commercial (for-profit) counterparts, developing internal capabilities such as a unique expertise, strong culture, and organizational leadership rather than physical assets was therefore crucial for them to sustain their strategic positions over time. Organizational culture has been classified as a key resource and a 'strategic asset' because it is difficult to imitate (Reed and DeFillippi 1990; Amit and Schoemaker 1993) and it takes time, skill, and capital to develop (Dierickx and Cool 1989). Charities in this study, particularly smaller ones, considered their organizational culture as one of their key positioning strengths. It sets the internal context within which strategic decisions are made (Webster 1994).

> As we are a small charity and we don't have projects for everyone to support, we have developed a unique culture that emphasized using our expertise in housing accommodation, quality services to beneficiaries, and long-term relationships with our donors to support our mission. (Fundraising Manager, Charity A)

External Environmental Factors

This study identifies external environmental factors as influences that are not within the direct control of the organization's management and that could affect its strategies unexpectedly (Learned et al. 1969; Andrews 1980; Johnson, Scholes, and Whittington 2006). On the basis of this research, three external factors that could influence the charity's positioning strategy are: governmental influence, other external environmental factors, and competitor influence.

Governmental Influence

Governmental influence was the most significant external factor that emerged from the case studies. It could influence the choice of a charity's core positioning strategy and positioning dimensions. Although the charities in this study received statutory income in varying degrees, they perceived the government to be less of a competitor for organizational resources. However, as highlighted in Chapter 6 and earlier in this chapter, the degree of governmental influence differed depending on the perceived role played by government in its relationship with the charity—whether as their policy maker (e.g., national policies and regulations in social care and community welfare services) or as a legitimizer of their activities.

This situation had a particular resonance in the UK, where the government policies in the last decade had emphasized partnership with, and increased the capacity of, charitable and voluntary organizations in the delivery of public services (HM Treasury 2002). This study thus suggests a complicated set of relationships between charities and government. The charities were able to work well in partnership with central and regional government agencies despite being reliant on government for funding and public service contracts because they had remained focused on their missions. This situation is illustrated by the comments of two case study interviewees:

> Governmental policies do not change our charity's overall strategic position directly, but only operational issues, for example, setting clearer policies for beach lifeguarding services at local levels, legitimizing the charity's role for this public service, and statutory requirements for search-and-rescue training qualifications that it provides to its crew and volunteers. (Beach Lifeguarding Officer, Charity C)

> As a voluntary and non-profit organization that handles large volumes of government contracts, being able to work with governmental funders and agencies gives us a high degree of legitimacy about our capabilities and expertise. (Development Director, Charity D)

One possible explanation for the collaborative relationship between charitable organizations and government is that the charities in this study were primarily engaged in the actual delivery of services to users/beneficiaries. Advocacy or campaigning activities were less of a priority in their missions, unlike other charities with those activities as their primary purpose for existence. Another reason was the strategic choices the case study organizational leaders had taken to ensure that their relationship with government—their policy maker and legitimizer—was less adversarial but more cooperative and collaborative. Although the charities perceived varying degrees of competitive intensity for service contracts and funding in their subsectors, they have chosen to strategically align their organizations in often less confrontational positions to sustain their survival (Wilson 1994).

The charities' particular relationship with central and local government agencies reflected the evolution of the UK government's policy of partnership with the voluntary sector in public service delivery over the past decade. As it was suggested in Chapter 3, this development was augmented by the 'Compact' (1998) that set out the formal framework for partnership working between the UK government and voluntary and charitable organizations (Home Office 1998; NCVO 2005a). Of particular significance was the establishment of 'Codes of Good Practice' for funding and procurement for statutory (national and local) contract and grant undertakings by both sides. Proposals to strengthen the 'Compact' governing formal relations between government at all levels and the voluntary sector in policy design, codes of practice, and public service delivery signalled the commitment made by both parties to develop strategic relationships (Osborne 2002; Osborne and McLaughlin 2004).

Other External Environmental Influences

These influences comprised of environmental factors (other than governmental influence) external to the charitable organization, which were outside the direct control of its management, such as economic conditions, technological, and socio-demographic changes. The findings from both the survey and case studies revealed that the external operating environment in which charities operate is becoming increasingly challenging and competitive, particularly in the arena of fundraising both for voluntary income and statutory funding. Such a situation could either provide opportunities for or impede the charities' strategic positioning (Bruce 1998; Hudson 2002). Factors such as an ageing and increasingly pluralistic population, shifts in demographics of service users and beneficiaries, and changes in the demands of funders/donors were the most frequently cited social-demographic influences in this study.

Moreover, changes in the national and international economic environments (recessionary or growth trends) and technological changes that had availed cost-effective electronic/Internet capabilities for fundraising and service delivery had affected those charities that relied heavily on voluntary income, such as Charity A and Charity C. Importantly, the influence of different environmental conditions had affected the charities' positioning dimensions more significantly than their core positioning strategies. The positioning dimensions through which the charities differentiated themselves from other voluntary organizations had to be reviewed in light of shifts in their corporate strategies as the charities adapted to changes in their evolving environmental conditions.

Competitor Influence

The growing competition for both financial and other resources is increasingly evident in many charity subsectors where a number of charities serve the same cause, offer similar types of services (such as general welfare for children or accommodation services for elderly persons), or operate in the same geographical or user segments as each other. CAF (2003) reports 23 per cent of the top five hundred British fundraising charities were in the general welfare and social care subsectors. Within these subsectors, for example, nearly 25 per cent of the charities targeted the children and young people welfare segment alone. However, the drivers of intra-sectoral competition could vary depending on the nature of services involved and their historical orientations. For instance, those charities that derived a high proportion of their income from statutory sources (e.g., Charity B and Charity D) had to compete with other charities and commercial (for-profit) firms for governmental contracts. More crucially, they also competed for both legitimacy and attention from government funders. In contrast, an increasingly discerning general public and media challenged charities that depended on voluntary sources of funding, such as individual donations and corporate sponsorships (e.g., Charity A and Charity C).

Although there are different schools of thought on the notion of charitable and non-profit organizations adopting competitive strategies (e.g., Saxon-Harrold 1990; Herman 1994; Courtney 2002; Bruce 2005; Pepin 2006; Williams 2006), this study has found little evidence to suggest that the positioning strategies of charities were created or pursued for a purely competitive motive. Whilst it may be difficult to achieve extremes in either perfect competitive strategies or truly collaborative ones, the findings suggest that, in terms of strategic positioning, there was a tendency for charities to strive towards a combination of competitive and cooperative/collaborative motives for both service delivery and fundraising because of their ingrained, values-driven mission for existence and their legal obligation to maintain their charitable purpose as dictated by charity laws. This situation is suggested in the following quotation:

> Increase in competition from other charities for non-government funding won't be a major influence on our mission and strategic position. If someone out there is able to offer their services better than we can, we are not going to be out of the drug treatment service. We're going to still want to provide that service because of our mission. (Head of Fundraising, Charity D)

Mediating Factors

The integrating model proposes that the external environmental factors described earlier may not necessarily impact directly on the charity's positioning strategy. Significantly, the external environmental factors could be mediated by other factors, which could amplify or reduce their influence. Mediators are conceptualized here as those factors that intervene between stimuli and response (Baron and Kenny 1986). The model suggests that an external antecedent (stimuli) may indirectly affect the response, such as the choice of or change in a particular positioning dimension, through the mediating factor (James and Brett 1984). Two groups of mediating factors were identified from the basis of this study: influential internal and external stakeholders and critical 'trigger' events.

Influential Internal and External Stakeholders

As it was reviewed in Chapter 2, the literature provides various definitions of a stakeholder depending on how broad or narrow the impact of its relationship is on the organization. It has been established earlier in this chapter that influential stakeholders in this study have been defined as those groups or organizations who possess the power and legitimacy to influence the organization's behaviour by virtue of their resource dependent relationships with it (Mitchell, Agle, and Wood 1997), and on whom the charity relies for its continuing survival (Clarkson 1995).

Stakeholders can be external or internal to the organization. Several authors have suggested that the number and type of stakeholders of a charitable and non-profit organization are greater and more varied compared to for-profit ones (Bryson 1995). Their degree of influence would vary depending on the charity's sources of income and legitimacy, as well as their power, visibility, and vocality (Leat 1995a). In the theoretical model in Figure 7.1 influential stakeholders are categorized as internal and external stakeholders who could mediate the impact of specific external environment forces on the choice of a positioning strategy in the charitable context. These two groups of stakeholders are discussed in the following.

Internal Influential Stakeholder (Key Decision-Maker) Among the distinguishing features of a charitable organization are the entirely non-executive and voluntary composition of its governing board of trustees and the unique relationship between the trustees and the chief executive (Leat 1995a). Hudson (2002) argues that there are overlapping responsibilities between the governance responsibilities of a charity's trustees and the management responsibilities of its chief executive. For instance, the case studies revealed that in relatively 'younger' and smaller charities (e.g., Charity A), the trustees were more actively involved in their planning and management activities. On the other hand, in larger and more established charities (e.g., Charity C and Charity D), the chief executives played more dominant roles in making decisions about the charities' corporate plans/strategies.

Leat (1995a) argues that the roles of the chair of the board of trustees and the chief executive are more important in a charitable organization than in a commercial (for-profit) organization. Together, they decide on changes to the charity's mission, corporate plans, and strategies. This phenomenon echoes Pfeffer and Salancik's (1978: 20) assertion that managers, as key decision-makers of an organization, can facilitate or constrain an organization's adaptation to different environmental conditions. The findings in this research suggest that the charity's organizational leaders often initiated a more formalized process of strategic positioning in the charity, and decided how resources were acquired, developed, and allocated to support its positioning strategy. They were particularly influential when they were knowledgeable in or supportive of business and management approaches in the charity's operations. The quotations that follow highlight the different perspectives of these two internal stakeholders' influence on the charity's strategic position:

> Since 2001, the board of trustees has been increasingly involved in planning, developing, and reviewing the strategic directions of the charity. A change in that direction could affect the way the charity positions itself. For example, if the corporate strategy decides that the charity begins to provide day accommodation only, this will influence where our competition is, our strengths and weaknesses, and consequently where our positioning lies. (Chief Executive, Charity A)

> Strong leadership in the charity shapes the corporate culture. A leadership change, especially a new chief executive, will affect the types of corporate strategies pursued, and could affect the charity's positioning. Our current chief executive is very mission-orientated. (Head of Fundraising, Charity D)

External Influential Stakeholder (Resource Dependency) External influential stakeholders can influence the choice of positioning dimensions by virtue of the resources they provide to charities. The extent of this influence would depend partly on the degree to which the charity depends on resources (in particular funding) from these stakeholders. Two groups of external stakeholders stood out in this study's findings: local government agencies that provided direct substantial financial resources (grants and public services contracts) and volunteers who provided essential services to charities.

It was revealed in this study that the government is regarded by charities as an increasingly influential external stakeholder because of its role as their funder (grants and contract income) besides being their policy maker and a legitimizer of their public service work. For instance, 38 per cent of the total annual income of general charities in the UK came from statutory grants and contract income in 2004–2005 compared to 27 per cent a decade ago (NCVO 1996, 2007). The degree of a government funder's influence would also depend on the service subsector the charity operated in. The top five hundred charities in the UK social care subsector received the highest proportion of total annual income (30 per cent) from central and local government grants and contract fees in 2003 (CAF 2004). The growth of these charities appeared to be influenced by governmental policies on development of social care, both at the national and local levels. On the other hand, charities operating in the international and environment subsectors tended to rely more on individual donations. They received 56 per cent and 43 per cent respectively from this voluntary source of income over the same period (CAF 2004). Moreover, the degree of influence by a statutory funder would also depend on the extent to which the charity leaders engaged with them as a partner or acted to maintain the charity's independence and autonomy.

However, the increasing trend for charities to deliver public services under government contracts does not necessarily imply that they are becoming overly dependent on this source of funding or are losing their independence (Blackmore 2004). On the contrary, it could suggest that charities are more accomplished in their understanding and adoption of strategic approaches to securing resources, while at the same time, maintaining credibility and legitimacy (Leat 1995b: 161).

Volunteers, other than the board of trustees, play a range of roles in charities, such as their participation in service delivery, fundraising, or organizational management. Osborne (1998: 16) argues that the defining characteristic of a voluntary organization is the 'voluntary value' that they hold. For charities, this means that they should show some form of public benefit, such as participation of volunteers in service delivery and in fundraising or as part of the volunteer management of the organization. However, the case studies in this present research revealed that the extent to which volunteers could influence the positioning dimensions of a charity would depend on the value that the organization placed on its volunteer ethos and how dependent it was on volunteers.

For instance, Charity C considered its volunteer base as more than an economic resource. It has relied heavily on volunteers to operate over 95 per cent of its emergency sea rescue and fundraising activities since its inception 180 years ago. A strong volunteer ethos was therefore a key element of its mission statement and an integral core value. Its volunteer ethos had shaped the charity's strategic position by differentiating it from other charities and private sector organizations providing similar services. This situation resonates with Alcock's (2003) perception of volunteers as the most important and often the 'sole' resource of community-based organizations and charities. In contrast, Charity D had increasingly relied on paid staff to deliver its drug treatment services instead of using volunteers. This decision was influenced by its corporate strategy to take advantage of the evolving government's policy to increase statutory funding and programmes for the treatment of drug misuse. However, there was little evidence in this study to suggest that paid staff were more or less committed to the charity's mission compared to volunteers.

> Our strategic position has changed structurally and operationally over the years. Overall, the organization is more sophisticated and professional today with more paid staff dealing with different aspects of treatment services, and less dependent on volunteers like in the early years

when it was more of a membership association charity. (Development Director, Charity D)

Critical 'Trigger' Events

This study found that unanticipated external or internal events, which the charity had little or no control over, could trigger changes in the charity's positioning activity. These events included a major change in organizational leadership, a sudden shift in governmental policy, or changes in the legal framework for the provision of public services. Quinn (1978: 9) terms such events as 'precipitating events,' which could cause the organization to respond with urgent, piecemeal, and interim decisions that inexorably shape its future strategic position.

As it was described in Chapter 6, this phenomenon was particularly prevalent in the four case studies over the past decade. For instance, the economic downturn in the UK in the 1990s and into the early 2000s had resulted in a decline in voluntary and legacy income for many charities, such as Charity A and Charity C that relied heavily on these income sources. Decline in the charities' investment returns had also negatively impacted their resource bases, which in turn triggered a review of their core positioning strategies and positioning dimensions.

Moreover, competition for government contracts in the delivery of public services (e.g., health care, social care, rural regeneration) increased during this period as more charities vied for contract income to compensate for the loss of their voluntary funds. Another example was a sudden leadership change in the charity, such as the arrival of a new chairman of the board of trustees or a new chief executive who brought strategic management thinking into the organization's planning approach. Such a change invariably triggered a change in the charity's positioning activities—or even initiated the process of positioning itself, evident in Charity B and Charity D.

In summary, this section has unveiled the theoretical model and explained the impact of various influencing factors on the components of a positioning strategy in the charitable context. It has been argued that the model and its constituents are better able to explain the factors influencing a positioning strategy in the charity context. The model integrates the factors that have emerged from the empirical stages (survey and case studies) in this research. These were compared with those that had been drawn up from the conceptualization stage. The next section discusses the underlying premises that support this model for the charitable context.

MAJOR PREMISES UNDERPINNING
THE THEORETICAL MODEL

This chapter concludes by highlighting four underlying premises of the theoretical model of influencing factors and discusses their relevance to strategic positioning in charities that provide public service (Chew and Osborne 2008b).

Interaction of External and Internal Influencing Factors

First, the model suggests that a complex combination of external and internal factors interact to influence the strategic positioning in charities. These factors are drawn from multiple theoretical perspectives. The empirical findings in this study support the assertion by other researchers (e.g., Henderson and Mitchell 1997; Fahy 2000) that no one particular theoretical perspective can adequately explain all influences on strategy development and choices. Hooley, Broderick, and Moller (1998) and Hooley and others (2001) suggest that both the competitive industry/market-orientation and resource-based perspectives offer important insights into the development of a positioning strategy. The marketing perspective argues that if a strategy becomes too embedded in the internal resources of an organization alone, it runs the risk of ignoring the demands arising from changing turbulent markets and external environments. On the other hand, the resource-based view asserts that marketing strategies are not likely to be effective if they do not exploit the organization's resource endowments and capabilities. The findings in this study lend broad support to these two perspectives in so far as to enable a differentiation between internal and external influences on a positioning strategy in charitable organizations.

However, this study argues that a third perspective, namely, the stakeholder/resource dependence perspective is equal, if not more crucial, in explaining other influencing factors. The model suggests that certain internal and external stakeholders can impose their influence on the charity's strategic direction, and consequently its position, in different ways. For instance, influential internal stakeholders, such as the arrival of a new chairman of the board of trustees or the chief executive, could trigger a change in the charity's positioning activities or initiate the process of positioning itself.

> Previously, before our current chairman came on board, there was a lack of structure, lack of process, and lack of accountability in the charity. He brought a more professional approach to running our operations and redefined our strategic position. (Marketing and Public Relations Manager, Charity A)

A dominant external stakeholder, such as a local government funding agency, could influence the type of positioning dimensions the charity uses to differentiate itself from other charities providing similar services. Positioning dimensions are developed and based on the organization's key strengths and available resources. The effect of resource dependency on influential external stakeholders could result in the charity developing distinctive capabilities, such as strong organizational culture, expertise in a particular service, or management skills, which are more difficult to imitate (Amit and Schoemaker 1993; Hall 1993; Fahy 2000), as highlighted by a case study interviewee:

> A high dependency on government contracts and funding may be a major weakness if our organization provides a narrow range of services. But we have developed a versatile range of services in the treatment of drug and alcohol misuse, and our expertise to clients has provided a degree of credibility and legitimacy for our work. (Branch Manager, Charity D)

The integrating model therefore offers a new perspective using alternative theoretical lenses in explaining the interaction of the various influencing factors on a positioning strategy in the charitable context.

Distinctiveness of the Theoretical Model in the Charitable Context

Second, the model depicts specific factors that are unique to the charitable context, which are not commonly depicted in commercial (for-profit) marketing/strategy literature, such as the charity's mission, governmental influences, and mediating stakeholders. The variations in the factors uncovered in the charitable context arise from three fundamentally distinct issues: positioning goals, the process of strategic positioning, and the role of marketing in this process.

Positioning Goals

The motivations for strategic positioning in charities were found to be multiple in this research and differed from the often singular purpose of gaining competitive advantage attributed to commercial (for-profit) organizations. The marketing literature (e.g., Lovelock and Weinberg 1989; Andreasen and Kotler 2003) suggests that a positioning strategy in non-profit organizations is a key outcome of the marketing planning process similar to commercial (for-profit) organizations. This assertion is based on the premise that positioning is used for competitive reasons (e.g., Porter 1985; Webster 1992; Hooley et al. 2001).

However, this study has revealed that charities adopt a particular positioning strategy due to a combination of competitive and cooperative/collaborative motives because of their ingrained, values-driven mission and the legal obligation to maintain their charitable purpose as dictated by charity laws. These conditions reflect the validity of Behn's (1988) argument that the broader charitable involvement in public services has evolved because neither the market nor government will provide these services or provide them more efficiently and effectively. For instance, the charitable organizations in this study have existed for their causes—mere survival for them was insufficient. They strived to sustain their causes by adapting to their changing environments, which included positioning themselves in *niches* to avoid competition (Mintzberg 1987) or by cooperating with other parties, even 'would-be competitors' in pursuit of their missions (Astley and Fombrun 1983).

The latter situation was found to persist in the case studies in this research. Charities cooperated with other organizations that were considered their competitors in pursuit of their organizational strategies, as illustrated in the two quotations that follow. Crucially, however, their core missions remained constant:

> We are in direct competition with two other non-profit organizations that are involved in life-saving activities at sea and beach. Despite this, at the corporate level, we have a cooperative partnership with them, for example, agreement for them to provide volunteer beach lifeguards on busy weekends and during holidays under our umbrella. (Beach Lifeguarding Officer, Charity C)

> A charitable foundation that specializes in giving large grants to community groups in this region is our competitor. But we also work in partnership with them. If there is a piece of research on an issue, we might fund it in partnership with them. If people come to us for grants of large amounts we point to their direction. In the same way, when they receive small grant applications they refer them to us. So, this works both ways for us. (Marketing and Communications Manager, Charity B)

Pepin (2006) argues that the particular institutional and policy contexts of British charitable organizations warrant a more cooperative/collaborative strategic approach in working with other organizations in the voluntary, public, and private sectors. The heterogeneity of potential influences from multiple stakeholders on these organizations would thus preclude their adopting generic competitive strategies, as used in the for-profit sector (Wilson 1994).

Process of Developing Positioning Strategy

Hudson (2002) and Johnson, Scholes, and Whittington (2006) argue that the organization's strategic position is an outcome of a review of the external environment and organizational capabilities in the organization-wide planning process. As highlighted earlier in this chapter, this strategic management perspective seems to be supported by the findings in this research. They revealed that developing an organizational-level positioning strategy in the charitable context was more likely to be embedded in their corporate strategy planning process than in the marketing planning process, as suggested in the marketing literature. The corporate location of strategic positioning activity in charities is demonstrated graphically by a chief executive in one of the case studies:

> The positioning direction and positioning statement of our charity were developed within the corporate strategy planning process, which are reflected in the mission statement and in its strategic intent today. (Chief Executive, Charity A)

The strategic positioning process in charities in this study was not always deliberate or preplanned, but an emergent response made by them to environmental influences and organizational change. Such an emergent strategy stimulated organizational learning and paved the way for a more conscious approach to strategy development at a later organizational stage (Mintzberg and Waters 1985). In larger and more established charities, such as Charity C and Charity D, there were extended periods of learning from experimentation and past experiences in their positioning activities (Brodtrick 1998). In relatively younger charities though, such as Charity A and Charity B, this process had evolved quite unconsciously and was unplanned, mainly in response to their rapidly changing external environments.

> There is an emerging process of strategy planning—where there were processes in place previously—some worked, some did not. The organization learned as it grew and improved on those that worked, and removed those that did not. Management techniques changed as the organization grew and staff changed. That forces some changes on the process of planning and positioning as well. The planning processes are now being strengthened—taking the best bits from our experiences and putting them together. (Corporate Planning Manager, Charity C)

The case study organizations' experiences reflect Behn's (1988) concept of management by 'groping along' where the organization avoided detailed planning processes but encouraged adaptation and adjustments to their strategic positions over time. Both emergent and deliberate positioning strategies were thus capable of becoming realized ones in the charities in this study. It is therefore argued here that the strategic positioning process in the charitable context is more complex and has not been adequately accommodated in the existing positioning literature.

Role of Marketing in Strategic Positioning

This study has found that marketing played a supporting rather than a leading role in the charitable organization's strategic positioning process, which was mainly in communicating the organization's strategic position to its various target audiences. This role contrasts to that portrayed in the marketing literature (e.g., Lovelock and Weinberg 1989; Kotler and

Andreasen 1996), where marketing plays a dominant role in strategic positioning (e.g., identifying the components of a positioning strategy, defining the organization's competitive position, allocating marketing resources to develop the organization's competitive advantage, and sustaining its strategic position).

This study has revealed that charities have begun to develop dedicated marketing functions in their organizations. However, the marketing role appeared to be an operational one in the strategic positioning process, that is, to communicate the positioning messages once they were defined by the senior management team and board of trustees, rather than taking the lead in the process itself.

Two possible reasons are offered to explain this variance. First, different charities in this study were at different stages in their organizational development, thus exhibiting varying degrees of orientation towards strategic management and marketing practice. The findings from both the postal survey and case studies thus found that charities had begun to undertake strategic marketing planning activities, albeit moderately. This situation is exemplified by the following comment by a case study interviewee:

> Marketing has positive contributions to the charity's organizational change, especially in developing consistent external communications, re-branding, and fundraising. But, these can be better, for example, we need to be clearer about the role of marketing for the organization. We need to clarify how marketing links throughout the organization. Also, we need to do more in marketing to our internal audiences about our corporate and strategic plans and how to deliver these well. (Development Director, Charity D)

The other reason is the contextual difference between charitable organizations and commercial (for-profit) organizations, which researchers and managers ignore at their peril. As argued previously, the positioning goals of charities were multiple rather than focused on a singular motive of gaining competitive advantage, which is a common attribute of commercial (for-profit) organizations. Andreasen, Goodstein, and Wilson (2005) argue that the potential barriers arising when transferring marketing knowledge to non-profit organizations are their lack of marketing skill and the difference in organizational characteristics between them compared to commercial (for-profit) organizations. Leat (1995a) and Rees (1998) suggest that the evolution of commercial management and marketing thought/approaches in voluntary and non-profit organizations is inevitable.

Yet Wright, Taylor, and Bryde (2005: 7) argue that the theoretical development of marketing for voluntary and public service organizations has been bolted on as a niche application and has failed to incorporate new paradigms of marketing for the non-profit context into the fundamentals of management theory. In this regard, this study has found that the marketing function was considered by charity managers as contributing positively to their organizations, albeit not yet at a strategic level in positioning as advocated in the extant marketing literature.

Influence of Mediating Factors

Third, the direct influence of external environmental factors on the charity's positioning strategy was mediated by the actions/decisions of influential internal stakeholders (e.g., the board of trustees/chief executive) and external stakeholders on which the charity depended for critical resources (e.g., a dominant funder and volunteers).

Another mediating influence may come from critical events, such as a sudden change in organizational leadership or an unexpected decline in financial resources. Such factors could trigger a review of the charity's key strengths and distinctive competences and initiate changes to its strategic positioning. The process of identifying and solidifying the charity's strategic position may therefore not always be formalized in the organization until a key decision-maker or a dramatic event triggers that urgency.

The proposed theoretical model does not, however, assume 'complete mediation,' which implies that *all* of the effects of the external influences on the positioning strategy are caused by the presence of the mediating factors (James and Brett 1984: 307). It is acknowledged here that under certain conditions the mediating factor(s) can assume a moderating role. For instance, a charity's dependency on government funding or volunteers as critical resources was found to be contingent on other factors, such as the subsector that it operates in, its organizational culture and size, or its funding pattern. These conditions are reflected in the following quotations made by interviewees in different case study organizations:

> Funding new types of services will affect the capacity and infrastructure of the charity to meet these requirements. When we are a large organization, we need to decide if we want to undertake some government contracts or not, for example, in the prisons tendering system where the commissioners for that funding decided stringent forms of paying out of services and will impose sanctions on us if we don't deliver the required standards. (Development Director, Charity D)

> Being independent, that is, not managed or funded by government, is absolutely vital for our charity so that it has no government messing around whatsoever. We are not politically tied and do not operate at the whims of government. That is one of the most frequently asked questions when we are fundraising on the streets. I feel passionate that we are independent and for the reasons that it does such a good job. (Branch Fundraising Officer, Charity C)

Pre-eminence of the Charity's Mission

Finally, the findings from both the survey and case studies revealed that the charity's mission played a crucial role in the organizational-level strategic positioning because it acted as both a positioning differentiator and as a primary influence on positioning strategy. Despite contrasting histories and features, the charities in this study have developed a strong sense of mission, vision, and values, which were communicated to their external and internal audiences. These provided the key direction for the development of the charities' strategic positions.

> Our charity's mission—what the charity stands for and what it aims to do—is the lynchpin to its positioning. If somebody asks "How are we different and what we do well?" I will read to them our mission statement. (Marketing and Communications Manager, Charity B)

Other research has suggested that a fundamental challenge for charitable organizations compared to commercial (for-profit) organizations is the tension between mission and the needs/demands of external stakeholders, in particular those whom the charities depend on for resources (e.g., Leat 1995b; Hudson 2002). This study, to the contrary, suggests that the primary target stakeholder for positioning by charities was their service users or beneficiaries. Donors and funders were considered secondary stakeholders in their strategic positioning activities.

NCVO (2004a) cautions that British charities that increasingly deliver public services under governmental contracts risk mission drift in their search for funding. It argues that, whilst charities have a wide range of stakeholders, the user/beneficiary should be the most important stakeholder driving their work and not the funder or government agency that provides contracts for delivery of public services (Blackmore 2004). In a similar vein, Alcock, Brannelly, and Ross (2004) suggest that voluntary and charitable organizations that undertake service delivery contracts for government need to consider the extent to which these contracts mesh with their organizational mission and are beneficial to their users or beneficiaries. Whilst this study acknowledged these concerns, it has found little evidence of such mission drift in the case studies. These charities had maintained their strategic positions, which were anchored in their missions, despite making structural, operational, and resource changes over time. It was also apparent that their organizational leaders were acutely aware of the potential threats of embarking on strategies that could stray from their missions and strategic positions:

> Our new five-year corporate plan has reinforced the organization's core positioning and was developed to ensure that the charity, its people and resources are focused in that direction and that we are not straying

too much into government funded service contracts. (Grants Manager, Charity B)

Therefore, charities that were strongly wedded to their core missions could embark on a broad search for funding. They have maintained their focus on serving their key target audience by developing strengths and distinctive competences that were unique to their organizations. However, they had to be flexible in implementing internal operational changes in pursuit of their missions, such as building new or strengthening well-established collaborative links with organizations in other sectors to support their strategic positions over time. These conditions are exemplified in the following two quotations:

> We need to be careful about too much government funding for charities. The amount of government funding that the charity received has had different effects on the organization. But, I don't think any government will have the strength to jeopardize the funding of key public services that charities are delivering. We don't have a problem with reviewing our mission, objectives, and values, but there needs to be reasons from within the organization to do that, other than financial ones. These should not be challenged or changed purely for chasing the money. (Regional Manager, Charity C)

> The kind of work we do is not fashionable but something that is needed. There are a lot of service providers who are concerned that if their type of service goes out of fashion things will have to change tomorrow. Although there is uncertainty after the government's Drug Strategy ends in 2008, I think there will always be certain public services that are needed and that will always be there regardless of whether they are funded by government or not. We are probably one of those types of services. (Branch Manager, Charity D)

The literature review in Chapter 2 has highlighted that a strategic position is neither static nor permanent, and it would need to be appraised as the organization adapts to external environmental changes (Porter 1996; Zineldin and Bredenlow 2001). Charities have been reminded to review their strategic positions regularly (Charity Commission 2004), especially in light of the changing needs of service users/beneficiaries and emerging funding sources, while at the same time preserving their charitable missions. However, this undertaking could be a difficult balancing act.

The resilience of the strategic positions of charities in this study had helped them avoid mission drift. Yet this rigidity could curtail the charities' flexibility in repositioning themselves in response to their changing environments in the future. This potential problem was evident in some of the case studies. For instance, Charity D had begun to face difficulty in raising voluntary income because of its heavy reliance on statutory funding due to its strategic position. Charity C encountered resistance from its volunteers when it expanded its emergency rescue services into beach lifeguarding as a response to declining voluntary income and an ageing donor base. Further research could provide a more comprehensive understanding of this emerging dimension of strategic positioning in the charitable context.

CONCLUSIONS

The discussion in this chapter has crucially demonstrated that the extant literature and scant research on strategic positioning are limited in their ability to accommodate the unique context of positioning in charitable organizations, and they do not adequately guide charity managers in developing their positioning strategy. This study has attempted to overcome some of these deficiencies by developing a theoretical model of factors influencing a positioning strategy in the charitable context. It integrates the multidimensional factors that have emerged from the empirical findings in this research. The factors and their relevance to strategic positioning in the charitable context were discussed in detail. Four underlying premises supporting the model's ability to accommodate the distinctiveness of the charitable context were explained. It must be acknowledged here that the model and its constituents would require validation with further research work. Suggestions in this area are the subject of the next and final chapter. This concluding chapter will also identify the major implications of the findings for the management of strategic positioning in voluntary and charitable organizations.

8 Implications and Future Development

This final chapter will summarize the major conclusions of the study's findings and highlight the implications of these findings for positioning theory and research. It will conclude by offering lessons for the management of strategic positioning in voluntary and non-profit organizations and by suggesting future research directions.

MAJOR CONCLUSIONS

Two main objectives have guided this study. Firstly, it sought to map the strategic positioning activities in charitable organizations within the wider voluntary sector, and secondly, it aimed to identify and explain the key factors that could influence the choice of a charity's positioning strategy. The key findings in answer to the research questions, which were established to achieve these objectives, have been presented in Chapters 5 and 6, and discussed in detail in Chapter 7. Based on these findings, we can conclude that charitable and voluntary organizations have begun to undertake strategic positioning for their organizations as part of their corporate strategic planning to differentiate themselves in an increasingly challenging and competitive external operating environment. The process of developing a charity's organizational-level positioning strategy is embedded in its corporate planning process, with the marketing function playing a role mainly in communicating the charity's strategic position once it has been agreed upon by the charity leaders. This finding contrasts with the contemporary marketing literature's depiction of positioning as a key marketing activity in the organization's strategic marketing planning (e.g., Lovelock and Weinberg 1989; Kotler and Andreasen 1996; Andreasen and Kotler 2003).

A distinctive combination of cooperative/collaborative and competitive motives drives charities to undertake their positioning activities. This differs from the predominantly adversarial motive for positioning by commercial (for-profit) organizations in order to gain a competitive advantage over their rivals (Porter 1985; Hamel and Prahalad 1989; Hooley, Broderick, and Moller 1998; Hooley, Saunders, and Piercy 1998). Moreover, the process of developing a positioning strategy in charities was found to be an emergent one, which provided serendipitous learning in strategy development for charity managers. This finding contradicts the 'design lens' or rational model of developing a positioning strategy where the strategy process is depicted as a conscious step-by-step one (Johnson, Scholes, and Whittington 2006).

The outcome of the strategic positioning process in charities is a positioning strategy that comprises three interrelated decision components: the choice of a generic or core positioning strategy—the broad positioning direction for the charity; the choice of primary and secondary target audiences (e.g., users/beneficiaries and donors/funders) to which the charity's positioning efforts are directed; and the choice of specific positioning dimensions, which the charity develops to differentiate itself from other providers delivering a similar service. Charitable organizations have a predisposition towards adopting differentiation and focus positioning strategies, which are supported by a range of positioning dimensions. However, the type of core positioning strategy and choice of positioning dimensions developed by different charities would depend on their organizational size, funding pattern, and historical orientation. Larger charities tend to adopt differentiation positioning, while small to mid-sized charities that depend more on nonvoluntary sources of income (e.g., statutory grants and service contract fees) tend to develop focus or niche positioning as their generic or core positioning strategy. The charity's mission, a close working relationship with statutory and other voluntary organizations, and a wide network of branches and volunteers are the positioning dimensions that are unique to charitable organizations.

The components of a charity's positioning strategy are influenced by a complex combination of organizational, external environmental, stakeholder, and mediating factors. Some of these influences appear to be similar to those depicted in the initial conceptual framework shown in Chapter 2—reflecting the existing theoretical perspectives on positioning. However, there are other factors that are unique to the charitable context, such as the charity's mission, varying forms of governmental influence, competing demands between users/beneficiaries and donors/volunteers, the charity's board of trustees/chief executive, and key trigger events. The most significant influence arises from the charity's mission, which plays a crucial role in shaping the charity's organizational-level strategic position because of its influence on the choice of the charity's core positioning strategy, the choice of its primary target audience (user/beneficiary), and as a positioning differentiator. The legal obligation imposed on charities to preserve their charitable purpose/status reinforces the pre-eminence of the charity's mission in enabling or curtailing changes to its strategic position over time. The variations in the influencing factors in the charitable context compared to those depicted in the literature for commercial (for-profit) organizations stem from three distinct differences: the positioning goals, the strategic positioning process, and the role of marketing in strategic positioning. These deviations from the existing literature reflect the particular institutional and organizational contexts of charities and underscore the danger of uncritically adopting generic marketing and management approaches by charitable and non-profit organizations.

IMPLICATIONS FOR THEORY AND RESEARCH

The major conclusions summarized earlier in this chapter suggest various implications for positioning theory and research in non-profit and non-market environments. Three implications for theory and research are offered here.

First, the literature review in Chapter 2 has revealed a paucity of empirical research on strategic positioning at the organizational level in voluntary and charitable contexts, and the extent to which existing theories and interpretations of positioning in the literature are applicable to these contexts. This study has provided such an empirical basis. The evidence from this study has revealed that charitable organizations are undertaking strategic positioning activities in ways that show likeness to some activities advocated in the existing literature (e.g., the use of particular generic positioning strategies and positioning dimensions), while demonstrating uniqueness in others (e.g., their positioning goals, process of developing a positioning strategy, and influencing factors on the choice of a positioning strategy).

This study has revealed that charities are positioning themselves in their changing external environments in distinctive ways that are not adequately explained by existing positioning theories. Interestingly, a low-cost positioning strategy and particular types of positioning dimensions were not employed by charities. It is argued here that their inherent resource dependency on external parties and tendency towards cooperative/collaborative relationships with their heterogeneous stakeholders would make it impractical or even impossible for them to adopt monopolistic forms of positioning (Wilson 1994; Bruce 1998). In contrast, they tended to adopt core positioning strategies that emphasized avoidance of direct competition (Mintzberg 1987) and have developed positioning dimensions that are less tangible and more enduring to support their strategic positions over time. These findings can be better explained by drawing upon alternative theoretical perspectives, such as the stakeholder and resource dependence theories (Pfeffer and Salancik 1978), instead of the marketing derivative alone that emphasizes mainly competitive positioning. This study therefore suggests that theory development in strategic positioning in the non-profit context has lagged behind practice. This study has also provided an alternative approach to conceptualizing strategic positioning and its related concepts of strategic position and positioning strategy in the charitable context by integrating different theoretical perspectives and disciplinary lenses on positioning, namely, those that have been derived from the strategic management, resource-based view, marketing, stakeholder, and the resource dependence literatures.

Each of these theoretical perspectives is useful but limited in its ability to fully explain strategic positioning in the charitable and non-profit contexts. Therefore, adopting a multidimensional approach is appropriate for theory building in complex organizational contexts, such as that of charitable organizations (Thomas and McGee 1986; Johnson, Scholes, and Whittington 2006). Moreover, it is argued here that there is an urgent need to develop more theoretical models and conceptual frameworks that take account of the particular organizational, political, and environment contexts of voluntary and non-profit organizations to guide research and inform management practice.

Second, and building on the first point, the literature review in Chapter 2 has also revealed that the underlying assumptions of strategic positioning depicted in the commercial (for-profit) literature (e.g., Porter 1980; Hooley, Broderick, and Moller 1998; Hooley, Saunders, and Piercy 1998; Hooley et al. 2001) have been adopted in the positioning literature for voluntary and non-profit organizations (e.g., Lovelock and Weinberg 1989; McLeish 1995; Kotler and Andreasen 1996; Andreasen and Kotler 2003). Strategic positioning in commercial (for-profit) organizations is predominately undertaken for mainly competitive reasons. The strategic intent of commercial organizations is to create and maintain a competitive positioning strategy that supports their positioning goal(s) and enables them to outperform their rivals (Hamel and Prahalad 1989). However, this study has revealed a complex combination of positioning goals in charitable organizations, which included cooperative, collaborative, and competitive elements. Whilst charitable organizations in this study recognized the intensifying competition in raising funds and securing public service contracts, their missions, organizational culture, core values, and accountability to various stakeholders have moulded their strategic positions.

In addition, the role of marketing in leading the strategic positioning process as is assumed in contemporary marketing literature (e.g., Kotler and Andreasen 1996; Andreasen and Kotler 2003) was found to be less significant in charities. Chapter 7 discussed two plausible reasons to explain this variation—the development of marketing practice in charities lagged behind that of commercial (for-profit) organizations, and the contextual differences between these organizations.

The role of marketing in strategic positioning in charities was found to be limited to a supporting role in this study, namely, in communicating their strategic positions to the target audiences. The marketing perspective of positioning for charities would therefore need to be reviewed in light of the empirical findings gained from this research. Further, as it was discussed in Chapter 3, the dissimilarities between the organizational contexts of charities and commercial (for-profit) organizations should signal to scholars and researchers the risks of advocating blanket management approaches for charitable organizations without careful consideration of their contextual variations (Leat 1995a; Rees 1998; Guy and Hitchcock 2000). These dissimilarities would require either a critical adaptation or reinterpretation of positioning models from the marketing literature for charitable and non-profit organizations.

Third, this study has revealed that strategic positioning is a complex concept and requires a multidimensional methodology to research it. Moreover, the complex nature of the charitable context suggests that no single theoretical perspective, and consequently no single factor, can adequately explain all influences on a charity's positioning strategy. A combination of perspectives and influencing factors are therefore needed to adequately accommodate the unique context of positioning for charities in practice. Consequently, this research has utilized a three-stage methodology, which comprised of a conceptualization stage, an exploratory postal survey stage, and a cross-sectional case studies stage, to develop an original theoretical model that integrates the influencing factors. Whilst this model does not claim causality in the influencing factors due to its exploratory nature, it nevertheless highlights the multifaceted interrelationships between them. This methodology provides an alternative approach to researching strategic positioning in the charitable context, especially for theory building. It offers a distinctive addition to contemporary positioning theory and could facilitate future research using this methodology in voluntary and non-profit management studies.

LESSONS FOR VOLUNTARY SECTOR MANAGERS IN THE PRACTICE OF STRATEGIC POSITIONING

This research suggests five key issues for the managers of voluntary and charitable organizations to consider in planning and developing their strategic positioning activities. First, it was noted in Chapters 1 and 3 that the profound changes taking place in the public policy context (in which voluntary and charitable organizations operate) could offer these organizations potential opportunities for growth and to be involved in policy development, while at the same time could pose threats to their distinctive competences. One recurring concern is about the risk of mission drift in charities, in the UK and elsewhere, that increasingly deliver public services under government contracts and their potential loss of independence to campaign for their causes (Leat 1995b; NCVO 2004a; Osborne and McLaughlin 2004; Alcock, Brannelly, and Ross 2004).

In a similar vein, Hudson (2003) suggests that US charities are facing increasing competitive pressure to earn their income through a wide range of business activities (e.g., earned income from users and government contracts) that are sometimes unrelated to their mission. Mission drift for charities means loss of focus on their charitable purpose and prioritizing their activities for dominant funders instead of serving their core beneficiaries

(Blackmore 2004; Charity Commission 2007a). The potential deviation from a charity's mission could also affect its fundraising efforts from voluntary sources and spur confusion among external audiences about the charity's purpose.

Encouragingly, this research found little evidence of mission drift or loss of independence in charitable organizations. They have developed strong strategic positions that were guided by their missions despite making structural, operational, and resource changes over time. This has enabled them to preserve their charitable values and independence, whilst building strategic relationships with their various stakeholders, including the government, in pursuance of their missions. However, it is acknowledged here that tensions persist in charities in balancing the conflicting demands of their various stakeholders, such as between uses/beneficiaries and donors/funders. It is also recognized that there is a further tension in charities between remaining committed to their core organizational mission and responding appropriately to changes in their external environment. An attention to strategic positioning by charities can help them rise to this difficult challenge. The findings in this study suggest that charities have begun to develop organizational strategic positions that best preserve their particular mission and that effectively differentiate them from other charities and non-profit organizations. However, they would need to be more proactive in shaping their strategic positions to meet both these objectives.

The second issue concerns the debate on the potential loss of independence of voluntary and charitable organizations (e.g., constraints in making strategic decisions and in campaigning for policy or legislative changes) in an increasingly government-driven agenda for delivery of public services, and the resulting emergence of partnership working and contractual arrangements with government. Blackmore (2004) argues that this debate is a flawed one—the key issue in this debate should not be about independence of charities *per se*, but about the degree of interdependence and how they manage strategic relationships with their various stakeholders, including government funders. Advocacy or campaigning should not be an assumed role for all charitable organizations. Hudson (2003: 203) suggests that the extent of advocacy in charitable organizations would depend on their inclination towards this role, the commitment of their leaders, and their capacity for research. However, the need to maintain independence in 'voice' and 'choice' in voluntary and charitable organizations is crucial to preserving their distinctive contribution in the delivery of public services (Chew and Osborne 2007).

As it was discussed in Chapter 3, there have been efforts to strengthen the formal working partnership (e.g., through the 'Compacts' in the UK) between the government, both at the national and local levels, and the voluntary sector in policy design and public service delivery (Osborne 2002; Osborne and McLaughlin 2004). It is important now for charitable organizations to take strategic positioning seriously, and in a way that safeguards their core values and independence while enabling them to build strategic relationships with public and private sector organizations in the provision of public services. Their contribution to public services is important, but so is their role in enabling and sustaining a civil society. Voluntary and charitable organizations therefore need to be proactive in shaping their strategic positions to meet both these objectives, rather than being passive recipients of a strategic position shaped for them by the transient needs and demands of the government (Chew and Osborne 2007, 2008a, 2008c).

Third, this study has uncovered a complex combination of cooperative, collaborative, and competitive motives underpinning the strategic positioning activities of charitable organizations. This unique combination of positioning goals underscores the distinctive nature of charities that strive to develop and sustain strategic relationships with counterparts in the wider voluntary sector and with organizations in the public and private sectors. However, the increasing number of organizations in the wider voluntary and non-profit sector, combined with the blurring of boundaries between this sector and the public and private sectors, is likely to increase competition for resources and public/media attention.

Moreover, new legal forms of hybrid organizations, such as the Community Interest Company, are emerging among voluntary and non-profit organizations in the new millennium (Department of Trade and Industry [DTI] 2002). These social enterprise hybrids aim to accommodate the increasing social enterprise activities among voluntary and charitable organizations that are involved in public service provision with government agencies (Chew 2008). Being more 'business-like' and undertaking profit-making activities are increasingly encouraged in charities and are defining characteristics of being socially enterprising (DTI 2002). This runs counter to their 'public benefit' worth and charitable purposes, which have to be demonstrated under existing charity laws. These new organizational entrants have exacerbated the shifting and blurring of boundaries between the various sectors.

The growing competitive pressure on resource attraction could drive charities to embark on strategic positioning for predominately adversarial reasons in the future. This could undermine charities' cooperative and collaborative spirit, which is one of their defining characteristics in comparison to commercial (for-profit) organizations. It has been suggested earlier in this chapter that whilst mission strongly shapes the charity's positioning goals, it is the charity leaders, namely, the board of trustees/chief executive, who could mediate the direct impact of competition and other external environmental influences on the organization's strategic choices. Charity managers will need to develop appropriate strategic positions for their organizations that best reflect their charitable missions, enabling them to effectively differentiate from other charities, while at the same time ensuring that the organizations are open to learning from the external environment and from their own experiences.

The fourth issue is about the positioning dimensions developed by charities to support their core positioning strategies. An organization's positioning dimensions reflect its key strengths and distinctive competences, which require dedicated resources in order to sustain over time (Porter 1985). These resources include assets (tangible and intangible) and capabilities that the organization builds over time (Barney 1991; Grant 1991).

This present study has revealed that the inherent resource dependency of charitable organizations on external parties for financial and other tangible resources was necessary for them to develop a greater amount of internal capabilities and intangible assets to differentiate themselves from other organizations providing similar services. These included their service expertise or know-how, leadership and management skills, a good reputation, a wide network of branches/volunteers, and strong relationships with partner organizations, which included local government agencies and other nonprofit organizations.

The resource-based view of strategic positioning (discussed in Chapter 2) argues that intangible assets and capabilities, such as reputation, skills, and organizational relationships, are superior sources of distinctive competences of an organization (Prahalad and Hamel 1990; Amit and Schoemaker 1993). These intangible types of resources often take time to create and replace, are difficult to purchase, and are more enduring compared to their tangible counterparts (Hall 1992, 1993). In the case of charitable organizations, developing, protecting, and retaining intangible resources to sustain their distinctive positioning strategies would require charity leaders to understand the links between intangible resources and their contributions to the charity's strategic positioning. More research can help to provide further insights and managerial guidance into the relationship between different types of organizational resources and positional advantage of organizations other than commercial (for-profit) ones.

Fifth, there is a trend towards polarization among charitable organizations in terms of their size and their ability to attract resources. The largest charities (annual income exceeding £10 million) continue to grow in their number and their share of total income at the expense of small charities (annual income below £1 million) and mid-sized ones in the UK charitable sector (NCVO 2004a). For instance, the annual incomes of large charities have increased 45 per cent over the past ten years (1995–2005), while those of smaller and mid-sized charities have experienced declines of 40 per cent and 31 per cent respectively during the same period (NCVO 2007; Charity Commission 2007b).

In terms of strategic positioning, the smallest and the largest charities continue to attract voluntary funding and support from individual donors (NCVO 2008). They are able to do so, either because of their dedicated base of local support (in the case of small charities) or because of their ability to raise funds and develop strong national brands (in the case of larger charities). In contrast, mid-sized charities tend to rely more heavily on non-voluntary income, especially statutory funding, as their main source of income compared to the smallest or largest charities (NCVO 2008). In an increasingly polarized charity market, strategic positioning could be an important management tool for resource attraction and brand building, particularly in mid-sized charities that may be increasingly squeezed out from the marketplace (Chew and Osborne 2007). These organizations need to develop their own distinctive strategic positions and decide whether to remain as niche providers of localized services or to become larger operators with a diversified portfolio of services that their users/beneficiaries would value.

In conclusion, this section has drawn out some major implications for the managers of voluntary and charitable organizations when planning and developing their strategic positioning activities. It is important to emphasize that whilst strategic positioning as a management tool is advocated by voluntary and charitable organizations to help them to differentiate themselves in an increasingly competitive operating environment, ultimately, the adoption of an appropriate positioning strategy and the consequences of that decision on the charity's mission, core values, and its existing position require the application of managerial judgement. This study has shown that despite the potential benefits asserted for charities from the partnership with the public sector in service delivery (e.g., as a way to expand their activities or a source of income), there are risks as well. Overall, charity managers need to sustain a strong mission-led strategic position for their organizations. But, they should also be prepared to respond effectively to market opportunities when these arise.

LESSONS FOR GOVERNMENT AND THE WIDER VOLUNTARY SECTOR

The modernization of public services by governments within and outside the UK and the role of voluntary and charitable organizations in public service delivery are expected to dominate the relationship between government and the voluntary sector in the third millennium. It is therefore important to explore the wider impact of strategic positioning arising from this study. Two key issues are suggested from this research.

The first and overriding issue concerns the influence of government on the strategic positioning choices of charities. A major concern raised (e.g., Leat 1995b; NCVO 2004a; Hudson 2003) is the potential influence of the government as a dominant funder on charitable organizations' strategic choices and their independence as part of the wider voluntary sector. This research has provided evidence that the nature and degree of governmental influence on a positioning strategy of charitable organizations differed depending on the perceived role that government played in their relationship with charities. It has also revealed a complex set of dependencies between charities and the government. Charities considered government as a 'necessary' partner because of its role as a policy maker and legitimizer of their activities, and less so as their competitor for organizational resources. Governmental influence on the strategic positions of charities would also depend on the type of services provided by them, the degree to which the charity leaders engaged with government as a partner in the delivery of public services, and the actions they took to maintain their charities' independence and strategic autonomy. This study revealed that so long as charities remained focused on their missions, they were able to work with various local/central government agencies as partners despite their dependency on them for funding and public service contracts. In this way, charities were able to develop cooperative and collaborative relationships with the statutory bodies. The resource dependency of charities on external parties makes it imperative for them to build long-term relationships with resource providers, including central and local governments (Chew and Osborne 2008c).

While the government is providing contractual financial support for voluntary and charitable organizations, it must also take seriously the need to ensure that the independence of these organizations is preserved. For instance, in the UK, national and local 'Compacts' have established guidelines on the formal working relationship between government and the voluntary organizations that are delivering public services under government contracts. However, more could be done to ensure that these guidelines are enforced at ground level. Mutual trust and interdependence are crucial in strengthening strategic relationships between the public, voluntary, and charitable sectors. This will enhance cross-sectoral engagement in implementing the government's modernization agenda for public services reform, while at the same time ensuring that the 'mission critical' activities of voluntary and charitable organizations are safeguarded (Chew and Osborne 2007).

The other issue concerns the role of representative or umbrella bodies of the voluntary sector (e.g., the ACEVO, CAF, and NCVO in the UK). They need to recognize their influence on the strategic positioning of individual voluntary and charitable organizations. The strategic positioning activity of these organizations, when aggregated up, can have a considerable impact on positioning of the wider voluntary sector. As it was highlighted earlier in this chapter, the growing differentiation between large, primarily service-based charities and small local community charities, with a possible squeeze on mid-sized charities, has been cited as a growing concern among charity practitioners (Office for Public Management [OPM] 2005).

This present study has investigated the strategic positioning experiences of the largest charities (annual income above £10 million) and mid-sized charities (annual income between £1 million and £10 million) in the UK. It has also revealed that these charities are adopting specific positioning strategies to differentiate themselves from others in an increasingly competitive environment. Indeed, Osborne (2003a: 237) observes that the government is focusing increasingly on a small number of larger charities, working in relational contracts with government, as its 'preferred suppliers.' Would the increased use of strategic positioning by large charities further strengthen their national brands and exacerbate the polarization between them and smaller and mid-sized charities? Or could the use of positioning help to define the uniqueness of different charitable organizations to support their individual causes, regardless of their size? Potential answers to these questions would arguably require further research to understand these issues fully.

Nevertheless, a key point to stress here is the necessity for the representative bodies of voluntary and charitable organizations to involve smaller charities in debates and consultations about their role in collectively shaping the future direction of the wider voluntary sector. Smaller charities (those that earn an annual income of less than £100,000) are the backbone of the voluntary sector. For instance, they make up 85 per cent of the 190,000 UK registered charities in 2006 (NCVO 2008). Whilst there have been recent efforts to engage smaller charities at the sectoral level to share management experiences and find solutions to common policy problems (e.g., through the Small Charities Coalition in the UK), such developments have arguably been slow to materialize.

Issues, such as having a collective 'voice' (to preserve the charities' role in advocacy and campaigning for their causes) and 'choice' (to ensure that they are able to decide, manage, and run their operations independent of funders' requirements), are particularly crucial for all voluntary and charitable organizations. 'Voice' and 'choice' are not just confined to the largest charities—charitable organizations of whatever size, shape, or form need to be provided the opportunity to contribute to preserving the voluntary sector's distinctiveness.

FUTURE RESEARCH AND DEVELOPMENT

While this study has achieved its research objectives, it opens up further questions and avenues for future investigation. Six areas for research development are needed.

First, there are two important caveats to the theoretical model that have been developed in this study. The model is based on strategic positioning at the organizational level in charitable organizations, which is distinct from but provides direction for positioning at the operational (product and brand) levels. In addition, the influencing factors and proposed relationships between them have been generalized from the empirical evidence. There could be other influencing factors that this study has not identified under specific circumstances (Hofer and Schendel 1978). Consequently, this model may not include all influencing factors. Whetten (1989) suggests that one of the elements of a good theoretical model is its ability to guide future research, e.g., in terms of testing the relationships between the various variables in the model. The model is 'ready for the classroom and is of little value in the laboratory,' if all links have been empirically verified (ibid.: 491). This model and its constituents provide various opportunities for future testing and refinement. This further work could involve:

- Conducting replication studies to test the legitimacy of the model and its constituents (Yin 2003). This test could be useful to overcome the criticisms of non-replicability and personal bias of the researchers in qualitative studies (Blaikie 2006: 250).
- Constructing specific hypotheses to test the causal connectiveness between the various influencing factors more robustly.
- Testing the generalizability of the model using similar methods of data collection and analysis across other voluntary and non-profit organizational contexts besides the general welfare and social care subsectors in order to validate the model and its constituents (Blaikie 2006: 255).
- Exploring further the impact of mediating factors on governmental influence, competition, and other external environmental influences in other charitable subsectors, such as health care, the environment, or the arts.

Second, it would be interesting to explore how strategic positioning at the organizational level affects positioning at the functional levels in more detail in areas such as in the fundraising, brand building, and services development of voluntary and charitable organizations. The role of marketing, particularly in communicating the charity's strategic position to its various audiences, could be examined further in this interaction. This future research could provide insights into the interaction of different parts of the theoretical model, and consequently help to refine it.

The third area concerns the utilization of the exploratory postal survey method in this study to produce an initial mapping of the strategic positioning activities in charities. It was noted in Chapter 4 that the development of two 'new' scales in this study to measure the extent of strategic marketing planning and positioning strategy activities was necessary because of the lack of existing scales for the charitable context. Whilst the use of the scales in this present exploratory study was not to establish causality, tests for internal reliability and external validity of the scales were undertaken to enhance these conditions. Nevertheless, it would be beneficial to subject these scales to more rigorous validation tests, such as using a larger-scale postal survey. Moreover, a larger sample based on probabilistic sampling could provide further generalizability in the types of core positioning strategies adopted by charities, the positioning dimensions used by them, and the factors that influence their positioning strategies.

Fourth, the process of developing a charity's positioning strategy was explored in this study using comparative cross-sectional case studies. This approach has provided a snap-shot view of the issues to be examined. Future longitudinal study into this process could be conducted in order to examine the critical trigger events that catalyze non-linear shifts in strategy and culture, the causal relationships between the influencing factors, and their effects on the strategic relationships between charities, the wider voluntary and public/private sectors in more detail.

Fifth, this study has portrayed a generally positive role of strategic positioning in the strategic planning and management of charitable organizations. However, it would be important to investigate the negative or 'dark' side of strategic positioning in non-profit organizations in future research. Chapter 7 and an earlier section of this chapter have highlighted several emerging tensions and problematic organizational effects that arose from the strategic positioning activities of charities, such as the risk of mission drift, the dangers of developing an overly rigid strategic position that restricts the charity's flexibility to respond to changing environmental conditions, and the dilemma facing charities adopting positioning strategies for adversarial motives, which run counter to their inherent cooperative and collaborative character. Future research could shed light onto these tensions by examining how charitable organizations are responding to these challenges in more breadth and needed depth. These experiences could provide further lessons for the management of strategic positioning in voluntary and non-profit organizations.

Finally, conducting comparative studies on voluntary and charitable organizations in different countries would be useful to test the national bounds of the conclusions of this research and the theoretical model of influencing factors on a charity's positioning strategy. It is important to establish the extent to which this study's findings and its model are capable of wider application, or if they are bounded by national characteristics. International studies on voluntary and charitable organizations have made important contributions to the development of non-profit theories and management models in both economically developed and developing societies. The works of Salamon and Anheier (1994), Anheier and Kendall (2001), Hudson (2003), Osborne (2003b), Anheier (2005), and Nyssens (2006) are excellent examples of such comparative studies. Future comparative research to map the strategic positioning activities, the types of positioning strategies adopted by voluntary and non-profit organizations in different national contexts, and the relationship between the various influencing factors would provide a more comprehensive picture of strategic positioning as it is applied in an international non-market setting.

FINAL CONCLUDING REMARKS

This book has presented an original approach to investigating an important topic of strategic positioning in charitable organizations within the wider voluntary sector. It began with the assertion that this topic has received a lack of theoretical and empirical attention in both mainstream marketing/ strategy literature and the non-profit management research to date. This present study has by no means implied that it would fill all the research and information gaps in the area of strategic positioning in the charitable and non-profit context. Nevertheless, the findings from this study represent small stepping-stones towards a better understanding of the concept and practice of strategic positioning as it applies to voluntary and charitable organizations. In light of these findings it is clear that there is a need for more empirical works on developing theoretical and management models that can better accommodate the context of charitable organizations. It is hoped that this book will spur further research into management approaches and techniques for non-profit and non-market contexts.

Appendix A
Key Terminologies Used in This Book

The terminologies used in this book are to facilitate understanding and generate insights into the topic being investigated. However, it is acknowledged that different terms serve different purposes. Not all are useful or appropriate for this study's research context. This perspective is shared by Anheier (2005).

> Behind the many terms are, of course, different purposes. Definitions are neither true nor false, and they are ultimately judged by their usefulness in describing a part of reality of interest to us. Specifically, a definition must be simpler than the reality it seeks to describe. (Anheier 2005: 39)

This book has adopted the definitions of the following key terms to denote the various entities in this research.

Commercial (for-profit) organizations operate in the private sector. They are distinct from non-profit or public sector organizations because of their difference in ownership (individual versus collective) and purpose (profit versus social) for their existence (Bovaird and Löffler 2003).

Non-profit organizations are generally referred to in this book as organizations that exist primarily for a social purpose or cause. They include a wide range of organizations such as registered charities, non-registered charities, voluntary and non-profit organizations other than charities that exist for private benefit and are non-commercial, and quasi-non-governmental organizations (quangos) (NCVO 2002b).

Private sector comprises commercial (for-profit) organizations that neither operate in the voluntary sector nor the public sector. Arguably, their primary purpose for existence is to generate economic gains (and profits) through their various activities. They include private companies, partnerships, and sole traders (Hudson 2002).

Public sector comprises organizations and agencies that are part of the government apparatus. These organizations/entities include central government, local authorities, health authorities, and various other governmental agencies that administer/fund public policy and public service delivery (Hudson 2002).

Public services are defined in this book as services that are provided to benefit everyone living in a society but are not necessarily delivered or funded by government and the public sector. Theoretically, these services are distinct from private sector services because they produce 'externalities' (Flynn 2002: 13). In other words, potential gains, such as from education and health services, accrue to people other than those who should benefit directly. However, whilst people should pay for these services collectively rather than individually (since everyone benefits), there are mixed arguments as to who should own the facilities that deliver public services and how these services should be funded. The traditional argument is that government and the public sector should provide all public services where the private sector fails to do so (Flynn 2002). This argument is unconvincing as, for instance in the case of UK public services, many charitable organizations have provided services that were for 'public benefit' long before statutory provision began (Blackmore, Bush, and Bhutta 2005; Charity Commission 2005b). The blurring of boundaries between voluntary, public, and private sectors in delivering public services, in particular through contracts from central and local governments, has exacerbated this argument further (see Chapter 3 for a fuller discussion).

Voluntary and non-profit organizations are referred to in this book as the range of voluntary organizations, including charities that operate in the voluntary sector in the UK and western societies. This term draws insights on the definitional work of Salamon and Anheier (1992a), and the concept of voluntarism described by Bourdillon (1945). Osborne (1996a, 1996b, 1997, 1998) suggests that the continued use of the voluntary concept in the definition of voluntary and non-profit organizations sustains the link between organizations in the non-profit sector and their underlying conceptual principle of voluntarism.

Voluntarism is a concept that views the ability of voluntary and non-profit organizations to be freely formed in a diverse society, thus allowing a voice for the minority and disadvantaged sectors of society (Brenton 1985, cited in Osborne 1997: 13). This definition is broad enough to include a wide range of truly voluntary organizations, such as charitable organizations or charities, whilst excluding those organizations that do not derive income from voluntarism. Therefore, the use of the two terms is appropriate for the purpose of this book, which encompasses the characteristics of British charities as part of the UK voluntary sector.

Voluntary sector comprises all voluntary and charitable organizations, including registered and non-registered charities that primarily exist to achieve social purposes rather than seek economic gains (Hudson 2002). This sector may be referred to in different terms in different national contexts, such as the private not-for-profit sector, third sector, independent sector, or *économie sociale* (Hudson 2002; Anheier 2005).

Volunteer refers to a person who gives time and skills to provide services to other people or to the wider community (NCVO 2004b). These services/

efforts are part of an organized volunteering activity. This conceptualization is synonymous with Darvill and Mundy's (1984) definition of volunteers, as people:

> who voluntarily provide an unpaid direct service for one or more other persons to whom the volunteer is not related. The volunteer normally provides his or her service through some kind of formal scheme rather than through an informal neighbouring arrangement. (Darvill and Mundy 1984: 3)

Whilst adopting this definition of 'volunteer,' this book acknowledges the presence of informal volunteering, which is frequently presented in the form of the family or neighbours (Osborne 1998: 10). Voluntary and charitable organizations are, in general, dependent on the services of formal volunteers to varying degrees. Volunteers are formally involved in a wide range of activities, such as fundraising, organizing events, helping to run an activity, delivering services, and as members of the board of trustees or management committee of charities (NCVO 2004b). Trustees and management committee members constitute a special category of volunteers in charities. The largely unpaid contribution of organized volunteers and trustees is a defining characteristic of the voluntary sector (NCVO 2002b). There were an estimated three million formal volunteers and 750,000 trustees in registered charities contributing to a monetary value of about £15.4 million in 2000 in the UK (ibid.: 79).

Voluntary income includes all forms of voluntary donations, gifts, and legacies from the public, revenue from charity shops, and grants from other charities and trusts. This study has adopted the CAF's definition of voluntary income, which was derived from the top five hundred fundraising charities in the UK. This was done in order to ensure consistency in the measures of income sources for this study because it has also utilized the CAF's (2003) directory of top five hundred fundraising charities as this research's sampling frame (see Chapters 4 and 5 in this book for fuller details). Since 1977, the CAF has tracked the income and expenditures of the largest registered fundraising charities in the UK, and reproduced the data in its annual directories, namely, *Charity Trends/Dimensions* (various years).

This definition of voluntary income closely followed the Charity Commission's (England and Wales) definition of voluntary income for registered charities. Osborne and Hems (1994) highlighted the difficulties in estimating the income and expenditure of UK charities, mainly because the charitable sector is highly diverse and there remains a lack of accurate and comparable information on all charities in the sector. In the same vein, indicators of voluntary income differ vastly in methodology and consistency, and comparisons over a longer timescale could be unreliable or impossible (Mintel 2001).

Statutory income of charities in this study follows the definition used by CAF (2003). It comprises of grants received from local and central government, and contract income for services delivered to central or local government. Statutory income is classified as part of non-voluntary income of charities by the CAF and NCVO.

Total annual income of charities in this study comprised of voluntary income and non-voluntary income. In addition to statutory income, non-voluntary income included grants from other bodies besides government, grants from subsidiaries and affiliates, trading fees, and income from rents and investments (CAF 2003).

Note: Chapter 4 in this book explains other terms that have been used in the research process of this study.

Notes

NOTES TO CHAPTER 3

1. Scottish charity law has been changed by the Charities and Trustees Investment [Scotland] Act, which received Royal Assent on 14 July 2005. The
   Northern Ireland Office is currently overseeing proposals to reform charity
   law and regulation in Northern Ireland (Home Office 2006).
2. Gift Aid is one of the tax-effective methods initiated by the UK Government in
   2003 to encourage more donations by individuals and corporations to charitable organizations. A tax relief on income tax or capital gains tax is given
   for cash donation (gift), where every £1 donated is worth £1.25 to the charity
   (rate from April 2008).
3. The Performance Improvement Hub is one of six national hubs of expertise
   to raise the skills of charities and other voluntary organizations in England.
   It is part of the UK government's ten-year ChangeUp Strategy to improve the
   infrastructure, skills, and performance of the voluntary and community sector
   (NCVO 2005a).

NOTES TO CHAPTER 6

1. The first US community foundation was established in Cleveland, Ohio. By
   2004, there was a network of over one thousand communities throughout
   the world (Charity B's annual report 2004 and corporate presentation 2004).
2. There were over sixty community foundations in the UK in 2004, generating
   more than £74 million in assets and distributing £38 million in local grants
   each year (Charity B's corporate presentation 2004).
3. The Included Community Fund is a major programme of grants for economic
   regeneration and capacity building in the voluntary sector awarded on behalf of
   Tyne Wear Partnership with funds from One NorthEast and the EU (interview
   with Charity B's marketing and public relations manager, November 2004).
4. Charity B managed and awarded grants from the Local Network Fund provided by the Department for Education and Skills to counter children poverty
   and to develop potential of children and young people in Tyne & Wear and
   Northumberland (Charity B's Annual Report 2004).
5. Charity C's lifeboat service in the UK received no statutory funding; the Irish
   Government makes a contribution to the charity's lifeboats in Ireland (Charity
   C's communication strategy publication 2004–2005).
6. Thirteen thousand lifeboat volunteers served as lifeboat crew, coxswains/
   helmsmen, branch officials, shore helpers and supporters; another thirty

thousand volunteers helped in fundraising activities at branches and guilds across the UK and Republic of Ireland in 2004 (Charity C's annual report 2004).

7. Charity C was in a partnership agreement with two life-saving associations in the UK to provide volunteer lifeguards, if needed (Charity C's Beach Life-guarding Report 2000–2004).

8. Charity D's volunteer recruitment and training schemes started in 1997. Originating from the charity's London office, it proved to be very successful and was replicated in other areas in England. However, funding became the main limiting factor to finance volunteering on a larger scale in the charity (data from interviews at Charity D's branch offices in May and June 2005).

References

Aaker, D. (1989) 'Positioning your product.' In *Readings in Marketing Strategy (Volume 2)*, ed. V. Cook, J. Larreche, and E. Strong. Redwood City: The Scientific Press, 193–199.

Aaker, D., and J. Myers. (1987) *Advertising Management*. London: Prentice-Hall.

Abdy, M., and J. Barclay. (2000) *Marketing Collaboration in the Voluntary Sector*. London: NCVO Publications.

———. (2001) 'Marketing collaborations in the voluntary sector.' *International Journal of Nonprofit and Voluntary Sector Marketing* 6 (3): 215–30.

Alcock, P. (2003) *Social Policy in Britain*. 2nd ed. London: MacMillan.

Alcock, P., T. Brannelly, and L. Ross. (2004) *Formality or Flexibility? Voluntary Sector Contracting in Social Care and Health*. Online. Available HTTP: http://www.ncvo-vol.org/asp/search/ncvo/main.aspx?siteID= 1&sID=18&subSID (accessed February 2006).

Alpert, L., and R. Gatty. (1969) 'Product positioning by behavioural life styles.' *Journal of Marketing* 33 (2): 65–9.

Amit, R., and P.J. Schoemaker. (1993) 'Strategic assets and organizational rent.' *Strategic Management Journal* 14 (1): 33–46.

Andreasen, A., R. Goodstein, and J. Wilson. (2005) 'Transferring "marketing knowledge" to the nonprofit sector.' *Californian Management Review* 47 (4): 46–67.

Andreasen, A., and P. Kotler. (2003) *Strategic Marketing for Non-Profit Organizations*. 6th ed. Upper Saddle River: Prentice-Hall.

———. (2008) *Strategic Marketing for Non-Profit Organizations*. 7th ed. Upper Saddle River: Pearson Prentice-Hall.

Andrews, F.M. (1984) 'Construct validity and error components of survey measures: A structural modeling approach.' *Public Opinion Quarterly* 48 (1): 409–42.

Andrews, K.R. (1971) *The Concept of Corporate Strategy*. Homewood, IL: Irwin.

———. (1980) 'The concept of corporate strategy.' In *The Strategy Process*, European edition, ed. H. Mintzberg, J.B. Quinn, and S. Ghoshal. London: Prentice-Hall, 55–63.

Anheier, H. (2005) *Nonprofit Organizations: Theory, Management, Policy*. London: Routledge.

Anheier, H.K., and J. Kendall, eds. (2001) *Third Sector Policy at the Crossroads: An International Nonprofit Analysis*. London: Routledge.

Ansoff, H.I. (1965) *Corporate Strategy*. New York: McGraw-Hill.

Arnott, D. (1992) Bases of Financial Services Positioning, Unpublished Thesis, Manchester Business School, Manchester.

Astley, W.G., and C.J. Fombrun. (1983) 'Collective strategy: Social ecology of organizational environments.' *Academy of Management Review* 8 (4): 576–87.

Attia, S. (2003) 'Achieving sustainable competitive positioning: the role of resources within environmental constraints.' Unpublished thesis, Aston Business School, Birmingham, UK.

Balabanis, G., R.E. Stables, and H.C. Phillips. (1997) 'Market orientation in the top 200 British charity organizations and its impact on their performance.' *European Journal of Marketing* 31 (8): 583–603.

Barnard, C. (1938) *The Function of the Executive*. Cambridge, MA: Harvard University Press.

Barney, J.B. (1991) 'Firm resources and sustained competitive advantage.' *Journal of Management* 17 (1): 99–120.

Baron, R.M., and D.A. Kenny. (1986) 'The moderator-mediator variable distinction in social psychological research: Conceptual, strategic and statistical considerations.' *Journal of Personality and Social Psychology* 51 (6): 1173–82.

Behn, R. (1988) 'Management by groping along.' *Journal of Policy Analysis and Management* 7 (4): 643–63.

Bell, J. (1999) *Doing Your Research Project*. 3rd ed. Buckingham: Open University Press.

Bennett, R. (2003) 'Factors underlying the inclination to donate to particular types of charity.' *International Journal of Nonprofit and Voluntary Sector Marketing* 8 (1): 12–29.

Beveridge, W. (1948) *Voluntary Action*. London: Allen and Unwin.

Bhat, S., and S. Reddy. (1998) 'Symbolic and functional positioning of brands.' *Journal of Consumer Marketing* 15 (1): 32–43.

Blackmore, A. (2004) *Standing Apart, Working Together: A Study of the Myths and Realities of Voluntary and Community Sector Independence*. London: NCVO Publications.

Blackmore, A., H. Bush, and M. Bhutta. (2005) *The Reform of Public Services: The Role of the Voluntary Sector*. London: NCVO Publications.

Blaikie, N. (2006) *Designing Social Research: The Logic of Anticipation*. 5th ed. Malden: Polity Press-Blackwell Publishers.

Blankson, C. (1999) Positioning and Life Cycle Stages in the UK Services Industry. Unpublished Thesis, Kingston University, London.

Blankson, C., and S. Kalafatis. (1999) 'Issues and challenges in the positioning of service brands: A review.' *Journal of Product and Brand Management* 8 (2): 106–18.

———. (2001) 'The development of a consumer/customer-derived generic typology of positioning strategies.' *Journal of Marketing Theory and Practice* 9 (2): 35–53.

Blois, K. (1993) 'Marketing and non-profit organisations.' *Marketing Research Papers* (MRP 93/12), Templeton College, The Oxford Centre of Management Studies.

Bourdillon, A. (1945) 'Introduction.' In *Voluntary Social Services: The Place in the Modern State*, ed. A. Bourdillon. London: Methuen, 1–10.

Bovaird, T., and E. Löffler, eds. (2003) *Public Management and Governance*. London: Routledge.

Bovaird, T., and A. Rubienska. (1996) 'Marketing in the voluntary sector.' In *Managing in the Voluntary Sector: A Handbook for Managers in Charitable and Non-Profit Organizations*, ed. S.P. Osborne. London: International Thomson Business Press, 68–86.

Brenton, M. (1985) *Voluntary Sector in British Social Services*. London: Longman.

Brodtrick, O. (1998) 'Organizational learning and innovation: Tools for revitalising public services.' *International Review of Administrative Sciences* 64 (1): 83–96.

Brooksbank, R. (1994) 'The anatomy of marketing positioning strategy.' *Marketing Intelligence and Planning* 12 (4): 10–14.

Brown, H., and J. Sims. (1976) 'Market segmentation, product differentiation and market positioning as alternative marketing strategies.' In *Educators Conference*

Proceedings Series No.39, ed. K. Bernhardt. Chicago: American Marketing Association, 483–87.

Bruce, I. (1995) 'Do not-for-profits value their customers and their needs?' *International Marketing Review* 12 (4): 77–84.

———. (1998) *Successful Charity Marketing: Meeting Need.* 2nd ed. London: ICSA Publishing–Prentice-Hall.

———. (1999) 'In my opinion.' *Management Today* (August): 14, ABI/INFORM Global.

———. (2005) *Charity Marketing: Meeting Need Through Customer Focus.* London: ICSA Publishing.

Bruner, G.C., and P.J. Hensel. (1996) *Marketing Scales Handbook: A Compilation of Multi-Item Measures (Volume II).* Chicago: American Marketing Association.

Bryman, A. (1992) *Quantity and Quality in Social Research.* London: Routledge.

———. (2001) *Social Research Methods.* Oxford: Oxford University Press.

Bryson, J.M. (1995) *Strategic Planning for Public and Non-Profit Organizations: A Guide to Strengthening and Sustaining Organizational Achievement.* Rev. ed. San Francisco, CA: Jossey-Bass.

———, ed. (1999) *Strategic Management in Public and Voluntary Services: A Reader.* Oxford: Pergamon.

Burt, E., and J. Taylor. (2004) 'Drawing voluntary organizations into the information polity: Information resources and macro politics.' *Public Policy and Administration* 19, no. 1 (Spring): 66–81.

Cabinet Office. (1999) 'Modernizing Government White Paper.' Government Cabinet Office. Online. Available HTTP: http://archive.cabinet-office.gov.uk/ moderngov/ (accessed February 2006).

Carson, D., A. Gilmore, C. Perry, and K. Gronhaug. (2001) *Qualitative Marketing Research.* London: Sage Publications.

Chang, S., and H. Singh. (2000) 'Corporate and industry effects on business unit competitive position.' *Strategic Management Journal* 21 (7): 739–52.

Charities Act. (1992) *HM Stationery Office Ltd.* Online. Available HTTP: http://www.opsi.gov.uk/acts/acts1992/Ukpga_19920041_en_1.htm (accessed July 2006).

———. (1993) *HM Stationery Office Ltd.* Online. Available HTTP: http://www.opsi.gov.uk/acts/acts1993/Ukpga_19930010_en_1.htm (accessed July 2006).

———. (2006) UK Cabinet Office, London: The Stationery Office.

Charities Aid Foundation (CAF). (2000) *Dimensions of the Voluntary Sector.* Kent: West Malling.

———. (2003) *Charity Trends.* 24th ed. London: CAF.

———. (2004) *Charity Trends.* 25th ed. London: CAF.

———. (2005) *Charity Trends.* 26th ed. London: CAF.

CAF/NCVO. (2003) *Inside Research, Issue 19 (August).* Online. Available HTTP: http://www.cafonline.org/research (accessed September 2004).

Charity Commission. (2001) *Recognizing New Charitable Purposes.* Online. Available HTTP: http://www.charity-commission.gov.uk/publications (accessed July 2006).

———. (2003) *Facts and Figures.* Online. Available HTTP: http://www.charity-commission.gov.uk (accessed September 2003).

———. (2004) *Facts and Figures.* Online. Available HTTP: http://www.charity-commission.gov.uk (accessed December 2004).

———. (2005a) *Charities and Trading.* Online. Available HTTP: http://www.charity-commission.gov.uk/publications/cc35.asp (accessed July 2006).

———. (2005b) *Policy Statement on Charities and Public Service Delivery.* Online. Available HTTP: http://www.charity-commission.gov.uk/supportingcharities/polstat.asp (accessed February 2006).

———. (2005c) Facts and Figures, 1997–2004. Available HTTP: <http://www.charity-commission.gov.uk (accessed December 2005).

———. (2006) *Facts and Figures*. Online. Available HTTP: http://www.charity-commission.gov.uk (accessed February 2007).

———. (2007a) *Charities and Public Service Delivery*. Online. Available HTTP: http://www.charity-commission.gov.uk/library/publications/pdfs/cc37text.pdf (accessed March 2007).

———. (2007b) *Facts and Figures*. Online. Available HTTP: http://www.charity-commission.gov.uk (accessed January 2008).

Chew, C. (2003) 'What factors influence the positioning strategies in voluntary non-profit organizations? Towards a conceptual framework.' *Local Governance* 29 (4): 288–323.

———. (2005) 'Strategic marketing planning and positioning in voluntary non-profit organizations: Empirical findings and implications for British charitable organizations.' *Research Working Paper* RP0506 (May), Aston Business School, Birmingham, UK.

———. (2006a) 'Exploring strategic positioning in UK voluntary non-profit organizations: Lessons from the experiences of two cases of British charitable organizations that provide public services.' *Research Paper* RP0624 (July), Aston University, Birmingham, UK.

———. (2006b) 'Positioning and its strategic relevance: Emerging themes from the experiences of British charitable organizations.' *Public Management Review* 8 (2): 333–50.

———. (2008) 'Social enterprise in disguise: Towards hybrid organizational forms of voluntary and charitable organizations in the UK.' Refereed paper presented at the International Research Society for Public Management Conference, 26–28 March, Queensland University of Technology, Brisbane, Australia.

Chew, C., and S.P. Osborne. (2007) 'Use it or lose it!' *Public Management and Policy Review* 37 (June): 11.

———. (2008a) 'Exploring strategic positioning in the UK charitable sector: Emerging evidence from charitable organizations that provide public services.' *British Journal of Management* (forthcoming).

———. (2008b) 'Identifying the factors that influence positioning strategies in UK charitable organizations that provide public services: Towards an integrating model.' *Nonprofit and Voluntary Sector Quarterly* (forthcoming).

———. (2008c) 'Strategic positioning in UK charities that provide public services: Implications of a new integrating model.' *Public Money and Management*, 28(5): 283–90.

Child, J. (1972) 'Organizational structures, environment and performance: The role of strategic choice.' *Sociology* 6, no. 1 (January): 1–22.

Chisolm, L.B. (1995) 'Accountability and nonprofit organizations and those who control them: The legal framework.' *Nonprofit Management and Leadership* 6 (2): 141–56.

Clarke, P., and P. Mount. (2001) 'Nonprofit marketing: The key to marketing's "midlife crisis"?' *International Journal of Nonprofit and Voluntary Sector Marketing* 6 (1): 78–91.

Clarkson, M.B.E. (1995) 'A stakeholder framework for analyzing and evaluating corporate social performance.' *The Academy of Management Review* 20 (1): 92–117.

Collis, D.J., and C.A. Montgomery. (1995) 'Competing on resources: Strategy in the 1990s.' *Harvard Business Review* 73 (3): 118–28.

Courtney, R. (2002) *Strategic Management for Voluntary Nonprofit Organizations*. London: Routledge.

Cousins, L. (1990) 'Marketing planning in the public and non-profit sectors.' *European Journal of Marketing* 24 (7): 15–30.

Cravens, D. (1975) 'Marketing strategy positioning.' *Business Horizons* (December): 53–61.

Cravens, D.W., and N.F. Piercy. (1994) 'Relationship marketing and collaborative networks in service organizations.' *International Journal of Service Industry Management* 5 (5): 39–53.

Crawford, C. (1985) 'A new positioning typology.' *Journal of Product Innovation Management* 4 (1): 243–53.

Cronbach, L.J. (1951) 'Coefficient alpha and the internal structure of tests.' *Psychometrika* 16 (3): 297–334.

Darvill, G., and B. Mundy. (1984) *Volunteers in the Personal Social Services*. London: Tavistock.

Davis Smith, J. (1995) 'The voluntary tradition: Philanthropy and self-help in Britain 1500–1945.' In *An Introduction to the Voluntary Sector*, ed. J. Davis Smith, C. Rochester, and R. Hedley. London: Routledge, 9–29.

Day, G.S. (1994) 'The capabilities of market driven organizations.' *Journal of Marketing* 58 (4): 37–52.

Deakin Commission. (1996) *Meeting the Challenge of Change: Voluntary Action Into the 21st Century*. London: NCVO Publications.

Deakin, N. (2001) 'Putting narrow-mindedness out of countenance.' In *Third Sector Policy at the Crossroads: An International Nonprofit Analysis*, ed. H.K. Anheier and J. Kendall. London: Routledge, 36–50.

Denzin, N.K. (1978a) 'The logic of naturalistic inquiry.' In *Sociological Methods: A Sourcebook*, ed. N.K. Denzin. New York: McGraw-Hill, 6–29.

———. (1978b) *The Research Act*. 2nd ed. New York: McGraw-Hill.

Department of Trade and Industry (DTI). (2002) *Social Enterprise: A Strategy for Success*. Online. Available HTTP: http://www.dti.gov.uk/social enterprise (accessed April 2007).

Deshpande, R., and F.E. Webster. (1989) 'Organizational culture and marketing: Defining the research agenda.' *Journal of Marketing* 53 (1): 3–15.

DeVaus, D.A. (1996) *Surveys in Social Research*. 4th ed. London: UCL Press.

Devlin, J., C. Ennew, and M. Mirza. (1995) 'Organizational positioning in retail financial services.' *Journal of Marketing Management* 11 (1): 119–32.

Diamantopolous, A. and Hart, S. (1993) 'Linking market orientation and company performance—Preliminary work on Kohli and Jaworski's framework.' *Journal of Strategic Marketing* 1(2): 93–122.

Dibb, S. and Simkin, L. (1993) 'The strength of branding and positioning of services.' *International Journal of Service Industry Management* 4(1): 25–35.

Dierickx, I., and K. Cool. (1989) 'Asset stock accumulation and sustainability of competitive advantage.' *Management Science* 35 (12): 1504–11.

Dillman, D.A. (1978) *Mail and Telephone Surveys: The Total Design Method*. New York: Wiley and Sons.

Directory of Social Change. (2002) *The Major Charities: An Independent Guide*. London: DSC.

Donaldson, T., and L.E. Preston. (1995) 'The stakeholder theory of the corporation: Concepts, evidence and implications.' *Academy of Management Review* 20 (1): 65–91.

Doyle, P., and J. Saunders. (1985) 'Market segmentation and positioning in specialized industrial markets.' *Journal of Marketing* 49, no. 2 (Spring): 24–32.

Doyle, P., and V. Wong. (1998) 'Marketing and competitive performance: An empirical study.' *European Journal of Marketing* 32 (5/6): 514–35.

Drucker, P. (1990) *Managing the Non-Profit Organization: Practices and Principles*. Oxford: Butterworth-Heinemann.

Easterby-Smith, M., R. Thorpe, and A. Lowe. (2002) *Management Research: An Introduction*. London: Sage Publications.

Ebrahim, A. (2003) 'Making sense of accountability: Conceptual perspectives for northern and southern nonprofits.' *Nonprofit Management and Leadership* 14 (2): 191–212.

Edwards, M., and D. Hulme. (1996) 'Too close for comfort? The impact of official aid on nongovernmental organizations.' *World Development* 24 (6): 961–73.

Eisenhardt, K.M. (1989) 'Building theories from case study research.' *Academy of Management Review* 14 (4): 532–50.

Eisenhardt, K., and D. Sull. (2001) 'Strategy as simple rules.' *Harvard Business Review* 79, no. 1 (January): 107–16.

Ellis, B., and J. Mosher. (1993) 'Six Ps for four characteristics: A complete positioning strategy for the professional services firm—CPAs.' *Journal of Professional Services Marketing* 9 (1): 129–45.

Ellson, T. (2004) *Culture and Positioning as Determinants of Strategy*. Basingstoke: Palgrave Macmillan.

Engels, J. (1980) *Advertising: The Process and Practice*. New York: McGraw-Hill.

Evans, E., and J. Saxton. (2003) *Five Key Trends and Their Impact on the Voluntary Sector*. London: nfpSynergy.

Fahy, J. (2000) 'The resource-based view of the firm: Some stumbling blocks on the road to understanding sustainable competitive advantage.' *Journal of European Industrial Training* 24 (2/3/4): 94–104.

Fahy, J., and A. Smithee. (1999) 'Strategic marketing and the resource-based view of the firm.' *Academy of Marketing Science Review*. Online. Available HTTP: http://www.amsreview.org./amsrev/theory/fahy 10-99.html (accessed March 2004).

Fill, C. (2002) *Marketing Communications: Contexts, Strategies and Applications*. Harlow: Prentice-Hall.

Fink, A. (1993a) *How to Ask Research Questions*. Thousand Oaks: Sage Publications.

Fink, A. (1993b) *The Survey Handbook*. Thousand Oaks: Sage Publications.

Flynn, N. (2002) *Public Sector Management*. 4th ed. Harlow: Pearson Education.

Foddy, W. (1993) *Constructing Questions for Interviews and Questionnaires: Theory and Practice in Social Research*. Cambridge: Cambridge University Press.

Freeman, R.E. (1984) *Strategic Management: A Stakeholder Approach*. Boston: Pitman.

Freeman, R.E., and D.L. Reed. (1983) 'Stockholders and stakeholders: A new perspective on corporate governance.' *California Management Review* 25 (3): 93–4.

Frumkin, P., and A. Andre-Clark. (2000) 'When mission, markets and politics collide: Values and strategy in the nonprofit human services.' *Nonprofit and Voluntary Sector Quarterly* 29 (1): 141–63.

Frumkin, P., and M.T. Kim. (2001) 'Strategic positioning and the financing of nonprofit organizations: Is efficiency rewarded in the contributions marketplace?' *Public Administration Review* 61 (3): 266–75.

Fry, R.E. (1995) 'Accountability in organizational life: problem or opportunity for nonprofits?' *Nonprofit Management and Leadership* 6 (2): 181–95.

Future Foundation. (1999) *The Millennial Family*. London: Future Foundation.

——. (2003) *The Giving Age: Inheritance in the Context of an Ageing Population*. London: The International Longevity Centre.

——. (2006) *The Networked Family*. London: nVision.

Gill, J., and P. Johnson. (1997) *Research Methods for Managers*. 2nd ed. London: Paul Chapman Publishing.

Gilmore, A., and D. Carson. (1996) '"Integrative" qualitative methods in a services context.' *Marketing Intelligence and Planning* 14 (6): 21–6.

Grant, R.M. (1991) 'The resource-based theory of competitive advantage: Implications for strategy formulation.' *California Management Review* 33 (3): 114–35.

Greenley, G.E. (1989) 'An understanding of marketing strategy.' *European Journal of Marketing* 23 (8): 45–58.

———. (1995) 'Market orientation and company performance.' *British Journal of Management* 6 (1): 1–13.

Greenley, G.E., and G.R. Foxall. (1997) 'Multiple stakeholder orientation in UK companies and the implications for company performance.' *Journal of Management Studies* 34 (2): 259–84.

———. (1998) 'External moderation of association among stakeholder orientations and company performance.' *International Journal of Research in Marketing* 15 (1): 51–69.

Guy, M., and J. Hitchcock. (2000) 'If apples were oranges: The public/nonprofit/business nexus in Peter Drucker's work.' *Journal of Management History* 6 (1): 30–47.

Hall, R. (1992) 'The strategic analysis of intangible resources.' *Strategic Management Journal* 1 (3): 135–44.

———. (1993) 'A framework linking intangible resources and capabilities to sustainable competitive advantage.' *Strategic Management Journal* 14 (8): 607–18.

Hamel, G., and C.K. Prahalad. (1989) 'Strategic intent.' *Harvard Business Review* 67, no. 3 (May–June): 63–76.

Hamel, G. and C. K. Prahalad. (1990) 'The core competence of the corporation.' *Harvard Business Review* 68, no. 3: 79–91.

———. (1994) *Competing For the Future.* Cambridge, MA: Harvard Business School Press.

Hammersley, M. (1992) 'Deconstructing the qualitative-quantitative divide.' In *Mixing Methods: Qualitative and Quantitative Research*, ed. J. Brannan. Hants: Avebury Press, 189–203.

Handy, C. (1990) *Understanding Voluntary Organizations.* London: Penguin.

Hankinson, P. (2001) 'Brand orientation in the top 500 fundraising charities in the UK.' *Journal of Product and Brand Management* 10 (6/7): 346–58.

———. (2002) 'The impact of brand orientation on managerial practice: A quantitative study of the UK's top 500 fundraising managers.' *International Journal of Non-Profit and Voluntary Sector Marketing* 7 (1): 30–44.

Hansen, G.S., and B. Wernerfelt. (1989) 'Determinants of firm performance: The relative importance of economic and organizational factors.' *Strategic Management Journal* 10, no. 5 (September–October): 399–411.

Harris, M., C. Rochester, and P. Halfpenny. (2001) 'Voluntary organizations and social policy: Twenty years of change.' In *Voluntary Organizations and Social Policy in Britain*, ed. M. Harris and C. Rochester. Hampshire: Palgrave, Chapter 1.

Harrison, T. (1987) *A Handbook of Advertising Techniques.* London: Kogan Press.

Hatch, M.J., and M. Schultz. (2001) 'Are the strategic stars aligned for your corporate brand?' *Harvard Business Review* 79, no. 2 (February): 129–34.

Henderson, R., and W. Mitchell. (1997) 'The interactions of organizational and competitive influences on strategy and performance.' *Strategic Management Journal* 18 (Summer Special Issue): 5–14.

Herman, R.D. (1994) 'Conclusion: Preparing for the future of nonprofit management.' In *The Jossey-Bass Handbook of Nonprofit Leadership and Management*, ed. R.D. Herman and associates. San Francisco: Jossey-Bass, 616–26.

Hibbert, S. (1995) 'The market positioning of British medical charities.' *European Journal of Marketing* 29 (10): 6–26.

Hibbert, S., and S. Horne. (1996) 'Giving to charity: Questioning the donor decision Process.' *Journal of Consumer Marketing* 13 (2): 4–13.

Hill, C.P. (1970) *British Economic and Social History 1700–1964.* 3rd ed. London: Edward Arnold.

HM Treasury. (2002) *The Role of the Voluntary and Community Sector in Service Delivery: A Cross Cutting Review (September).* London: HM Treasury.

Hofer, C.W., and D. Schendel. (1978) *Strategy Formulation: Analytical Concepts*. St. Paul, MN: West Publishing Co.

Hoinville, G., R. Jowell, et al. (1978) *Survey Research Practice*. London: Heinemann Educational Books.

Home Office. (1998) *Home Office Annual Report 1998–1999*, Online. Available HTTP: http://www.homeoffice.gov.uk (accessed September 2006).

———. (2005a) *Drugs Treatment*. Online. Available HTTP: http://www.drugs.gov.uk/treatment/strategy/ (accessed May 2006).

———. (2005b) *Tackling Drugs, Changing Lives: Turning Strategy into Reality (December)*. Online. Available HTTP: http://www.drugs.gov.uk/drug-strategy/ (accessed May 2006).

———. (2006) *Final Regulatory Impact Assessment—Charities Bill (Chapter 1)*. Online. Available HTTP: //http://communities.homeoffice.gov.uk/ activecomms/ charity-law-and-reg/reform-charity-legislation/ (accessed July 2006).

Hooley, G. (2001) 'Positioning.' In *Encyclopedia of Marketing*, ed. M. Baker. London: Thomson Learning, 309–15.

Hooley, G., A. Broderick, and K. Moller. (1998) 'Competitive positioning and the resource-based view of the firm.' *Journal of Strategic Marketing* 6 (2): 97–115.

Hooley, G., G. Greenley, J. Fahy, and J. Cadogan. (2001) 'Market-focused resources, competitive positioning and firm performance.' *Journal of Marketing Management* 17 (5/6): 503–20.

Hooley, G., J.A. Saunders, and N.F. Piercy. (1998) *Marketing Strategy and Competitive Positioning*. 2nd ed. Harlow: Prentice-Hall.

———. (2004) *Marketing Strategy and Competitive Positioning*. 3rd ed. Harlow: Prentice-Hall.

Horne, S., and A. Laing. (2002) 'Editorial: non-profit marketing—ghetto or trailblazer?' *Journal of Marketing Management* 18 (9/10): 829–32.

Hudson, M. (2002) *Managing without Profit: The Art of Managing Third-Sector Organizations*. 2nd ed. London: Directory of Social Change.

———. (2003) *Managing at the Leading Edge: New Challenges in Managing Nonprofit Organizations*. London: Directory of Social Change.

Hult, T. and Ketchen, D. (2001) 'Does market orientation matter? A test of the relationship between positional advantage and performance.' *Strategic Management Journal* 22(9): 899–906.

James, L.R., and J.M. Brett. (1984) 'Mediators, moderators, and tests for mediation.' *Journal of Applied Psychology* 69 (2): 307–21.

Jick, J.D. (1979) 'Mixing qualitative and quantitative methods: Triangulation in Action.' *Administrative Science Quarterly* 24 (4): 602–11.

———. (1983) 'Mixing qualitative and quantitative methods: Triangulation in action.' In *Qualitative Methodology*, ed. J. Van Maanen. Beverly Hills: Sage Publications, 135–48.

Johnson, G., K. Scholes, and R. Whittington. (2006) *Exploring Corporate Strategy*. 7th ed. Harlow: Financial Times–Prentice-Hall.

Juga, J. (1999) 'Generic capabilities: Combining positional and resource-based views for strategic advantage.' *Journal of Strategic Marketing* 7 (1): 3–18.

Kalafatis, S.P., M.H. Tsogas, and C. Blankson. (2000) 'Positioning strategies in business markets.' *Journal of Business and Industrial Marketing* 15 (6): 416–32.

Katz, D., and R.L. Kahn. (1978) *The Social Psychology of Organizations*. London: Wiley and Sons.

Kearns, K.P. (1996) *Managing for Accountability: Preserving the Public Trust in Nonprofit Organizations*. San Francisco: Jossey-Bass.

Keaveney, P., and M. Kaufmann, eds. (2001) *Marketing for the Voluntary Sector: A Guide to Measuring Marketing Performance*. London: Kogan Page.

Kemp Commission. (1997) *Heart and Hand, Report of the Commission on the Future of the Voluntary Sector in Scotland*. Edinburgh: SCVO Publications.

Kendall, J., and M. Knapp. (1995) 'A loose and baggy monster: Boundaries, definitions and typologies.' In *An Introduction to the Voluntary Sector*, ed. J.D. Smith, C. Rochester, and R. Hedley. London: Routledge, 66–75.

———. (1996) *The Voluntary Sector in the UK*. Manchester: Manchester University Press.

Kennedy, S. (1998) 'The power of positioning: A case history from the Children's Society.' *Journal of Nonprofit and Voluntary Sector Marketing* 3 (3): 224–30.

Key, S. (1999) 'Towards a new theory of the firm: A critique of stakeholder "theory." ' *Management Decision* 37 (4): 317–28.

Key Note. (1997) *Charities: 1997 Market Report*. Hampton, Middlesex: Key Note Ltd.

Knights, D., and H. Willmott. (1987) 'Organizational culture as management strategy: A critique and illustration from the financial services industry.' *International Studies of Management and Organization* 17 (3): 40–63.

Kohli, A.K., and B.J. Jaworski. (1990) 'Market orientation: The construct, research propositions, and managerial implications.' *Journal of Marketing* 54 (April): 1–18.

Kotler, P. (1980) 'Strategic planning and the marketing process.' *Business* (May/June): 3.

———. (1994) *Marketing Management: Analysis, Planning, Implementation and Control*. 8th ed. Englewood Cliffs: Prentice-Hall.

———. (1999) *How to Create, Win and Dominate Markets*. New York: The Free Press.

———. (2000) *Marketing Management*. Millennium ed. Upper Saddle River: Prentice-Hall.

Kotler, P., and A.R. Andreasen. (1996) *Strategic Marketing for Non-profit Organizations*. 5th ed. Upper Saddle River: Pearson Education/Prentice-Hall.

Landry, C., D. Morley, R. Southwood, and P. Wright. (1985) 'What a way to run a railroad.' In *Strategic Management in Voluntary Nonprofit Organizations*, ed. R. Courtney. London: Routledge, Chapter 3.

Lane, J., A. Passey, and S. Saxon-Harrold. (1994) 'The resourcing of the charity sector: An overview of its income and expenditure.' In *Researching the Voluntary Sector: A National, Local and International Perspective*, 2nd ed., ed. S.K.E. Saxon-Harrold and J. Kendall. London: CAF, 3–15.

Langerak, F. (2003) 'The effect of market orientation on positional advantage and organization performance.' *Journal of Strategic Management* 11 (June): 93–115.

Lauffer, A. (1984) *Strategic Marketing for Not-For-Profit Organizations: Programs and Resource Development*. New York: The Free Press.

Learned, E.P., C.R. Christensen, K.R. Andrews, and W.D. Guth. (1969) *Business Policy*. Homewood, IL: Irwin.

Leat, D. (1995a) *Challenging Management, VOLPROF*. London: City University Business School.

———. (1995b) 'Funding matters.' In *An Introduction to the Voluntary Sector*, ed. J.D. Smith, C. Rochester, and R. Hedley. London: Routledge, Chapter 7.

Leat, D., G. Smolka, and J. Unell. (1981) *Voluntary and Statutory Collaboration Rhetoric or Reality?* London: Bedford Square Press.

Legge, K. (1994) 'Managing culture: Fact or fiction.' In *Personnel Management: A Comprehensive Guide to Theory and Practice in Britain*, ed. K. Sission. Oxford: Blackwell, 397–433.

Levitt, B., and J. March. (1988) 'Organizational learning.' *Annual Review in Sociology* 14:319–40.

Liao, Mei-Na, S. Foreman, and A. Sargeant. (2001) 'Market versus societal orientation in the non-profit context.' *International Journal of Nonprofit and Voluntary Sector Marketing* 6 (3): 254–68.

Lindblom, C. (1959) 'The science of muddling through.' *Public Administration Review* 19:79–88.

Lovelock, C., S. Vandermerwe, and B. Lewis. (1996) *Services Marketing: A European Perspective.* Upper Saddle Road: Prentice-Hall.

Lovelock, L., and C. Weinberg. (1989) *Public and Nonprofit Marketing.* 2nd ed. Redwood City: The Scientific Press.

Lyons, M. (1996) 'On a clear day . . .: Strategic management challenges for the non-profit sector.' In *Managing in the Voluntary Sector: A Handbook for Managers in Charitable and Non-profit Organizations,* ed. S.P. Osborne. London: International Thomson Business Press, 87–109.

MacMillan, I.C. (1983) 'Competitive strategies for not-for-profit agencies.' *Advances in Strategic Management* 1:61–82.

Maggard, J.P. (1986) 'Positioning revisited.' *Journal of Marketing* 40 (1): 63–6.

Mahoney, J.T., and J.R. Pandian. (1992) 'The resource-based view within the conversation of strategic management.' *Strategic Management Journal* 13 (5): 363–80.

Maple, P. (2003) *Marketing Strategy for Effective Fundraising.* London: Directory of Social Change.

Mason, D. (1984) *Voluntary Non-profit Enterprise Management.* New York: Plenum Press.

Matell, M.S., and J. Jacoby. (1972) 'Is there an optimal number of alternatives for Likert-scale items?' *Journal of Applied Psychology* 56:506–9.

McCarthy, M., and D. Norris. (1999) 'Improving competitive position using branded ingredients.' *Journal of Product and Brand Management* 8 (4): 267–85.

McGill, M., and L. Wooten. (1975) 'Management in the third sector.' *Public Administration Review* 35, no. 5 (September–October): 444–72.

McGuire, L. (2003) 'Transferring marketing to professional public services—an Australasian perspective.' *Local Governance* 29 (1): 55–77.

McLeish, B.J. (1995) *Successful Marketing Strategies for Nonprofit Organizations.* New York: Wiley and Sons.

Miles, M., and M. Huberman. (1994) *Qualitative Data Analysis.* 2nd ed. Thousand Oaks: Sage Publications.

Miles, R., and C. Snow. (1978) *Organizational Strategy, Structure and Process.* New York: McGraw-Hill.

Miller, R. L. and W. F. Lewis (1991) 'A stakeholder approach to marketing management using the value exchange model.' *European Journal of Marketing* 25(8): 55–68.

Mingers, J., and J. Brocklesby. (1995) 'Multimethodology: Towards a framework for mixing methodologies.' *Research Papers* (No. 188), Warwick Business School University of Warwick, Coventry, UK.

Mintel. (2001) *Charities: Market Intelligence Report (August).* London: Mintel International Group.

Mintzberg, H. (1978) 'Patterns in strategy formation.' *Management Science* 24, no. 9 (May): 934–48.

———. (1987) 'Crafting strategy.' *Harvard Business Review* 65, no. 4 (July–August), 66–75.

———. (1995) 'Five p's for strategy.' In *The Strategy Process,* European ed., ed. H. Mintzberg, J.B. Quinn, and S. Ghoshal. London: Prentice-Hall, 3–21.

Mintzberg, H., and J. Waters. (1985) 'Of strategies deliberate and emergent.' *Strategic Management Journal* 6, no. 3 (July–September): 257–72.

Mitchell, R.K., B.R. Agle, and D.J. Wood. (1997) 'Towards a theory of stakeholder identification and salience: Defining the principle of who and what really counts.' *Academy of Management Review* 22, no. 4 (October): 853–86.

Mitchell, V. (1996) 'Assessing the reliability and validity of questionnaires: An empirical example.' *Journal of Applied Management Studies* 5 (2): 199–207.

Moore, M. (2000) 'Managing for value: Organizational strategy in for-profit, non-profit, and governmental organizations.' *Nonprofit and Voluntary Sector Quarterly* 29, no. 1 (Supplement): 183–204.

Narver, J.C., and S.F. Slater. (1990) 'The effect of market orientation on business Profitability.' *Journal of Marketing* 54 (4): 20–35.

National Council for Voluntary Organizations (NCVO). (1994) 'Looking to the Millennium.' Speech by Stuart Etherington, CAF Conference on Redefining Charity, 10 November.

———. (1996) *The UK Voluntary Sector Statistical Almanac 1996*. London: NCVO Publications.

———. (1999) *The Next Five Years Through the Eyes of the Sector*. Online. Available HTTP: http: www.ncvo-vol.org.uk (accessed August 2003).

———. (2002a) *Report of the Treasury's Cross-Cutting Review of the Role of the Voluntary Sector in Public Services—A Briefing and Analysis (September)*. Online. Available HTTP: http:// www.ncvo-vol.org.uk/asp/search/ncvo/main. aspx?siteID=1&sID=18&subSID=... (accessed December 2005).

———. (2002b) *The UK Voluntary Sector Almanac 2002*. London: NCVO Publications.

———. (2003) *Voluntary Sector Strategic Analysis 2003/04*. London: NCVO Publications.

———. (2004a) *The UK Voluntary Sector Almanac 2004*. London: NCVO Publications.

———. (2004b) *Voluntary Sector Strategic Analysis 2004/05*. London: NCVO Publications.

———. (2005a) *Delivery of Public Services* (May). Online. Available HTTP: http:// www.ncvo-vol.org.uk/asp/search/microsites/main.asp (accessed February 2006).

———. (2005b) *Voluntary Sector Strategic Analysis 2005/06*. London: NCVO Publications.

———. (2006a) *The UK Voluntary Sector Almanac 2006*. London: NCVO Publications.

———. (2006b) *Voluntary Sector Strategic Analysis 2006/07*. London: NCVO Publications.

———. (2007) *The UK Voluntary Sector Almanac 2007*. London: NCVO Publications.

———. (2008) *The UK Civil Society Almanac 2008*. London: NCVO Publications.

National Statistics (2006) *Social Trends*. Online. Available HTTP: http://www. statistics.gov.uk/CCI/nscL.asp?ID=6545 (accessed September 2006).

Neuman, W.L. (2006) *Social Research Methods: Qualitative and Quantitative Approaches*. 6th ed. Boston: Pearson Education.

Nutt, P.C., and R.W. Backoff. (1992) *Strategic Management for Public and Third Sector Organizations: A Handbook for Leaders*. San Francisco: Jossey-Bass.

Nyssens, M. (2006) *Social Enterprise: At the Crossroads of Market, Public Policies and Civil Society*. London: Routledge.

Octon, C.M. (1983) 'A re-examination of marketing for British non-profit organizations.' *European Journal of Marketing* 17 (5): 33–43.

Office for Public Management (OPM). (2005) *Beyond Profit: Future Scenarios Towards 2010*. Online. Available HTTP: http://www.charity-ommission.gov.uk/ spr/ default.asp (accessed July 2006).

Office of the e-Envoy. (2003) *Policy Framework for a Mixed Economy in the Supply of e-Government Services: A Consultation Document*. London: Cabinet Office.

Ogbonna, E. (1993) 'Managing organizational culture: fantasy and reality.' *Human Resource Management Journal* 3 (2): 42–54.

Osborne, S.P., ed. (1996a) *Managing in the Voluntary Sector: A Handbook for Managers in Charitable and Non-Profit Organizations*. London: International Thomson Business Press.

———. (1996b) 'What is "voluntary" about the voluntary and non-profit sector?' In *Managing in the Voluntary Sector: A Handbook for Managers in Charitable and Non-Profit Organizations*, ed. S.P. Osborne. London: International Thomson Business Press, 5–17.

———. (1997) 'The voluntary and non-profit sector and the provision of social welfare services in Britain.' *Research Paper* (RP9711), Aston University, Birmingham, UK.

———. (1998) *Voluntary Organizations and Innovation in Public Services*. London: Routledge.

———. (2002) 'The voluntary and non-profit sector in the UK: Key trends and emerging issues in the relationship between the sector and the state.' *The Nonprofit Review* 2 (1): 11–21.

———. (2003a) 'A dance to the music of time: Evolving relationships between government and the voluntary and community sector over time.' *Local Governance* 29 (4): 227–43.

———, ed. (2003b) *The Voluntary and Non-Profit Sector in Japan: The Challenge of Chang*. London: Routledge.

Osborne, S.P., and L. Hems. (1994) 'Establishing the income and expenditure of charitable organizations in the UK: Methodology and summary of findings.' *Non-Profit Studies* 1 (1): 7–17

Osborne, S.P., and K. McLaughlin. (2004) 'The cross-cutting review of the voluntary sector: Where next for local government-voluntary sector relationships?' *Regional Studies* 38 (5): 573–82.

Osborne, S.P., and K. Ross. (2001) 'Regeneration: The role and impact of local development agencies.' In *Voluntary Organizations and Social Policy in Britain: Perspective on Change and Choice*, ed. M. Harris and C. Rochester. London: Palgrave, 81–91.

Pallant, J. (2001) *SPSS Survival Manual: A Step by Step Guide to Data Analysis Using SPSS for Windows (Version 10)*. Buckingham: Open University Press.

Paton, R., and C. Cornforth. (1992) 'What's different about managing in voluntary and non-profit organizations?' In *Issues in Voluntary and Non-Profit Management*, ed. J. Batsleer, C. Cornforth, and R. Paton. Wokingham: Addison-Wesley, 36–46.

Patton, M.Q. (1987) *How to Use Qualitative Methods in Evaluation*. Newbury Park, CA: Sage Publications.

Penrose, E. (1959) *The Theory of the Growth of the Firm*. Oxford: Oxford University Press.

Pepin, J. (2006) 'Choices have consequences, collaboration: Strategic issues, processes and benefits.' Paper presented at NCVO Third Sector Foresight Project and Performance Hub Seminar, 16 October, London.

Peteraf, M. (1993) 'The cornerstone of competitive advantage: A resource-based view.' *Strategic Management Journal* 14 (3): 179–92.

Pfeffer, J., and G.R. Salancik. (1978) *The External Control of Organizations: A Resource Dependency Perspective*. New York: Harper and Row.

Pharoah, C. (2003) 'Are there strings attached to government's shillings?' *Third Sector* 2 (July): 12.

Porter, M. (1980) *Competitive Strategy*. New York: The Free Press.

————. (1985) *Competitive Advantage*. New York: The Free Press.

————. (1991) 'Towards a dynamic theory of strategy.' *Strategic Management Journal* 12 (Winter): 95–117.

————. (1996) 'What is strategy?' *Harvard Business Review* 74 (6): 61–78.

Prahalad, C.K., and G. Hamel. (1990) 'The core competence of the corporation.' *Harvard Business Review* 68 (3): 79–91.

Quarter, J., and B.J. Richmond. (2001) 'Accounting for social value in non-profits and for-profits.' *Nonprofit Management and Leadership* 12, no. 1 (Fall): 75–85.

Quinn, J.B. (1978) 'Strategic change: "Logical incrementalism."' *Sloan Management Review* 20 (1): 7–21.

Reddy, A., and D. Campbell. (1993) 'Positioning hospitals: A model for regional hospitals.' *Marketing Health Services* 13 (1): 40–4.

Reed, R., and R.J. DeFillippi. (1990) 'Causal ambiguity, barriers to imitation and sustainable competitive advantage.' *The Academy of Management Review* 15 (1): 88–109.

Rees, P. (1998) 'Marketing in the UK and US not-for-profit sector: The import mirror view.' *The Service Industries Journal* 18, no. 1 (January): 113–31.

Remenyi, D., B. William, A. Money, and E. Swartz. (1998) *Doing Research in Business and Management*. London: Sage Publications.

Ries, A., and J. Trout. (1986) *Positioning: The Battle of Your Mind*. International ed. Singapore: McGraw-Hill.

Robson, C. (1993) *Real World Research*. Oxford: Blackwell.

Rodgers, B. (1949) *Cloak of Charities: Study of Eighteenth Century Philanthropy*. London: Methuen.

Salamon, L.M. (1987) 'Partners in public service: Towards a theory of government-nonprofit relations.' In *The Nonprofit Sector: A Research Handbook*, ed. W.W. Powell. New Haven: Yale University Press, 99–117.

Salamon, L.M., and H.K. Anheier. (1992a) 'In search of the nonprofit sector I: The question of definitions.' *Voluntas* 3 (2): 125–51.

————. (1992b) 'In search of the nonprofit sector II: The problem of classification.' *Voluntas* 3 (3): 267–309.

————. (1994) *The Emerging Sector: The Non-Profit Sector in Comparative Perspective—An Overview*. Baltimore: John Hopkins University.

Sargeant, A. (1995) 'Do UK charities have a lot to learn?' *Fund Raising Management* 26 (5): 14–16.

————. (1999) *Marketing Management for Non-Profit Organizations*. Oxford: Oxford University Press.

Saunders, M., P. Lewis, and A. Thornhill. (2000). *Research Methods for Business Students*. 2nd ed. Essex: Pearson Education.

Sawhill, J., and D. Williamson. (2001) 'Mission impossible? Measuring success in nonprofit organizations.' *Nonprofit Management and Leadership* 11 (3): 371–86.

Saxon-Harrold, S.K.E. (1990) 'Competition, resources and strategy in the British non-profit sector.' In *The Third Sector: Comparative Studies of Non-Profit Organizations*, ed. H.K. Anheier and W. Seibel. Berlin: Walter de Gruyter, 123–39.

Saxton, J. (1996) 'Strategies for competitive advantages in non-profit organizations.' *Journal of Non-Profit and Voluntary Sector Marketing* 1 (1): 50–62.

————. (2003) 'Is that a business or a charity that I see?' *Third Sector* (15 October). London: Haymarket Management (cited in *Times Public Agenda*, 21 October).

Seddon, N. (2007) *Who Cares? How State Funding and Political Activism Change Charity*. London: Civitas.

Shapiro, B.P. (1973) 'Marketing for non-profit organizations.' *Harvard Business Review* 50 (September–October): 123–132.

Schein, E.H. (1992) *Organizational Culture and Leadership*. 2nd ed. San Francisco: Jossey-Bass.

Simon, H.A. (1960) *The New Science of Management Decision*. Upper Saddle River: Prentice-Hall.

Skaggs, B., and M. Youndt. (2004) 'Strategic positioning, human capital and performance in service organizations: A customer interaction approach.' *Strategic Management Journal* 25 (1): 85–99.

Smith, R., and R. Lusch. (1976) 'How advertising can position a brand.' *Journal of Advertising Research* 16 (1): 37–43.

Society Guardian. (2005) *Future for Public Services (July)*. Online. Available HTTP: http://www.societyguardian.co.uk/futureforpublicservices (accessed February 2006).

Stake, R. (1995) *The Art of Case Study Research*. Thousand Oaks: Sage Publications.

———. (2000) 'Case Studies.' In *Handbook of Qualitative Research*, 2nd ed., ed. N.K. Denzin and Y.S. Lincoln. Thousand Oaks: Sage Publications, 435–53.

Strategy Unit. (2002) *Private Action, Public Benefit: A Review of Charities and the Wider Not-For-Profit Sector (September)*. London: Government Cabinet Office.

Taylor, J., and E. Burt. (2005) 'Voluntary organizations as e-democratic actors: Political identity, legitimacy and accountability and the need for new research.' *Policy and Politics* 33 (4): 601–16.

Taylor-Gooby, P. (1994) 'Charities in recession: Hard times for the weakest?' In *Researching the Voluntary Sector: A National, Local and International Perspective*, 2nd ed., ed. S.K.E. Saxon-Harrold and J. Kendall. London: CAF, 101–12.

Thomas, H., and J. McGee. (1986) 'Introduction: Mapping strategic management research.' In *Strategic Management Research: A European Perspective*, ed. J. McGee and H. Thomas. London: Wiley and Sons, 1–18.

Thompson, J.D. (1967) *Organizations in Action*. New York: McGraw-Hill.

Trout, J., and A. Ries. (1972) 'Positioning cuts through chaos in the marketplace.' *Advertising Age* (May): 52–60.

Vazquez, R., L.I. Alvarez, and M.L. Santos. (2002) 'Market orientation and social services in private non-profit organizations.' *European Journal of Marketing* 36 (9/10): 1022–46.

Webster, F.E. (1992) 'The changing role of marketing in the corporation.' *Journal of Marketing* 56 (October): 1–17.

———. (1994) *Market-Driven Management: Using the New Marketing Concept to Create a Customer-Oriented Company*. New York: Wiley and Sons.

Wenham, K., D. Stephens, and R. Hardy. (2003) 'The marketing effectiveness of UK environmental charity websites compared to best practices.' *International Journal of Nonprofit and Voluntary Sector Marketing* 8, no. 3 (August): 213–23.

Wernerfelt, B. (1984) 'A resource-based view of the firm.' *Strategic Management Journal* 5 (2): 171–80.

Whetten, D. (1989) 'What constitutes a theoretical contribution?' *Academy of Management Review* 14 (4): 490–95.

Williams, I. (2006) 'What does competition and collaboration mean in the voluntary and community sector?' Paper presented at NCVO Third Sector Foresight Project and Performance Hub Seminar, October, London.

Wilson, D.C. (1994) 'The voluntary sector in the 1990s and beyond.' In *Researching the Voluntary Sector: A National, Local and International Perspective*, 2nd ed., ed. S.K.E. Saxon-Harrold and J. Kendall. London: CAF, 72–82.

Wolfenden, Lord. (1978) *The Future of Voluntary Organizations, Report of the Wolfenden Committee*. London: Croom Helm.

Wortman, M.S. (1982) 'Strategic management and changing leadership roles.' *Applied Behavioural Science* 18 (3): 371.

Wray, R.B. (1994) 'Branding, product development and positioning the charity.' *Journal of Brand Management* 1 (5): 363–70.

Wright, G.H., A. Taylor, and D. Bryde. (2005) 'Quality, markets and customers in public services.' Paper presented at Panel on Marketing in the Public and Non-Profit Sectors at the 9th International Research Symposium on Public Management, 6–9 April, Milan.

Yin, R.K. (1994) *Case Study Research: Design and Methods.* 2nd ed. London: Sage Publications.

———. (2003) *Case Study Research: Design and Methods.* 3rd ed. London: Sage Publications.

Zeithaml, V., and M. Bitner. (1996) *Services Marketing.* Singapore: McGraw-Hill,

Zineldin, M. (1996) 'Bank strategic positioning and some determinants of bank selection.' *The International Journal of Bank Marketing* 14 (6): 12–24.

Zineldin, M., and T. Bredenlow. (2001) 'Performance measurement and management control positioning strategies, quality and productivity: A case study of a Swedish bank.' *Managerial Auditing Journal* 6 (9): 484–89.

Index